CREATED BY JOSS WHEDON

GREG **PAK**   LALIT KUMAR **SHARMA**   RAMON **BACHS**
DANIEL **BAYLISS**   FRANCESCO **SEGALA**   JOANA **LAFUENTE**

firefly™

NEW SHERIFF IN THE 'VERSE PART TWO

Published by

Series Designer
Marie Krupina

Collection Designer
Scott Newman

Assistant Editor
Gavin Gronenthal

Executive Editor
Jeanine Schaefer

Special Thanks to **Sierra Hahn**, **Becca J. Sadowsky**, and **Nicole Spiegel** & **Carol Roeder**.

Ross Richie CEO & Founder
Joy Huffman CFO
Matt Gagnon Editor-in-Chief
Filip Sablik President, Publishing & Marketing
Stephen Christy President, Development
Lance Kreiter Vice President, Licensing & Merchandising
Arune Singh Vice President, Marketing
Bryce Carlson Vice President, Editorial & Creative Strategy
Kate Henning Director, Operations
Spencer Simpson Director, Sales
Scott Newman Manager, Production Design
Elyse Strandberg Manager, Finance
Sierra Hahn Executive Editor
Jeanine Schaefer Executive Editor
Dafna Pleban Senior Editor
Shannon Watters Senior Editor
Eric Harburn Senior Editor
Sophie Philips-Roberts Associate Editor
Amanda LaFranco Associate Editor
Jonathan Manning Associate Editor
Gavin Gronenthal Assistant Editor
Gwen Waller Assistant Editor

Allyson Gronowitz Assistant Editor
Ramiro Portnoy Assistant Editor
Kenzie Rzonca Assistant Editor
Shelby Netschke Editorial Assistant
Michelle Ankley Design Coordinator
Marie Krupina Production Designer
Grace Park Production Designer
Chelsea Roberts Production Designer
Samantha Knapp Production Design Assistant
José Meza Live Events Lead
Stephanie Hocutt Digital Marketing Lead
Esther Kim Marketing Coordinator
Breanna Sarpy Live Events Coordinator
Amanda Lawson Marketing Assistant
Holly Aitchison Digital Sales Coordinator
Morgan Perry Retail Sales Coordinator
Megan Christopher Operations Coordinator
Rodrigo Hernandez Operations Coordinator
Zipporah Smith Operations Assistant
Jason Lee Senior Accountant
Sabrina Lesin Accounting Assistant

FIREFLY: NEW SHERIFF IN THE 'VERSE Volume Two, January 2021. Published by BOOM! Studios, a division of Boom Entertainment, Inc. © 2020 20th Century Studios. Originally published in single magazine form as FIREFLY No. 16-20. © 2020 20th Century Studios. BOOM! Studios™ and the BOOM! Studios logo are trademarks of Boom Entertainment, Inc., registered in various countries and categories. All characters, events, and institutions depicted herein are fictional. Any similarity between any of the names, characters, persons, events, and/or institutions in this publication to actual names, characters, and persons, whether living or dead, events, and/or institutions is unintended and purely coincidental. BOOM! Studios does not read or accept unsolicited submissions of ideas, stories, or artwork.

BOOM! Studios, 5670 Wilshire Boulevard, Suite 400, Los Angeles, CA 90036-5679. Printed in China. First Printing.

ISBN: 978-1-68415-660-3, eISBN: 978-1-64668-145-7

We can't die, Bendis. And

BECAUSE
SO VERY

Here lies my beloved Zoë, my autumn flower, s

WE'

I brought you some supper. But if you'd p

FOR BU

It's a real burden

BEING RIGHT
SO OFTEN.

米
酒
过
旅

Time for some
THRILLING
HEROICS.
喧闹 起来
y?
ARE
TTY.
ss attractive now she's all corpsified and gross...
E HERE
SINESS.
ure I have a few very catchy ones prepped. Sin and hellfire. One has lepers.
That sounds like something out of science fiction.
YOU LIVE ON A
SPACE SHIP, DEAR.
闹 起来
Curse your sudden but
INEVITABLE
BETRAYAL.

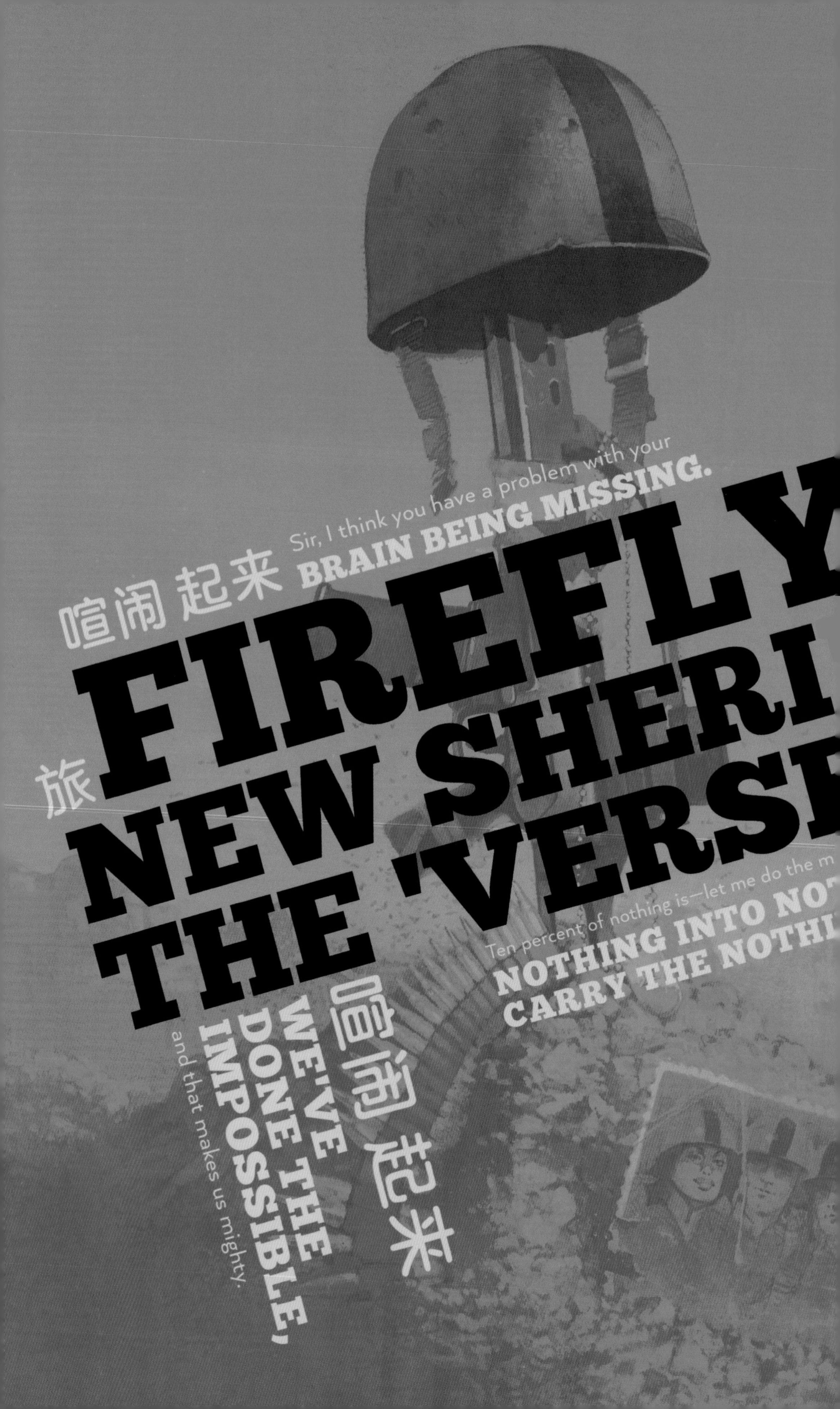

喧闹起来
Sir, I think you have a problem with your
BRAIN BEING MISSING.
旅
FIREFLY
NEW SHERI
THE 'VERS
Ten percent of nothing is—let me do the m
NOTHING INTO NOT
CARRY THE NOTHI
喧闹起来
WE'VE
DONE THE
IMPOSSIBLE,
and that makes us mighty.

Well, you were right about this being a bad idea.
THANKS FOR SAYIN', SIR.
F IN

Created by
Joss Whedon

New Sheriff in the 'Verse Part Two

Written by
Greg Pak

Illustrated by
Lalit Kumar Sharma
Ramon Bachs, Chapter Four
Daniel Bayliss, Chapter Eight

Colored by
Francesco Segala
Joana Lafuente, Chapter Ten

Lettered By
Jim Campbell

Cover by
Marc Aspinall

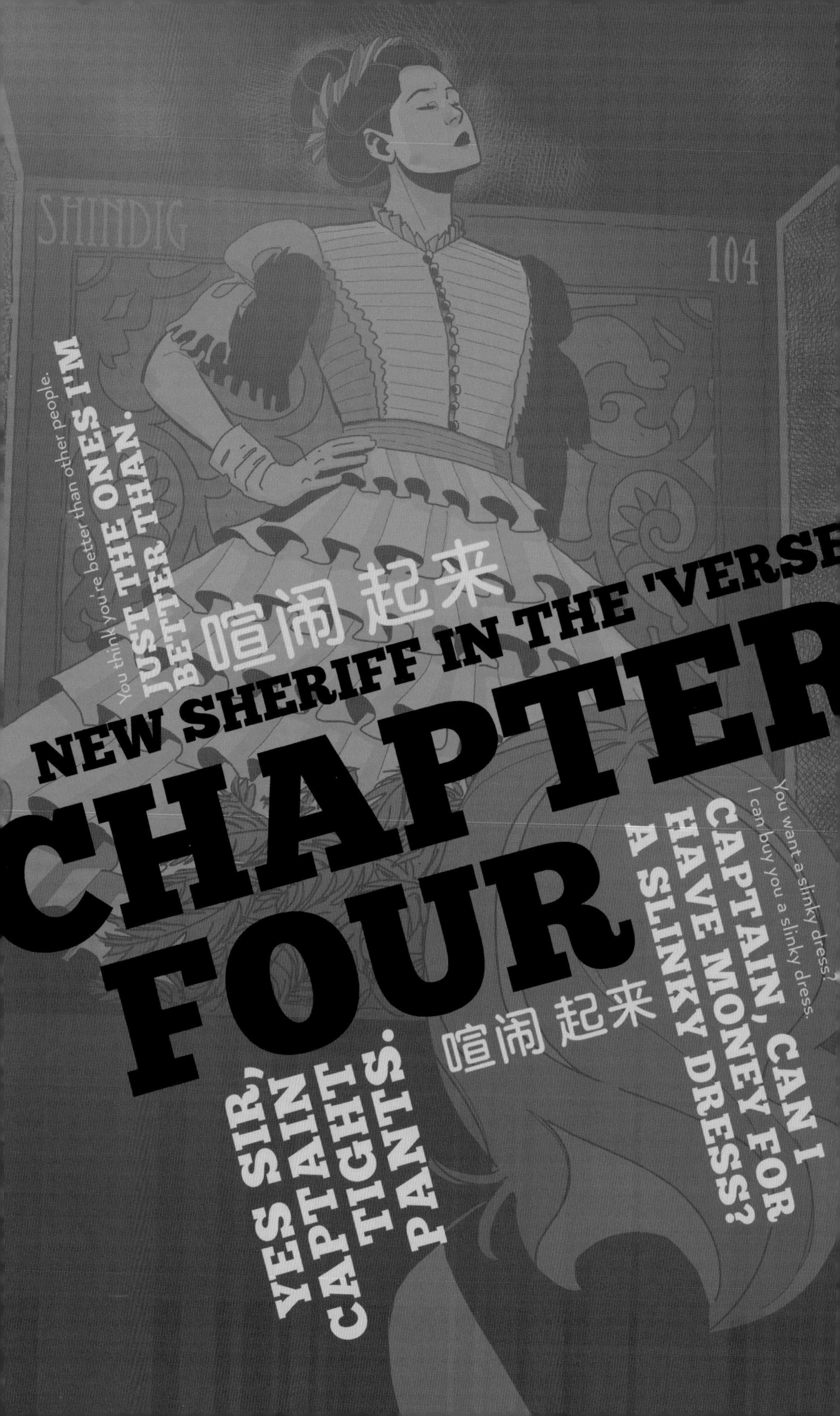
SHINDIG
104
You think you're better than other people.
JUST THE ONES I'M BETTER THAN.
喧闹 起来
NEW SHERIFF IN THE 'VERSE
CHAPTER FOUR
You want a slinky dress? I can buy you a slinky dress.
CAPTAIN, CAN I HAVE MONEY FOR A SLINKY DRESS?
喧闹 起来
YES SIR, CAPTAIN TIGHT PANTS.

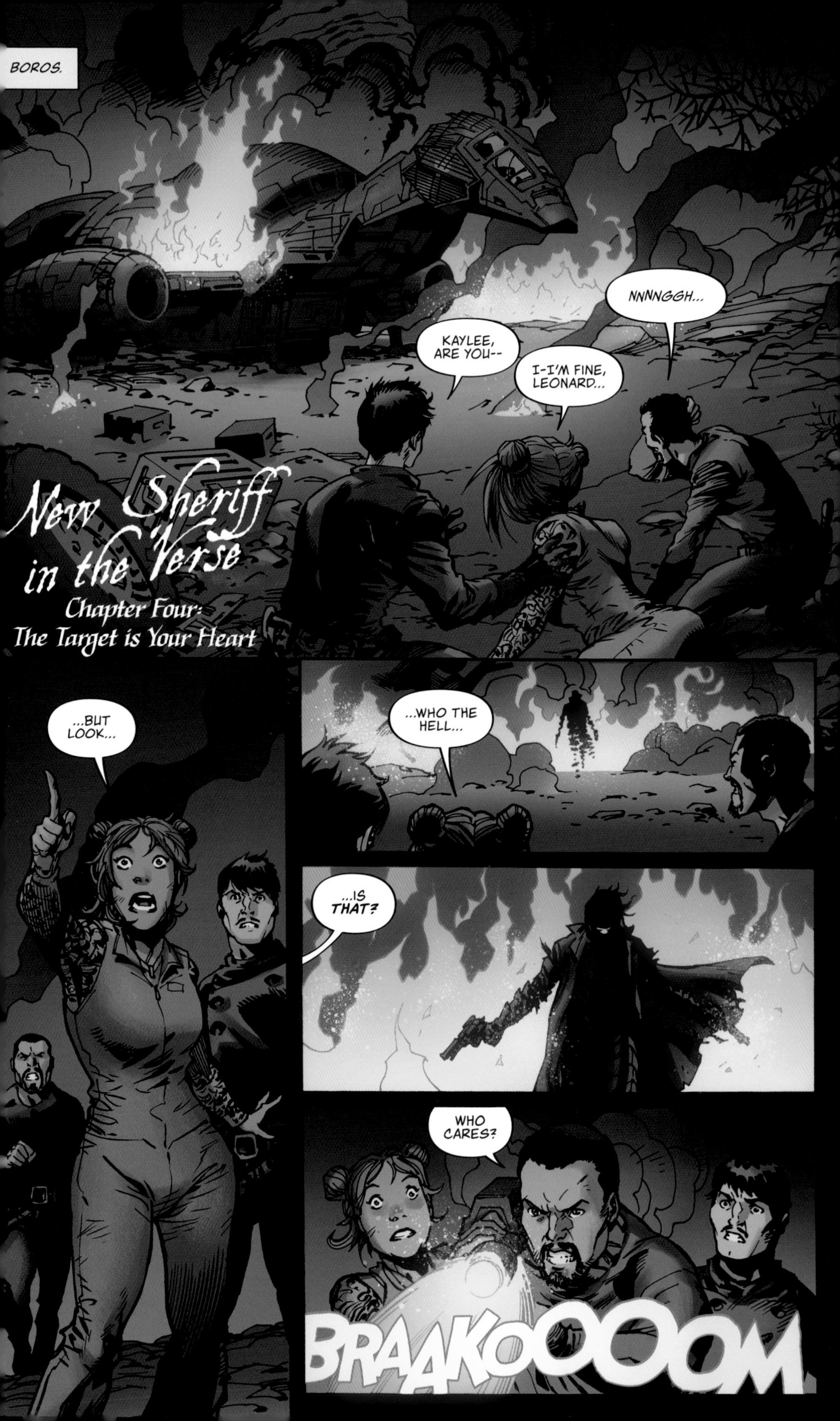
BOROS.
NNNNGGH...
KAYLEE, ARE YOU--
I-I'M FINE, LEONARD...
New Sheriff in the 'Verse
Chapter Four: The Target is Your Heart
...BUT LOOK...
...WHO THE HELL...
...IS THAT?
WHO CARES?
BRAAKOOOOM

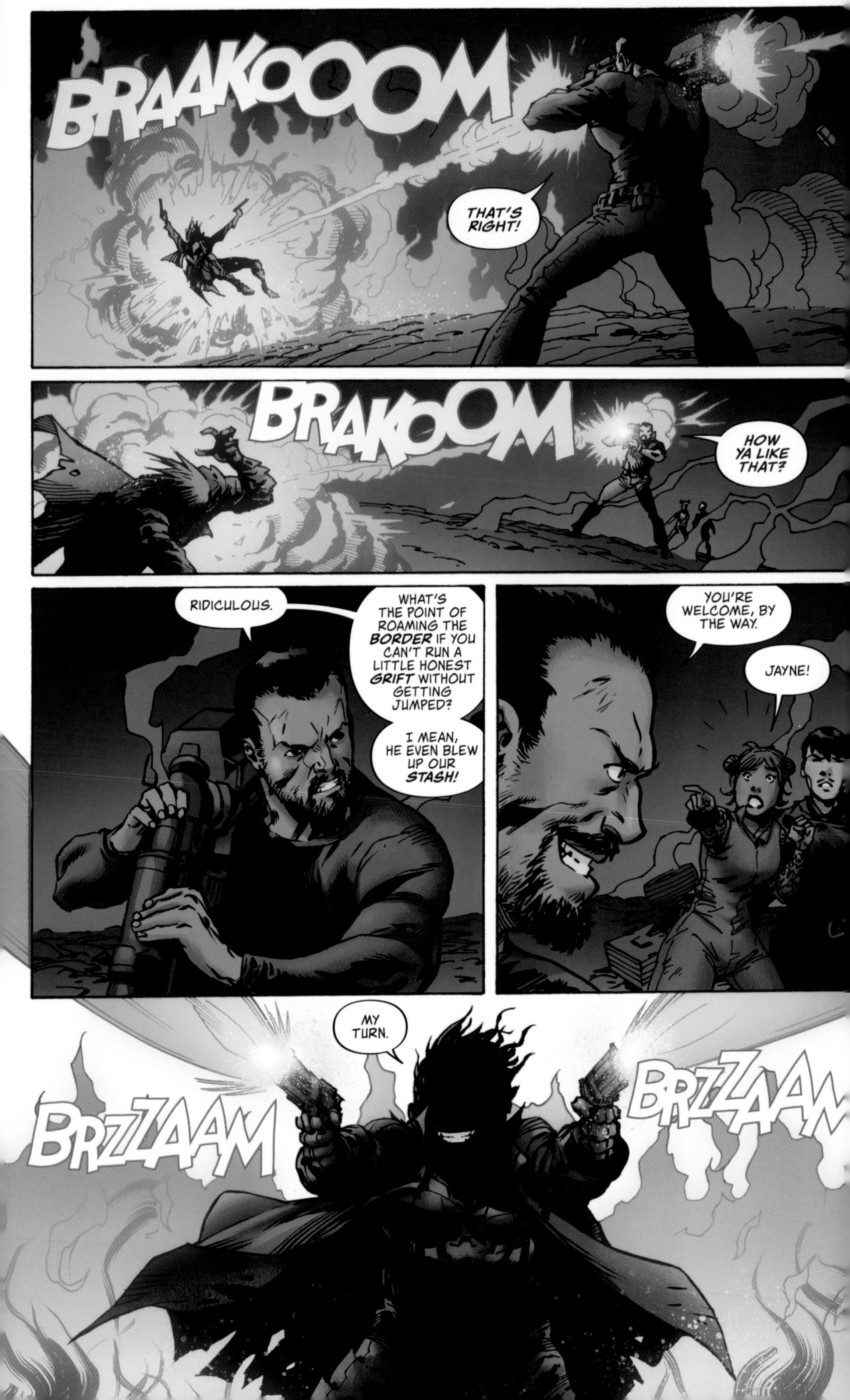
BRAAKOOOM
THAT'S RIGHT!
BRAKOOM
HOW YA LIKE THAT?
RIDICULOUS.
WHAT'S THE POINT OF ROAMING THE BORDER IF YOU CAN'T RUN A LITTLE HONEST GRIFT WITHOUT GETTING JUMPED?
I MEAN, HE EVEN BLEW UP OUR STASH!
YOU'RE WELCOME, BY THE WAY.
JAYNE!
MY TURN.
BRZZAAM
BRZZAAM

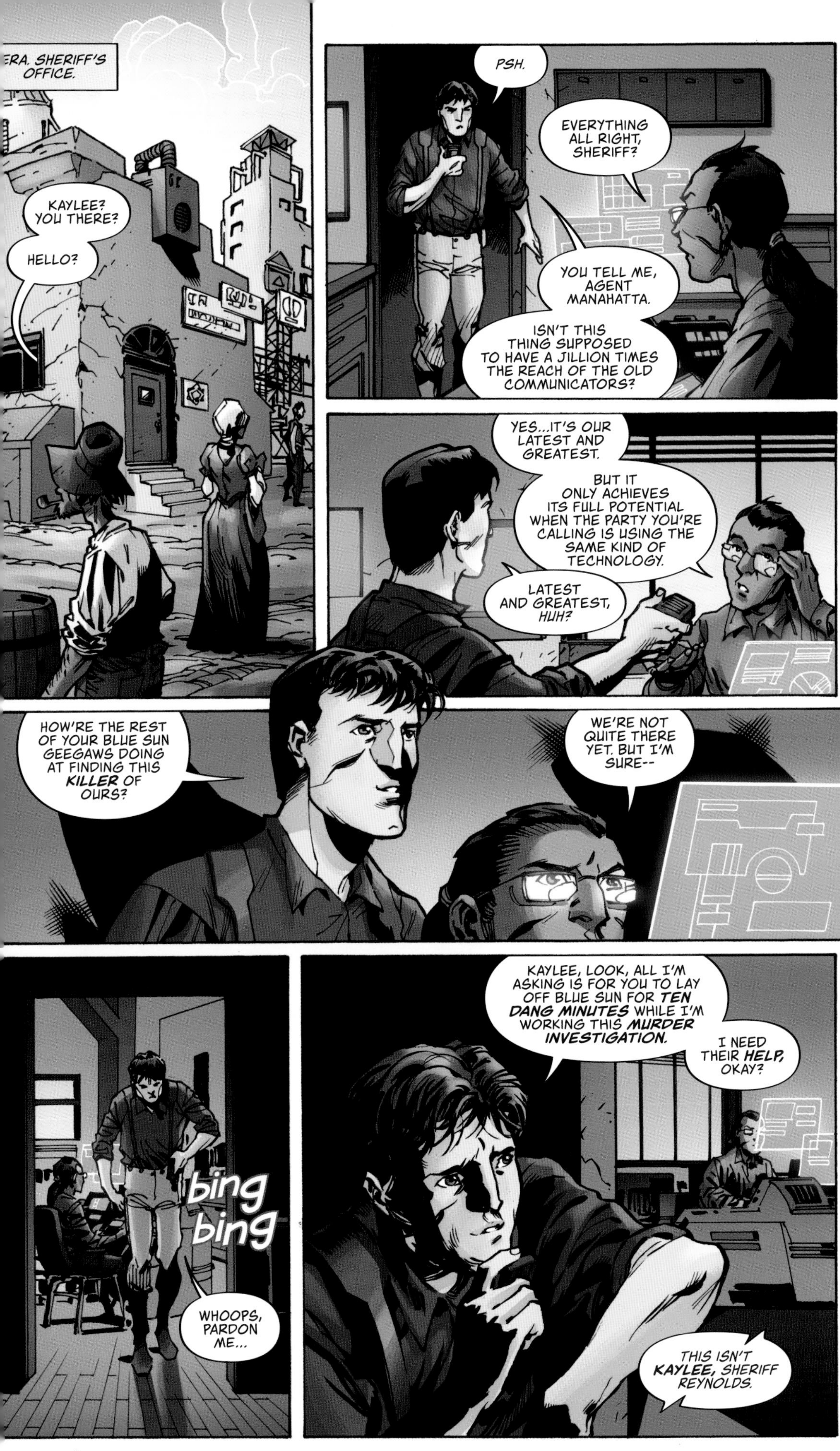

ERA. SHERIFF'S OFFICE.
KAYLEE? YOU THERE?
HELLO?
PSH.
EVERYTHING ALL RIGHT, SHERIFF?
YOU TELL ME, AGENT MANAHATTA.
ISN'T THIS THING SUPPOSED TO HAVE A JILLION TIMES THE REACH OF THE OLD COMMUNICATORS?
YES...IT'S OUR LATEST AND GREATEST.
BUT IT ONLY ACHIEVES ITS FULL POTENTIAL WHEN THE PARTY YOU'RE CALLING IS USING THE SAME KIND OF TECHNOLOGY.
LATEST AND GREATEST, *HUH?*
HOW'RE THE REST OF YOUR BLUE SUN GEEGAWS DOING AT FINDING THIS ***KILLER*** OF OURS?
WE'RE NOT QUITE THERE YET. BUT I'M SURE--
bing bing
WHOOPS, PARDON ME...
KAYLEE, LOOK, ALL I'M ASKING IS FOR YOU TO LAY OFF BLUE SUN FOR ***TEN DANG MINUTES*** WHILE I'M WORKING THIS ***MURDER INVESTIGATION.***
I NEED THEIR ***HELP,*** OKAY?
THIS ISN'T ***KAYLEE,*** *SHERIFF REYNOLDS.*

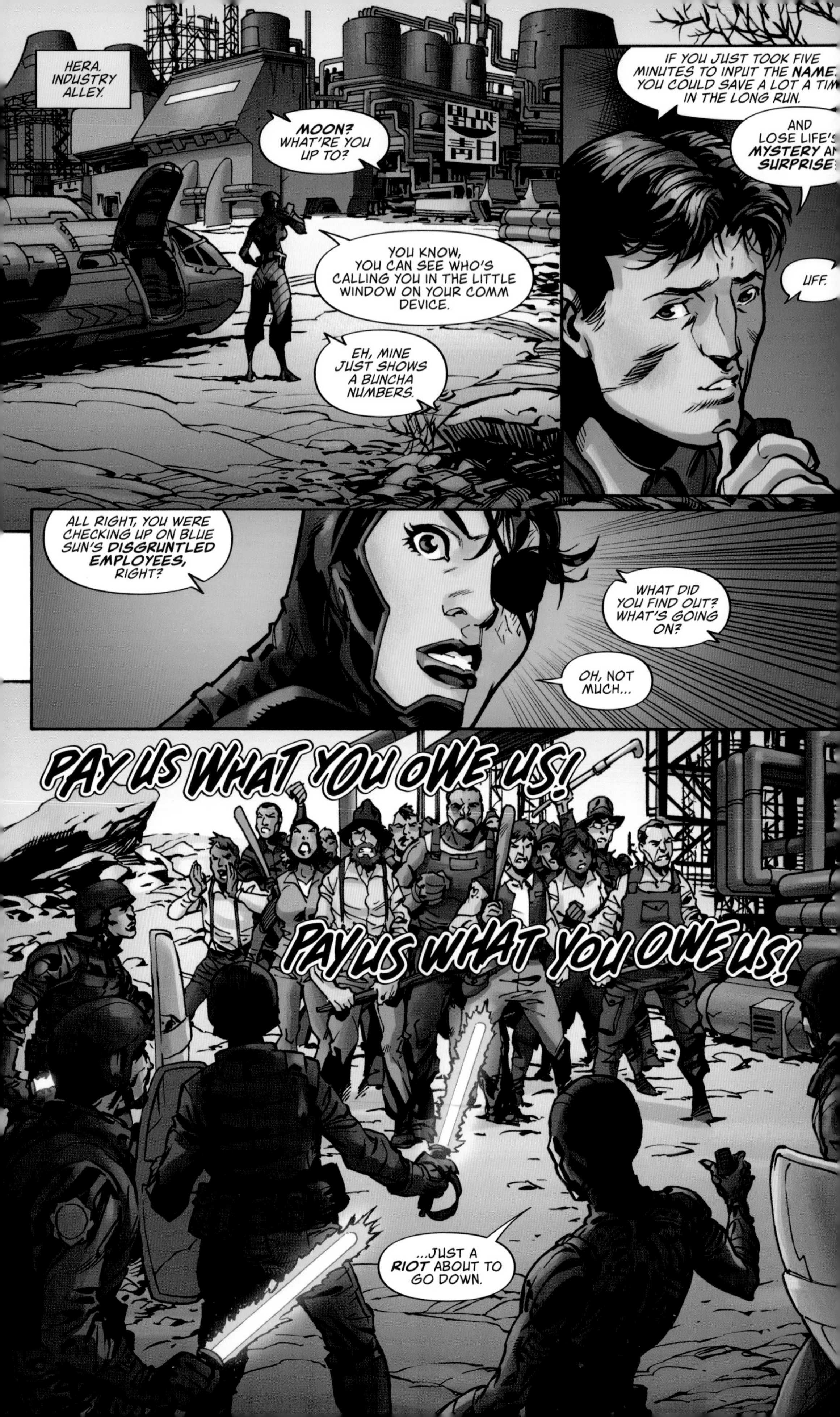
HERA. INDUSTRY ALLEY.
MOON? WHAT'RE YOU UP TO?
IF YOU JUST TOOK FIVE MINUTES TO INPUT THE NAME, YOU COULD SAVE A LOT A TIM IN THE LONG RUN.
AND LOSE LIFE'S MYSTERY AN SURPRISE
YOU KNOW, YOU CAN SEE WHO'S CALLING YOU IN THE LITTLE WINDOW ON YOUR COMM DEVICE.
UFF.
EH, MINE JUST SHOWS A BUNCHA NUMBERS.
ALL RIGHT, YOU WERE CHECKING UP ON BLUE SUN'S DISGRUNTLED EMPLOYEES, RIGHT?
WHAT DID YOU FIND OUT? WHAT'S GOING ON?
OH, NOT MUCH...
PAY US WHAT YOU OWE US!
PAY US WHAT YOU OWE US!
...JUST A RIOT ABOUT TO GO DOWN.

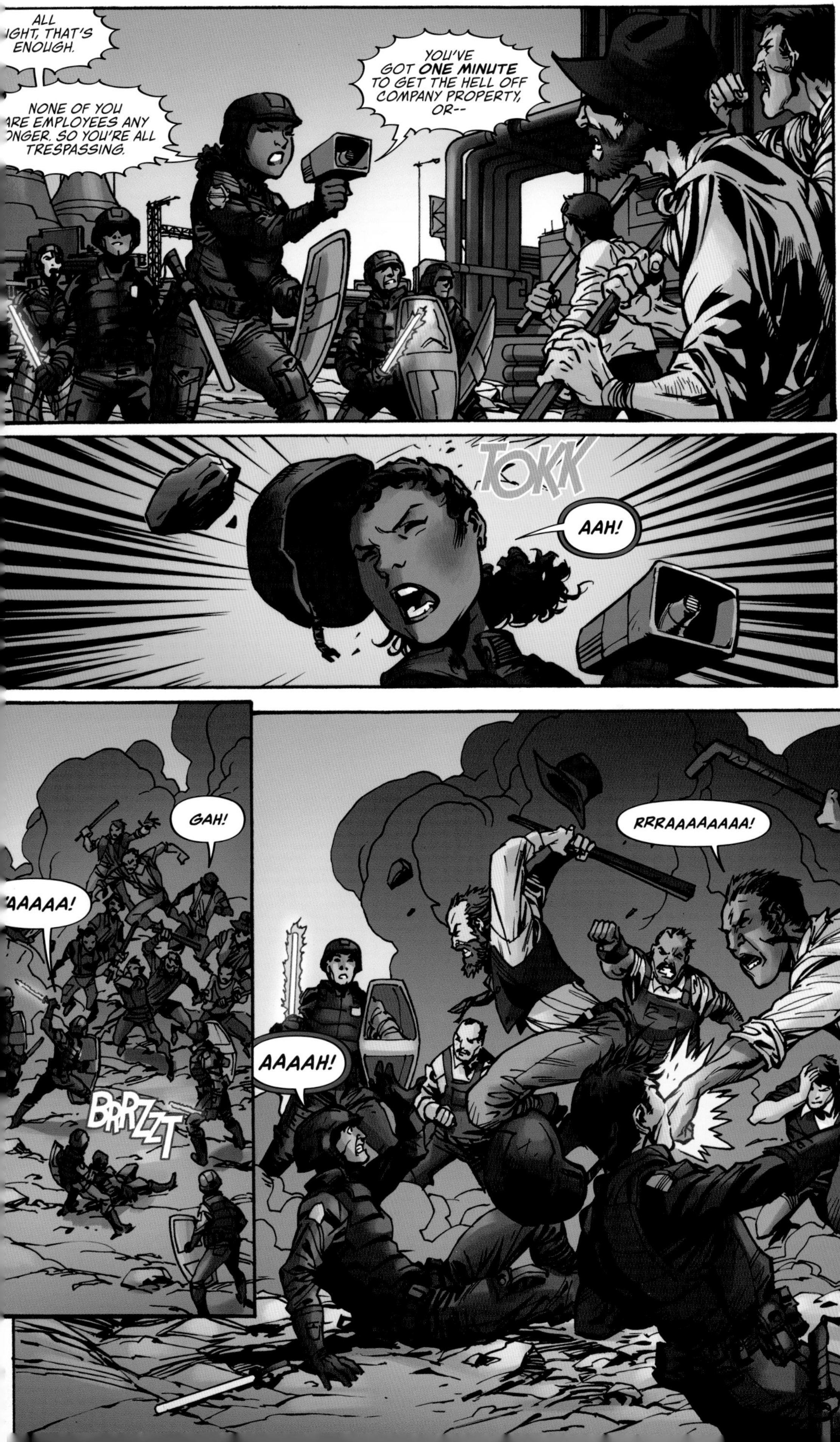
ALL
IGHT, THAT'S
ENOUGH.
NONE OF YOU
ARE EMPLOYEES ANY
ONGER. SO YOU'RE ALL
TRESPASSING.
YOU'VE
GOT ONE MINUTE
TO GET THE HELL OFF
COMPANY PROPERTY,
OR--
TOKK
AAH!
GAH!
AAAAA!
BRRZZT
RRRAAAAAAAA!
AAAAH!

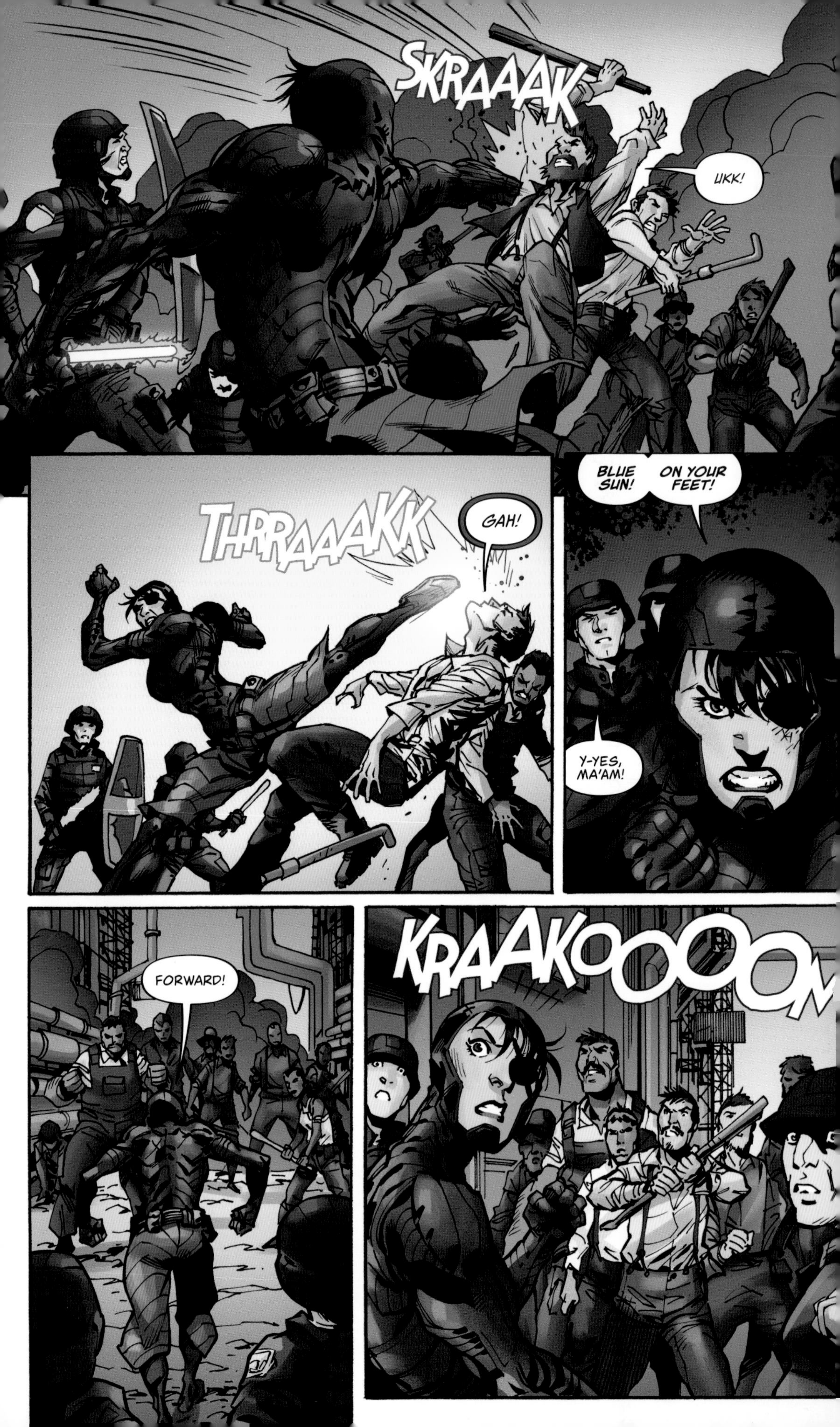
SKRAAAK
UKK!
THRRAAAKK
GAH!
BLUE SUN!
ON YOUR FEET!
Y-YES, MA'AM!
FORWARD!
KRAAKOOOOOM

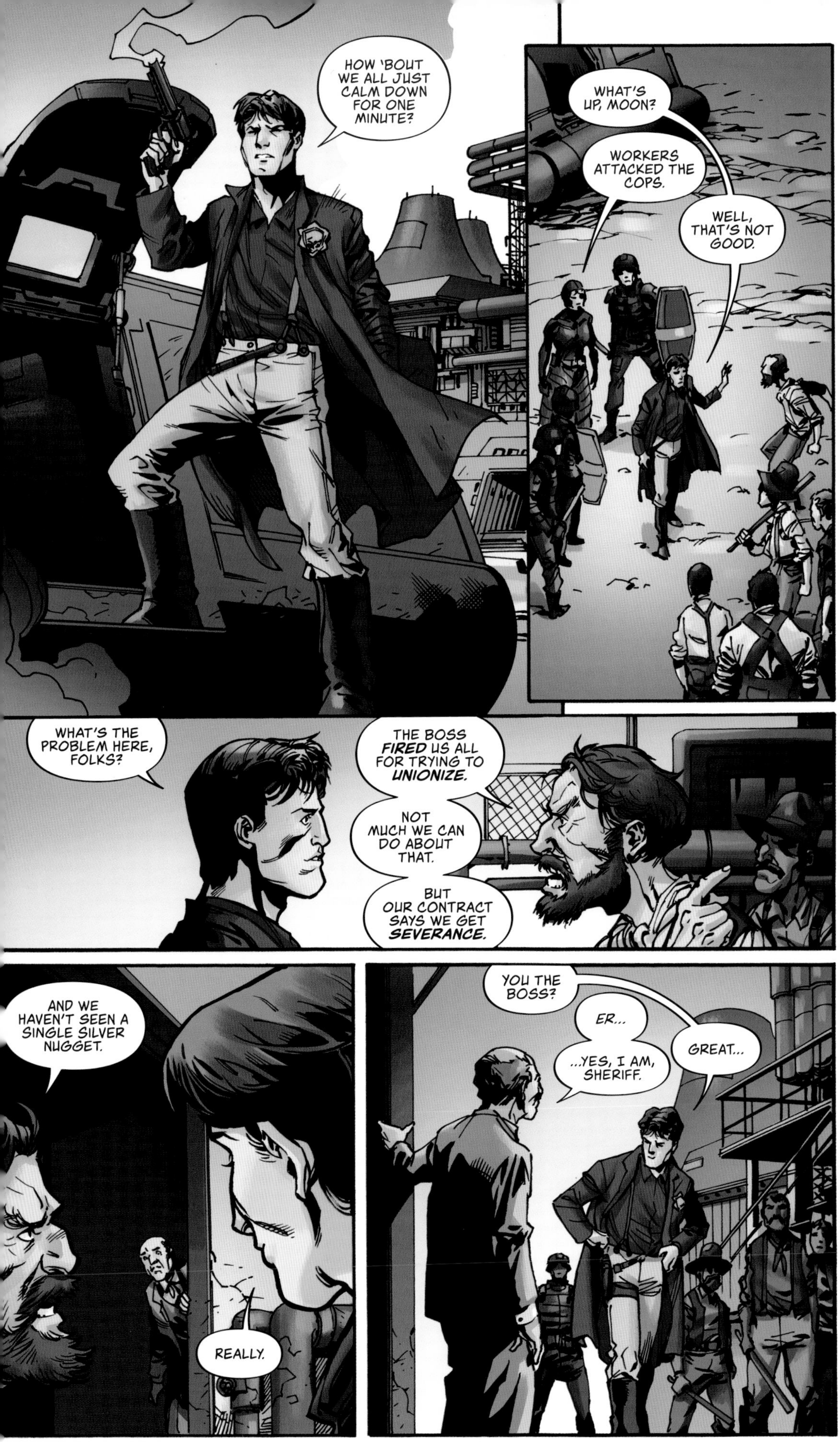
HOW 'BOUT WE ALL JUST CALM DOWN FOR ONE MINUTE?
WHAT'S UP, MOON?
WORKERS ATTACKED THE COPS.
WELL, THAT'S NOT GOOD.
WHAT'S THE PROBLEM HERE, FOLKS?
THE BOSS FIRED US ALL FOR TRYING TO UNIONIZE.
NOT MUCH WE CAN DO ABOUT THAT.
BUT OUR CONTRACT SAYS WE GET SEVERANCE.
AND WE HAVEN'T SEEN A SINGLE SILVER NUGGET.
REALLY.
YOU THE BOSS?
ER...
...YES, I AM, SHERIFF.
GREAT...

...LOOKS LIKE WE GOT THE RIGHT MAN TO FIX ALL OUR PROBLEMS, THEN.

HA HA, YES, AND THAT WOULD BE *YOU*, SHERIFF!

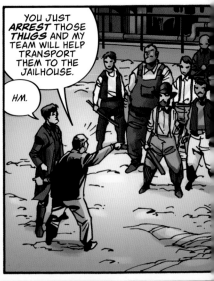

YOU JUST *ARREST* THOSE *THUGS* AND MY TEAM WILL HELP TRANSPORT THEM TO THE JAILHOUSE.

HM.

I DON'T THINK SO.

PARDON ME?

HERE'S WHAT'S GONNA HAPPEN...

...YOU'RE GONNA GO IN YOUR OFFICE AND FIND WHATEVER *CASH* YOU GOT SQUIRRELED AWAY...

...AND THEN YOU'RE GONNA COME BACK OUT HERE AND PAY THESE WORKERS WHAT YOU OWE THEM.

I-I WILL DO NO SUCH THING!

I DON'T KNOW WHAT THEY TOLD YOU, BUT I RUN A *CLEAN HOUSE*!

I DON'T OWE THEM A *THING*!

WELL, IF THAT'S THE CASE, MAYBE *I'LL* GO IN YOUR OFFICE AND GO THROUGH YOUR *BOOKS* LINE BY LINE AND SEE JUST HOW *CLEAN* YOUR HOUSE REALLY *IS*.

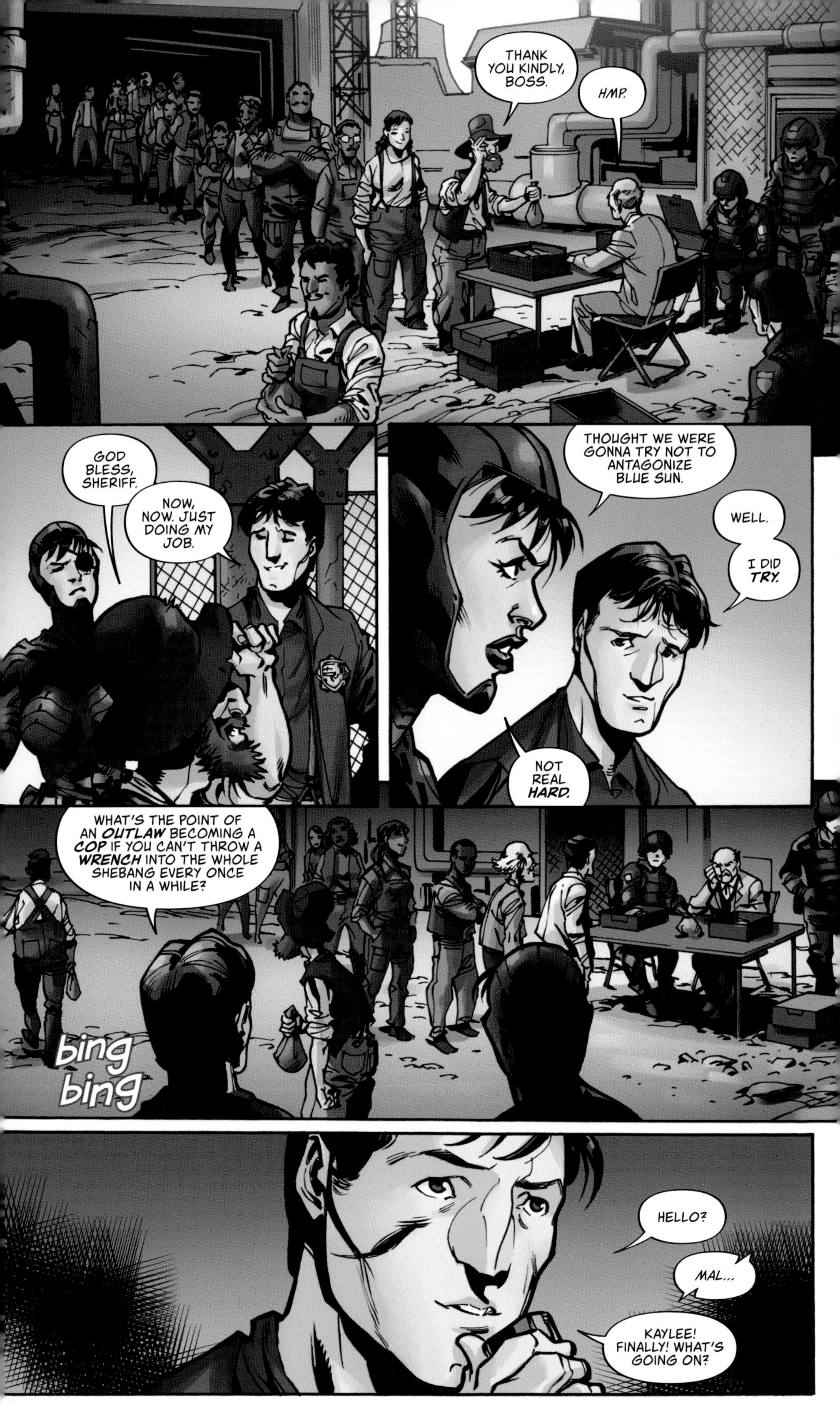
THANK YOU KINDLY, BOSS.
HMP.
GOD BLESS, SHERIFF.
NOW, NOW. JUST DOING MY JOB.
THOUGHT WE WERE GONNA TRY NOT TO ANTAGONIZE BLUE SUN.
WELL.
I DID TRY.
NOT REAL HARD.
WHAT'S THE POINT OF AN OUTLAW BECOMING A COP IF YOU CAN'T THROW A WRENCH INTO THE WHOLE SHEBANG EVERY ONCE IN A WHILE?
bing bing
HELLO?
MAL...
KAYLEE! FINALLY! WHAT'S GOING ON?

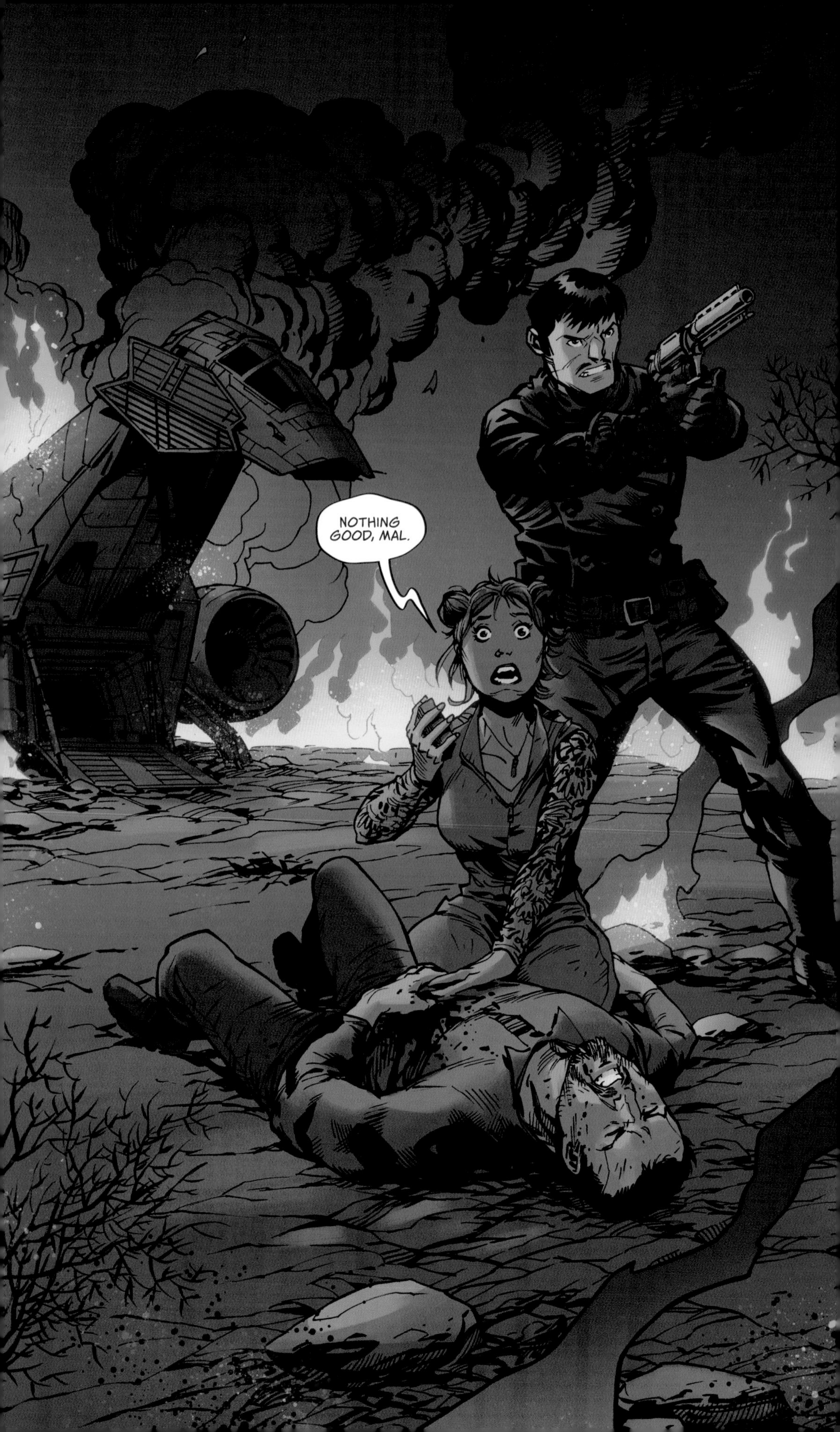
NOTHING GOOD, MAL.

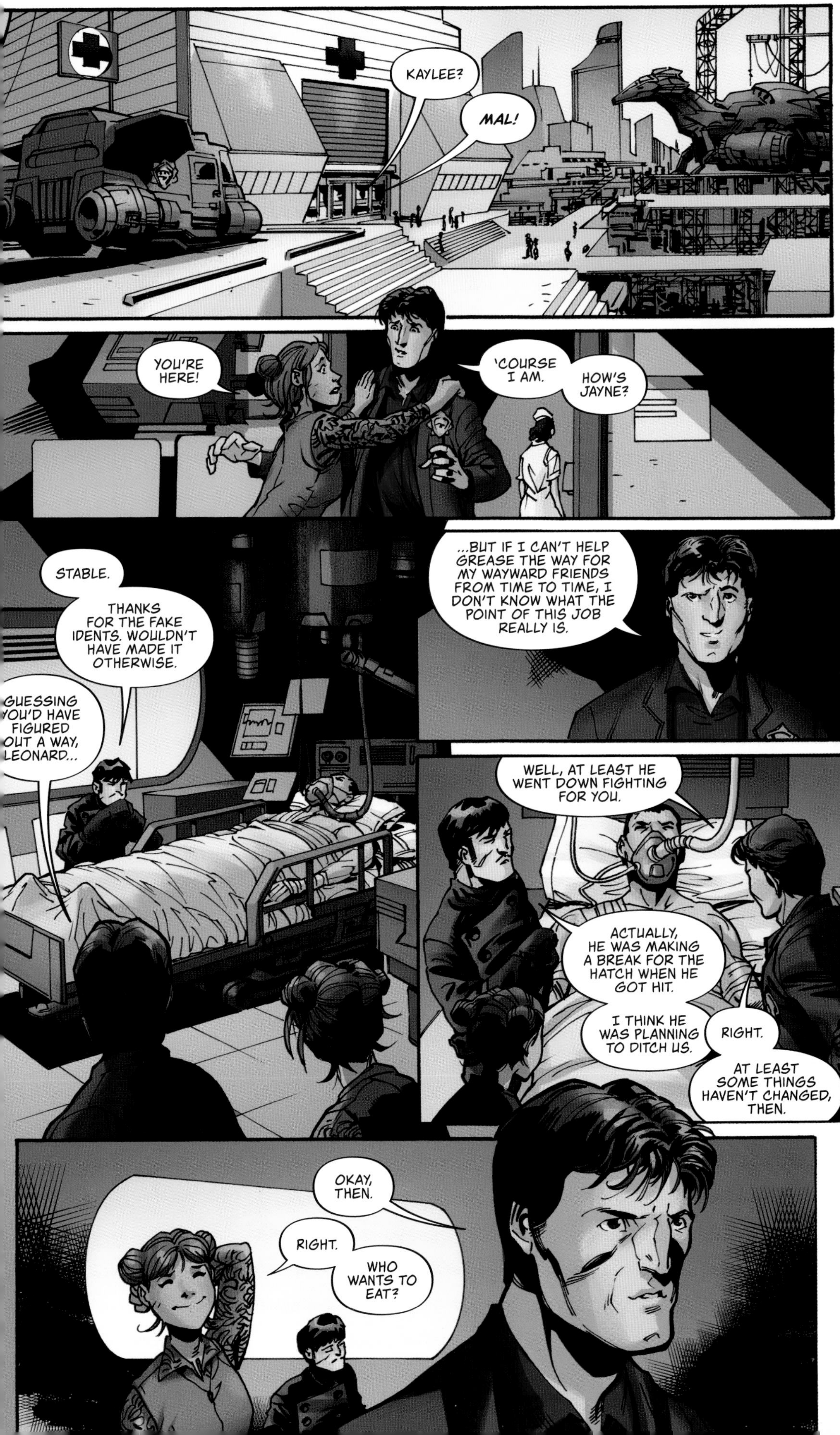

KAYLEE?
MAL!
YOU'RE HERE!
'COURSE I AM.
HOW'S JAYNE?
STABLE.
THANKS FOR THE FAKE IDENTS. WOULDN'T HAVE MADE IT OTHERWISE.
GUESSING YOU'D HAVE FIGURED OUT A WAY, LEONARD...
...BUT IF I CAN'T HELP GREASE THE WAY FOR MY WAYWARD FRIENDS FROM TIME TO TIME, I DON'T KNOW WHAT THE POINT OF THIS JOB REALLY IS.
WELL, AT LEAST HE WENT DOWN FIGHTING FOR YOU.
ACTUALLY, HE WAS MAKING A BREAK FOR THE HATCH WHEN HE GOT HIT.
I THINK HE WAS PLANNING TO DITCH US.
RIGHT.
AT LEAST SOME THINGS HAVEN'T CHANGED, THEN.
OKAY, THEN.
RIGHT.
WHO WANTS TO EAT?

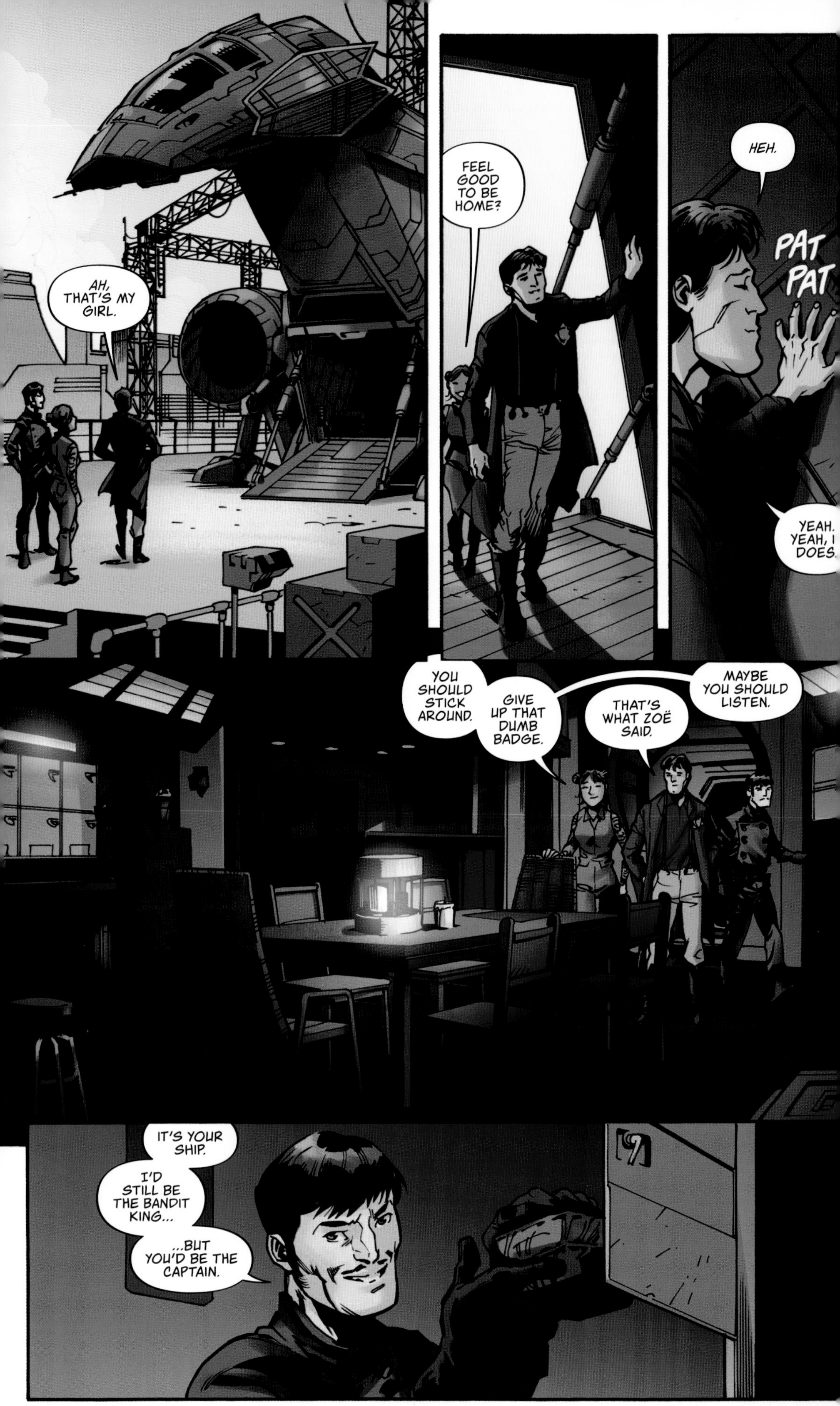
AH, THAT'S MY GIRL.
FEEL GOOD TO BE HOME?
HEH.
PAT PAT
YEAH. YEAH, I DOES.
YOU SHOULD STICK AROUND.
GIVE UP THAT DUMB BADGE.
THAT'S WHAT ZOË SAID.
MAYBE YOU SHOULD LISTEN.
IT'S YOUR SHIP.
I'D STILL BE THE BANDIT KING...
...BUT YOU'D BE THE CAPTAIN.

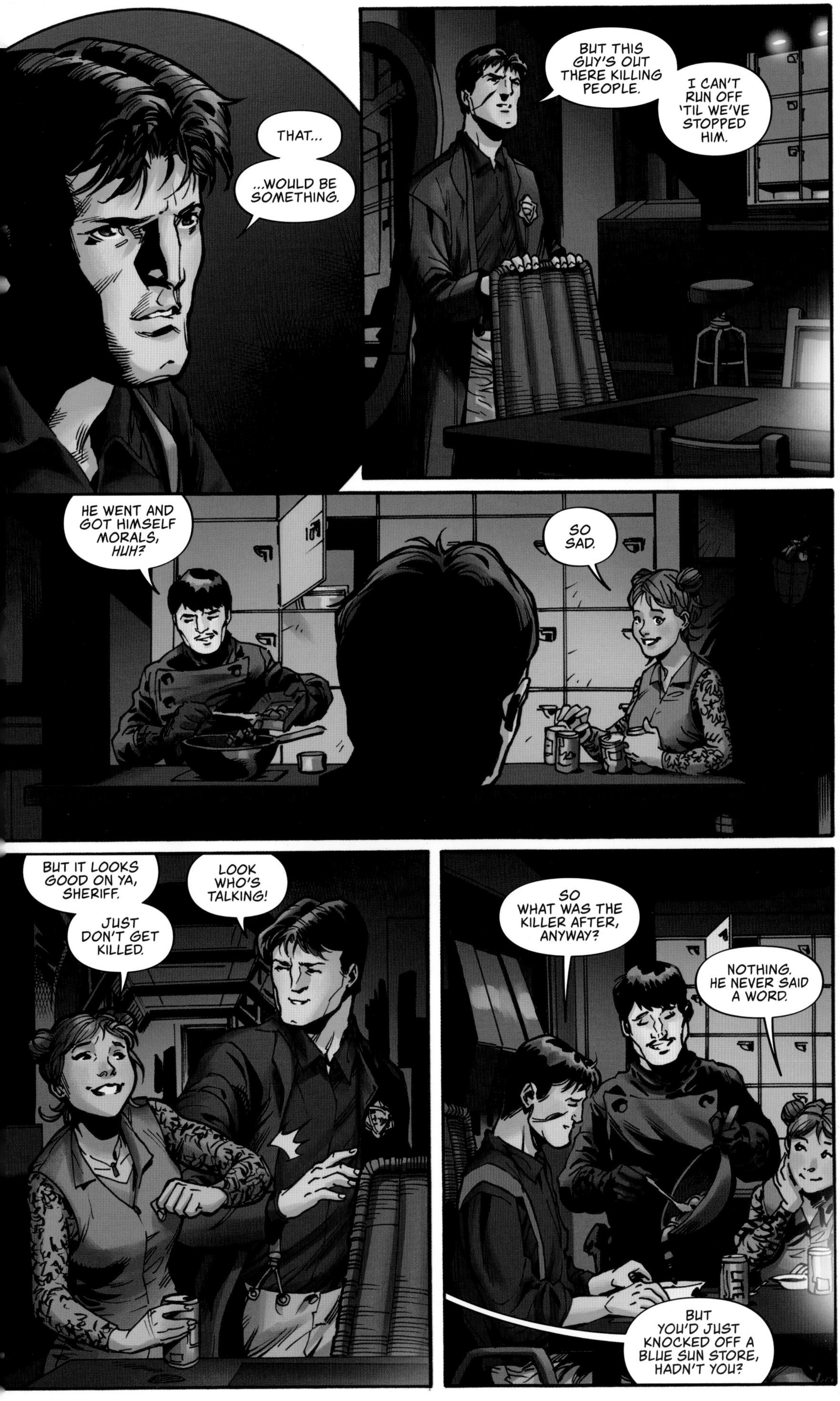
THAT...
...WOULD BE SOMETHING.
BUT THIS GUY'S OUT THERE KILLING PEOPLE.
I CAN'T RUN OFF 'TIL WE'VE STOPPED HIM.
HE WENT AND GOT HIMSELF MORALS, *HUH?*
SO SAD.
BUT IT LOOKS GOOD ON YA, SHERIFF.
JUST DON'T GET KILLED.
LOOK WHO'S TALKING!
SO WHAT WAS THE KILLER AFTER, ANYWAY?
NOTHING. HE NEVER SAID A WORD.
BUT YOU'D JUST KNOCKED OFF A BLUE SUN STORE, HADN'T YOU?

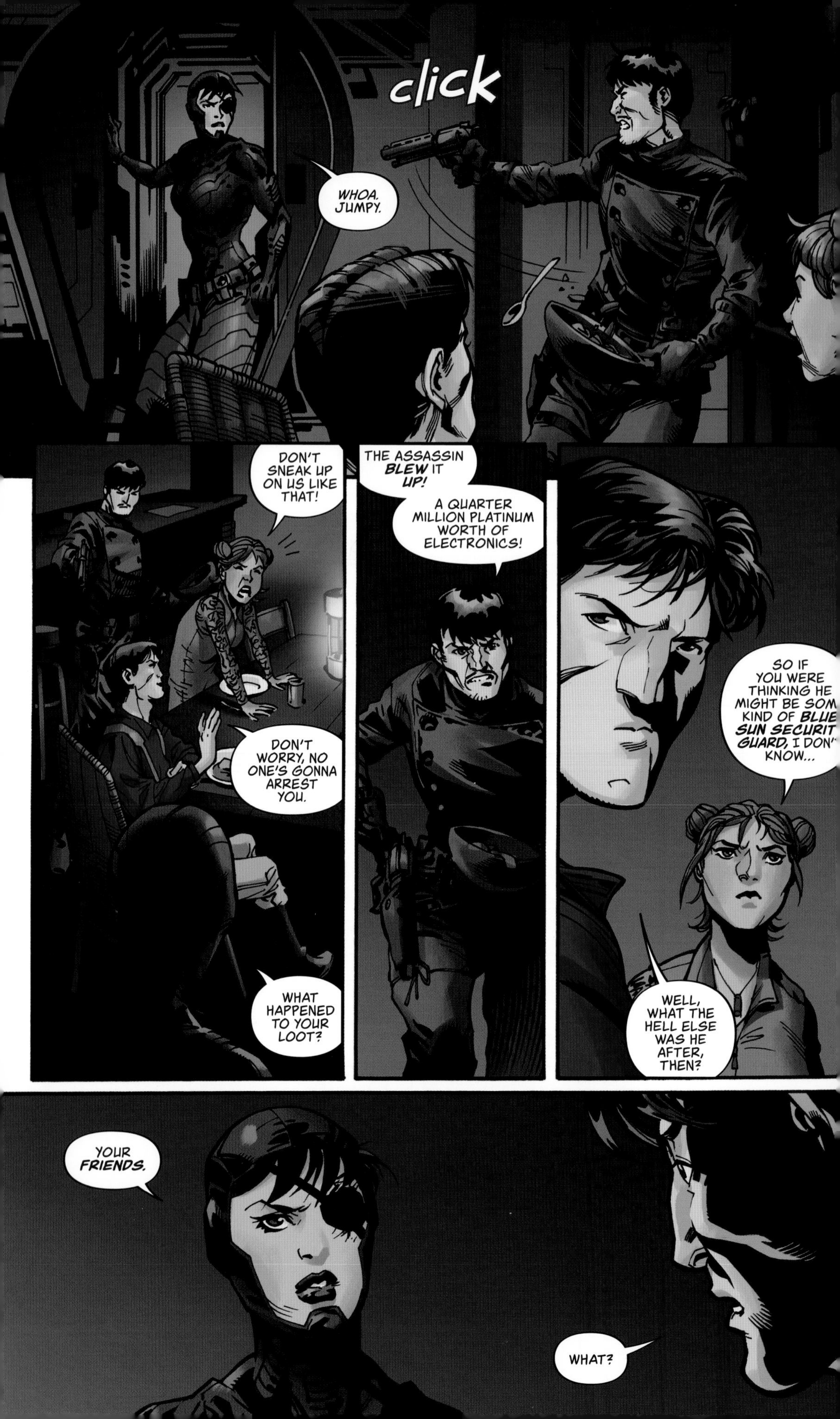
click
WHOA. JUMPY.
DON'T SNEAK UP ON US LIKE THAT!
DON'T WORRY, NO ONE'S GONNA ARREST YOU.
WHAT HAPPENED TO YOUR LOOT?
THE ASSASSIN BLEW IT UP!
A QUARTER MILLION PLATINUM WORTH OF ELECTRONICS!
SO IF YOU WERE THINKING HE MIGHT BE SOM KIND OF BLUE SUN SECURIT GUARD, I DON' KNOW...
WELL, WHAT THE HELL ELSE WAS HE AFTER, THEN?
YOUR FRIENDS.
WHAT?

THEY'RE YOUR FRIENDS. I DON'T KNOW HOW HE FOUND OUT.

BUT THAT'S THE ONLY OBVIOUS CONNECTION HERE.

YOU THINK...

...YOU THINK THIS IS ABOUT *ME?*

*OU'VE BEEN AKING THINGS A LOT EVER SINCE YOU BECAME SHERIFF...

AND EVER SINCE WAY *BEFORE* THEN.

...PROBABLY GOT A LOT OF ENEMIES OUT THERE.

BUT HE HAD THE CHANCE TO KILL ME! AND HE DIDN'T!

AND WHAT ABOUT THE OTHER PEOPLE HE'S BEEN KILLING? I MEAN, WHAT'S THE POINT?

MAYBE... HE'S JUST CRAZY.

I DUNNO. I'VE NEVER SEEN A CRAZY PERSON THIS *ORGANIZED.*

YOU'VE NEVER BEEN A *SHERIFF* BEFORE.

YOU'RE POKING *BIGGER BEARS* NOW...

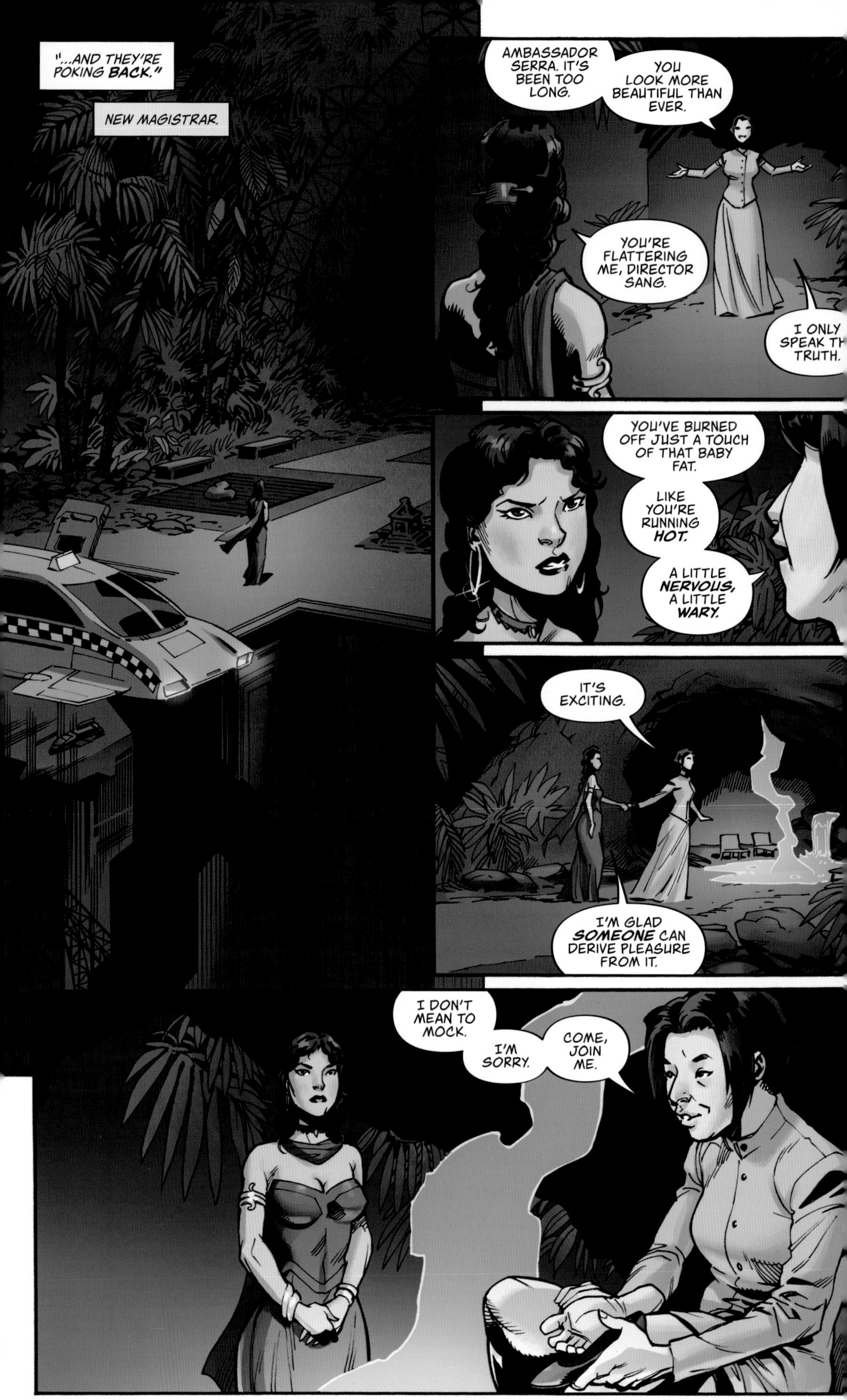
"...AND THEY'RE POKING **BACK.**"
NEW MAGISTRAR.
AMBASSADOR SERRA. IT'S BEEN TOO LONG.
YOU LOOK MORE BEAUTIFUL THAN EVER.
YOU'RE FLATTERING ME, DIRECTOR SANG.
I ONLY SPEAK TH TRUTH.
YOU'VE BURNED OFF JUST A TOUCH OF THAT BABY FAT.
LIKE YOU'RE RUNNING **HOT.**
A LITTLE **NERVOUS,** A LITTLE **WARY.**
IT'S EXCITING.
I'M GLAD **SOMEONE** CAN DERIVE PLEASURE FROM IT.
I DON'T MEAN TO MOCK.
I'M SORRY.
COME, JOIN ME.

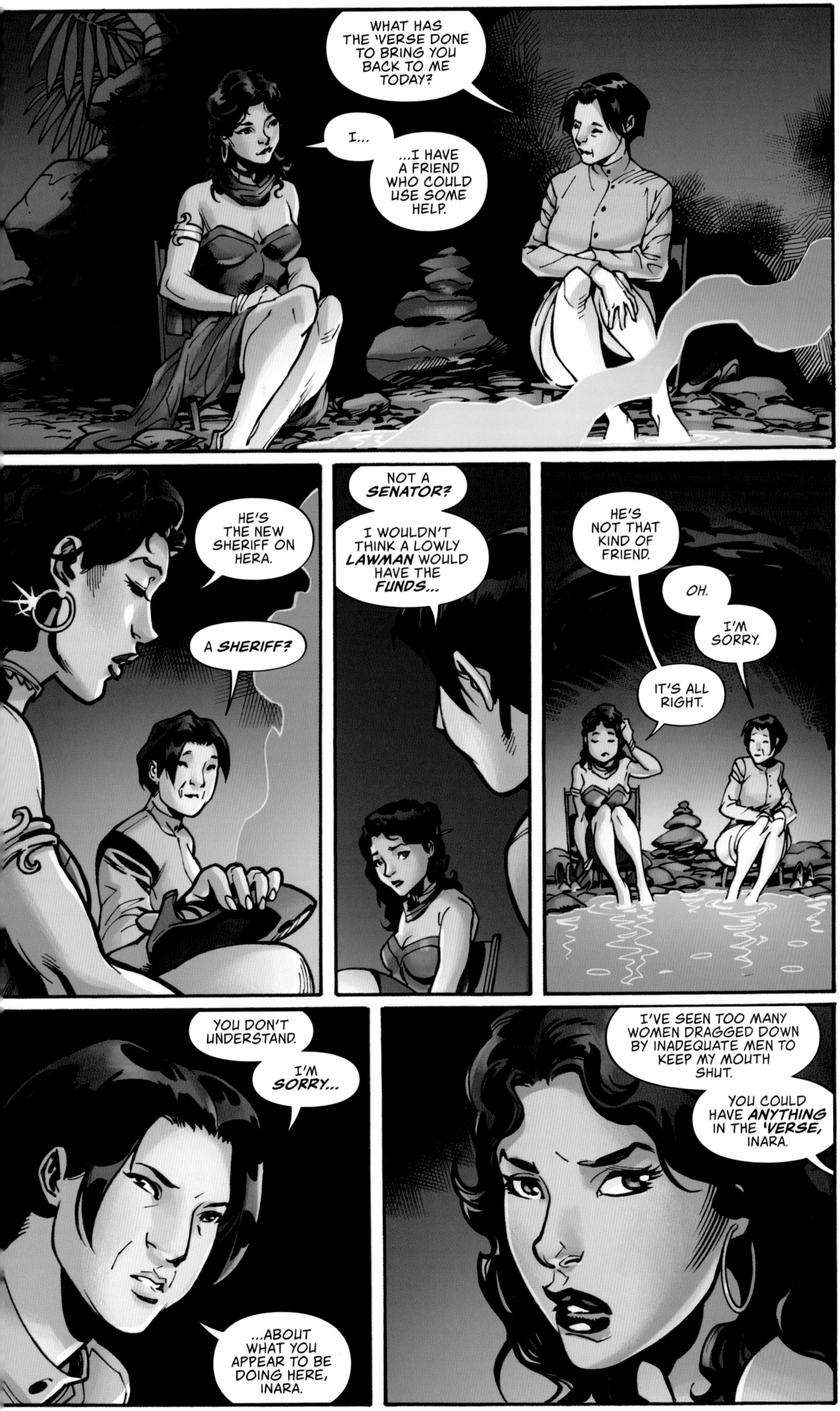

WHAT HAS THE 'VERSE DONE TO BRING YOU BACK TO ME TODAY?
I...
...I HAVE A FRIEND WHO COULD USE SOME HELP.
HE'S THE NEW SHERIFF ON HERA.
A SHERIFF?
NOT A SENATOR?
I WOULDN'T THINK A LOWLY LAWMAN WOULD HAVE THE FUNDS...
HE'S NOT THAT KIND OF FRIEND.
OH.
I'M SORRY.
IT'S ALL RIGHT.
YOU DON'T UNDERSTAND.
I'M SORRY...
...ABOUT WHAT YOU APPEAR TO BE DOING HERE, INARA.
I'VE SEEN TOO MANY WOMEN DRAGGED DOWN BY INADEQUATE MEN TO KEEP MY MOUTH SHUT.
YOU COULD HAVE ANYTHING IN THE 'VERSE, INARA.

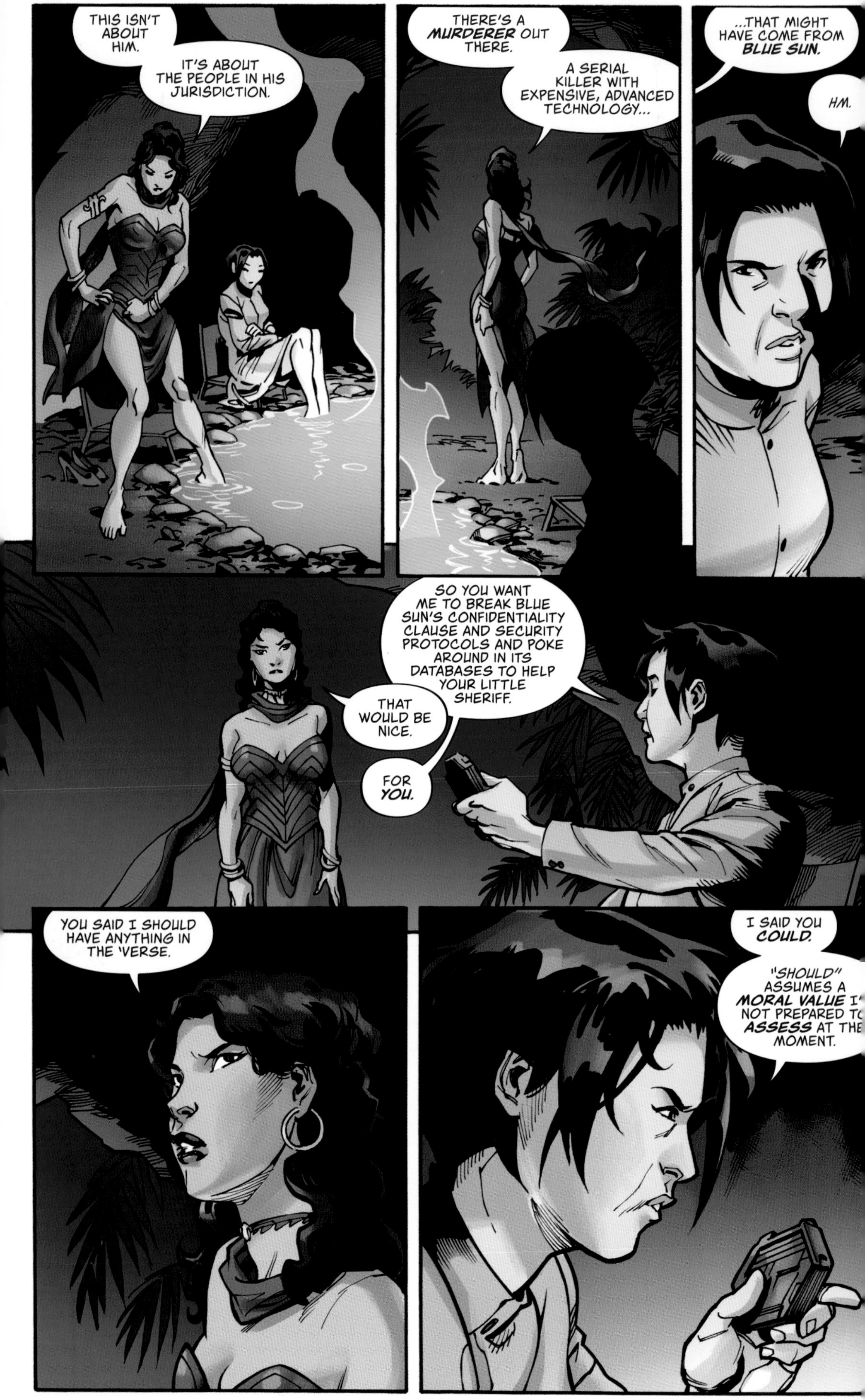

THIS ISN'T ABOUT HIM.
IT'S ABOUT THE PEOPLE IN HIS JURISDICTION.
THERE'S A MURDERER OUT THERE.
A SERIAL KILLER WITH EXPENSIVE, ADVANCED TECHNOLOGY...
...THAT MIGHT HAVE COME FROM BLUE SUN.
HM.
SO YOU WANT ME TO BREAK BLUE SUN'S CONFIDENTIALITY CLAUSE AND SECURITY PROTOCOLS AND POKE AROUND IN ITS DATABASES TO HELP YOUR LITTLE SHERIFF.
THAT WOULD BE NICE.
FOR YOU.
YOU SAID I SHOULD HAVE ANYTHING IN THE 'VERSE.
I SAID YOU COULD.

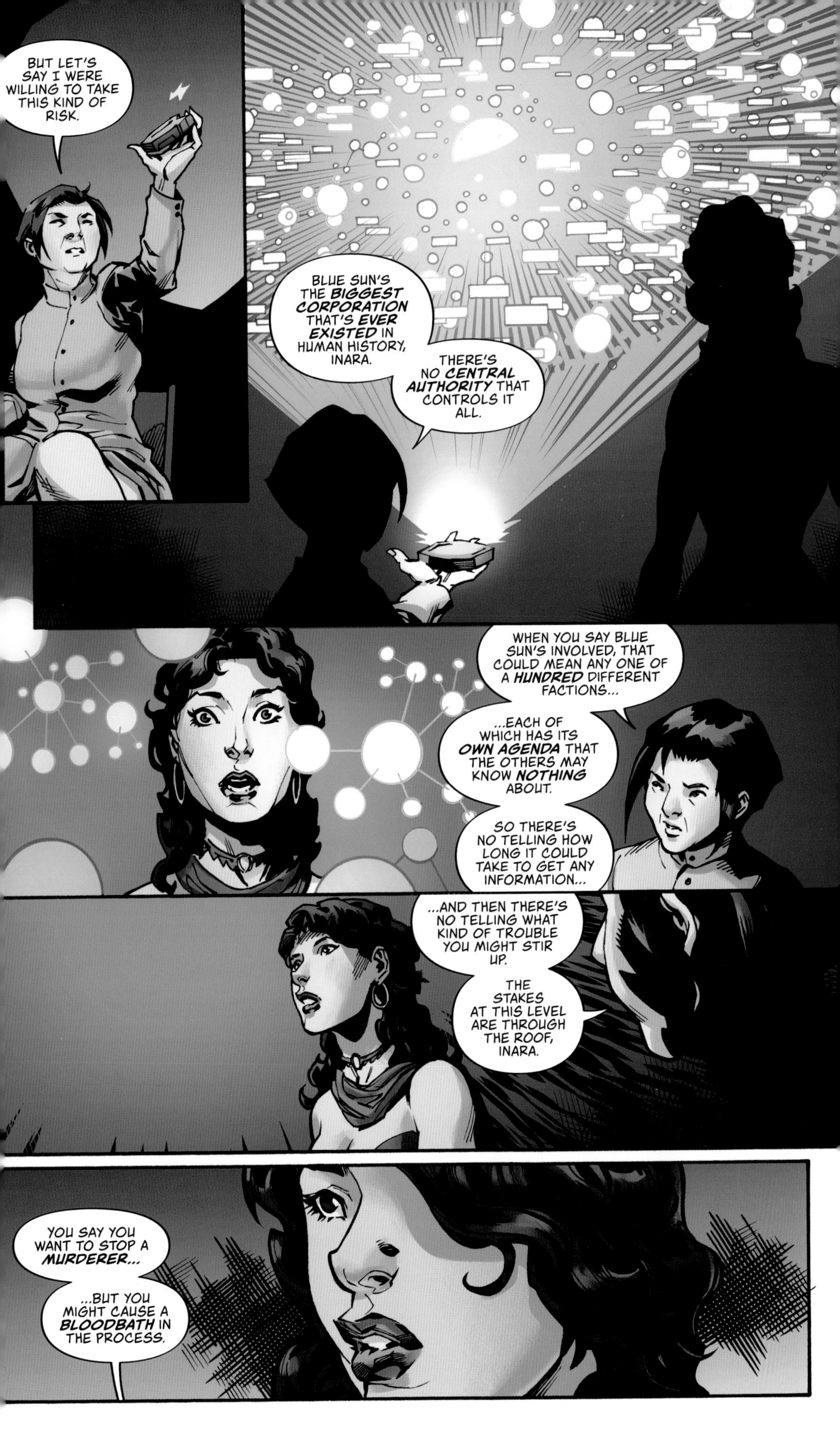
BUT LET'S SAY I WERE WILLING TO TAKE THIS KIND OF RISK.
BLUE SUN'S THE BIGGEST CORPORATION THAT'S EVER EXISTED IN HUMAN HISTORY, INARA.
THERE'S NO CENTRAL AUTHORITY THAT CONTROLS IT ALL.
WHEN YOU SAY BLUE SUN'S INVOLVED, THAT COULD MEAN ANY ONE OF A HUNDRED DIFFERENT FACTIONS...
...EACH OF WHICH HAS ITS OWN AGENDA THAT THE OTHERS MAY KNOW NOTHING ABOUT.
SO THERE'S NO TELLING HOW LONG IT COULD TAKE TO GET ANY INFORMATION...
...AND THEN THERE'S NO TELLING WHAT KIND OF TROUBLE YOU MIGHT STIR UP.
THE STAKES AT THIS LEVEL ARE THROUGH THE ROOF, INARA.
YOU SAY YOU WANT TO STOP A MURDERER...
...BUT YOU MIGHT CAUSE A BLOODBATH IN THE PROCESS.

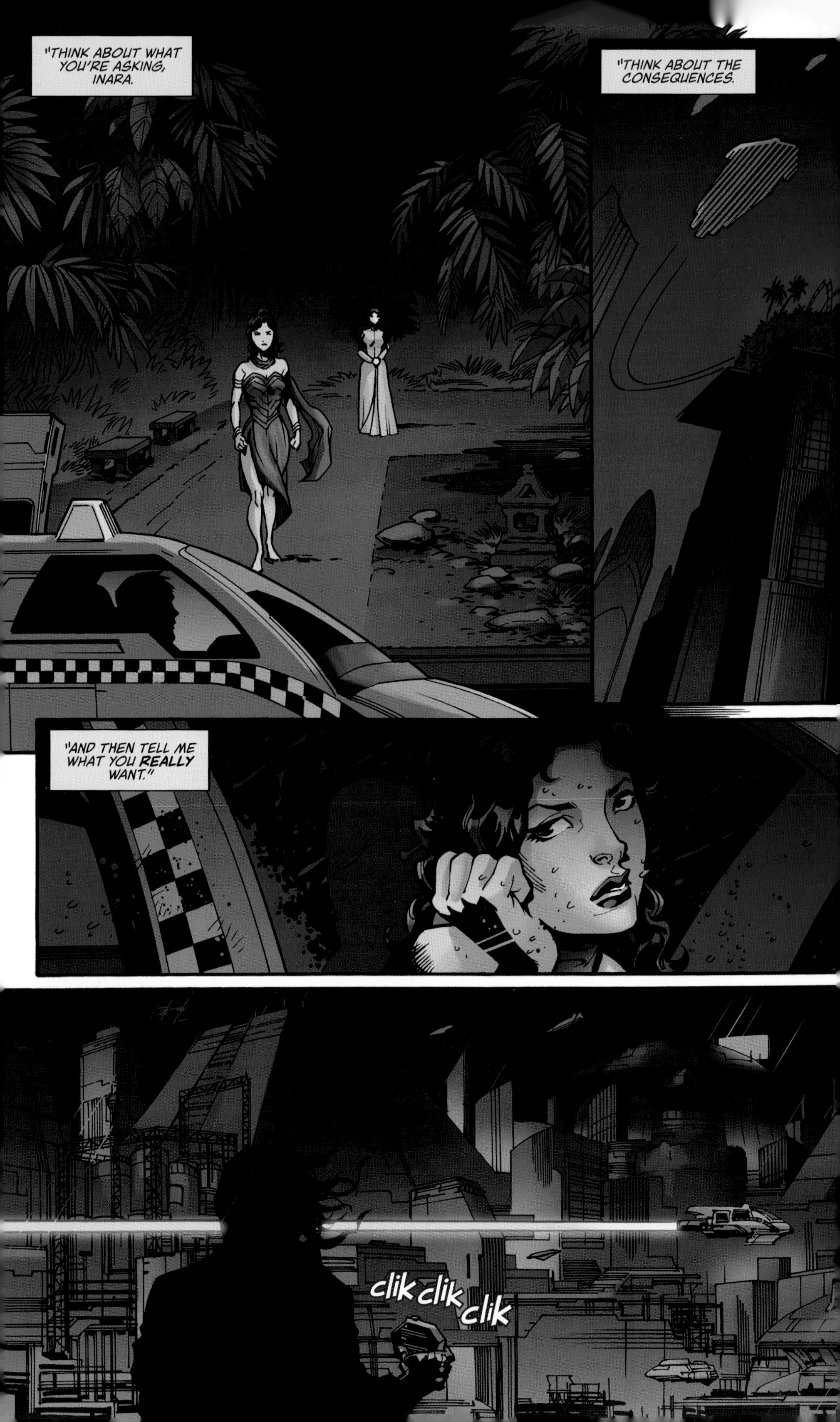
"THINK ABOUT WHAT YOU'RE ASKING, INARA.
"THINK ABOUT THE CONSEQUENCES.
"AND THEN TELL ME WHAT YOU REALLY WANT."
clik clik clik

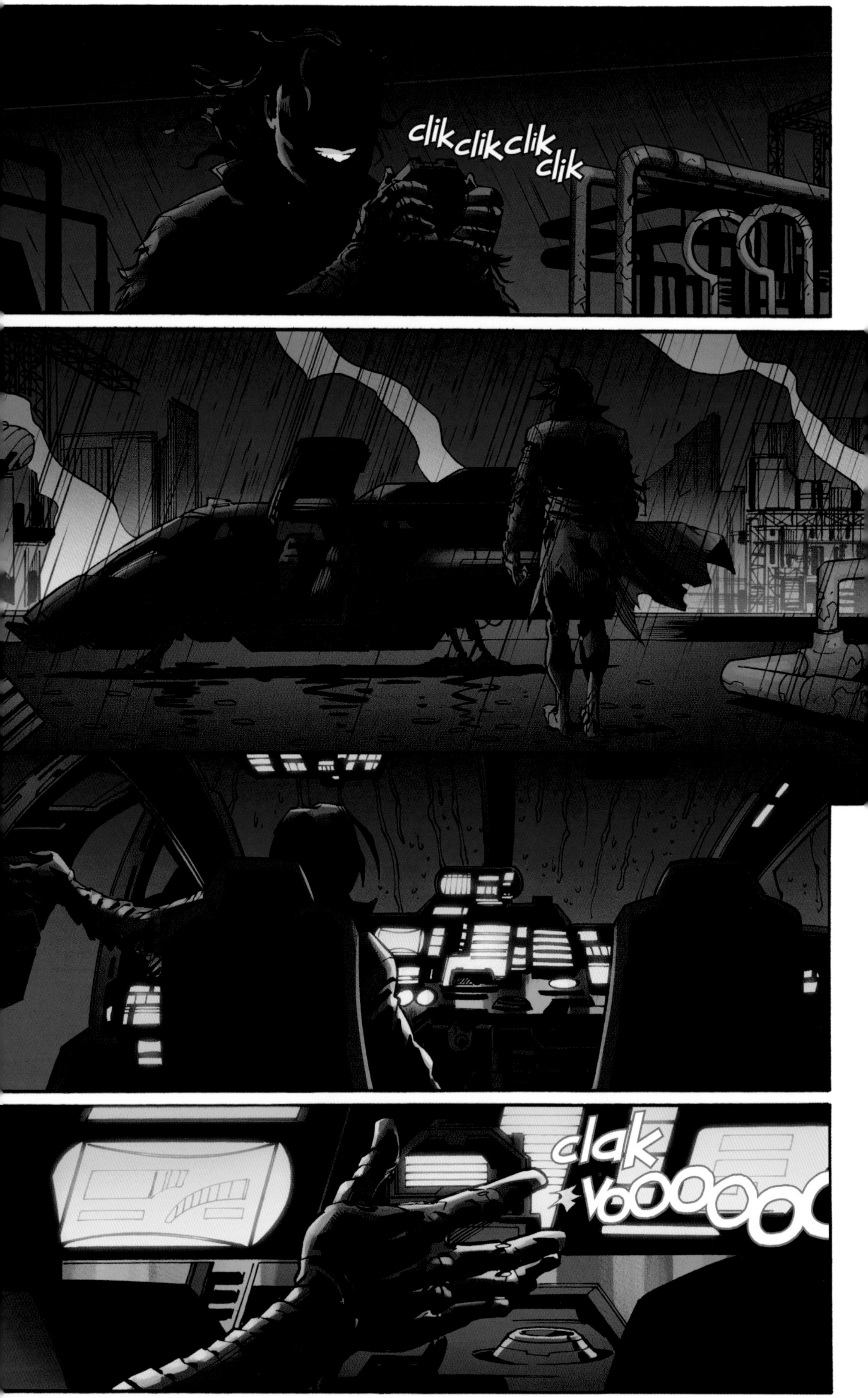
clikclikclik
clik
clak
VOOOOOO

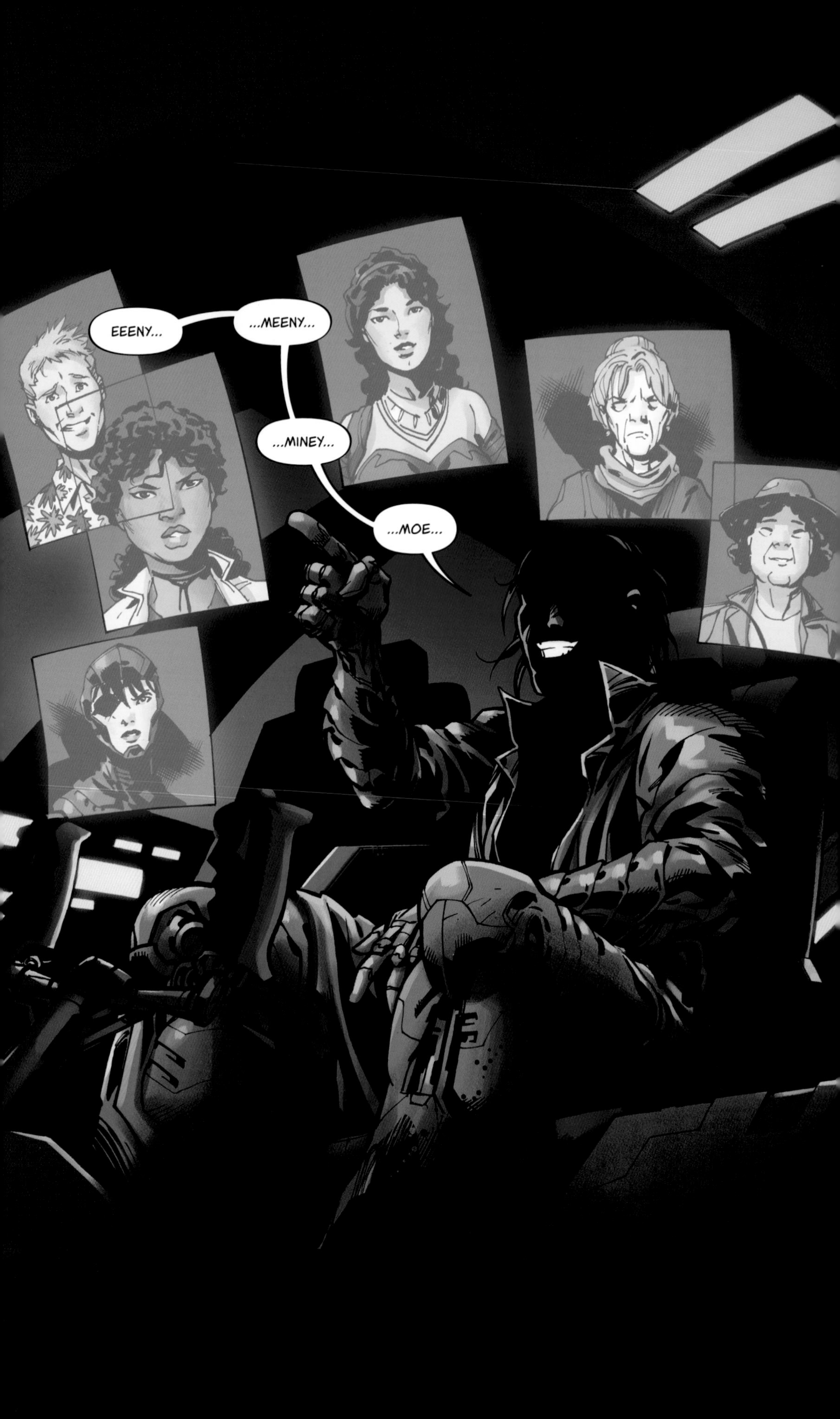
EEENY...
...MEENY...
...MINEY...
...MOE...

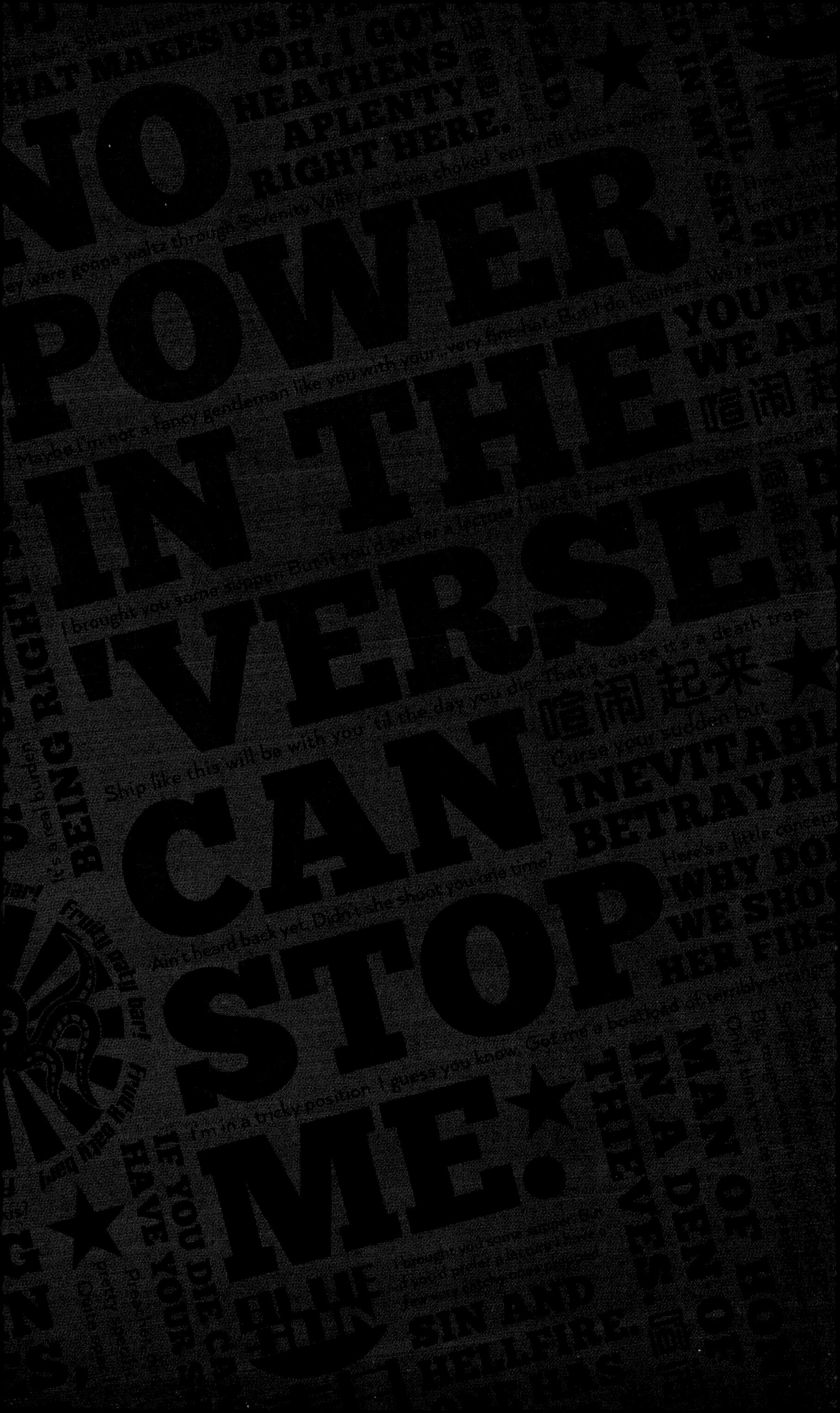
NO POWER IN THE 'VERSE CAN STOP ME.
OH, I GOT HEATHENS APLENTY RIGHT HERE.
INEVITABL BETRAYAL
SIN AND HELLFIRE
喧闹起来

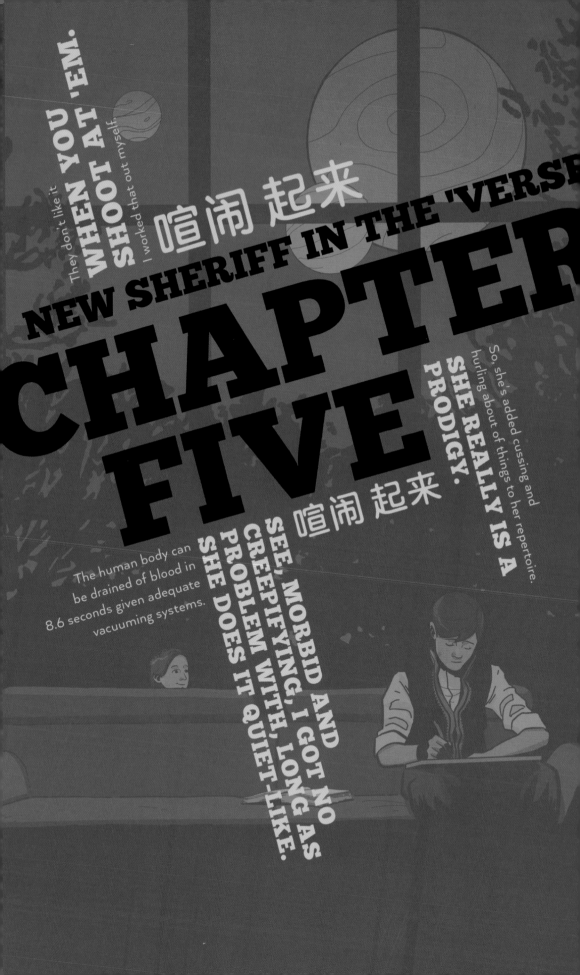

They don't like it
WHEN YOU
SHOOT AT 'EM.
I worked that out myself.

喧闹 起来

NEW SHERIFF IN THE 'VERSE

CHAPTER FIVE

So, she's added cussing and
hurling about of things to her repertoire.

SHE REALLY IS A
PRODIGY.

喧闹 起来

The human body can
be drained of blood in
8.6 seconds given adequate
vacuuming systems.

SEE, MORBID AND
CREEPIFYING, I GOT NO
PROBLEM WITH, LONG AS
SHE DOES IT QUIET-LIKE.

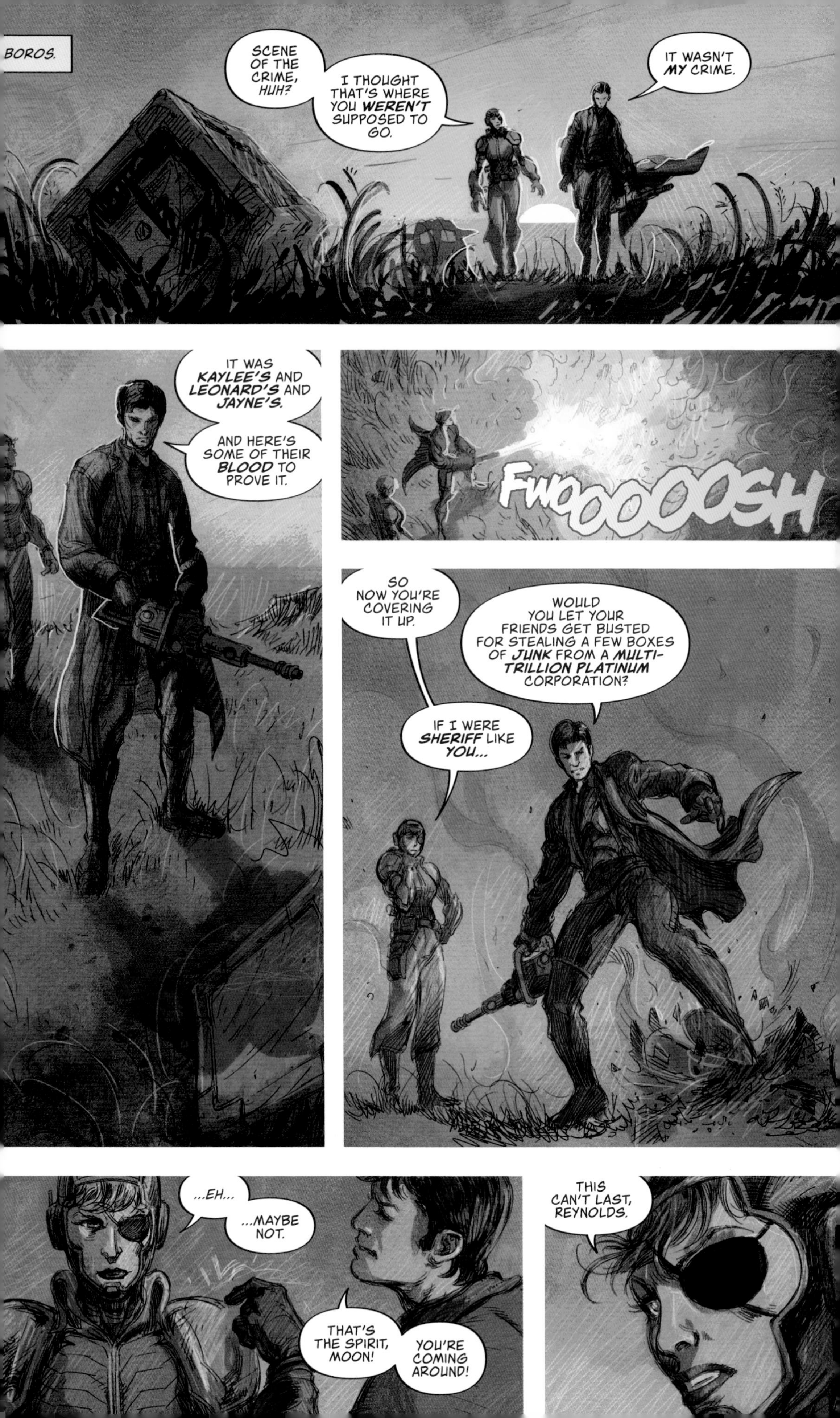
BOROS.
SCENE OF THE CRIME, HUH?
I THOUGHT THAT'S WHERE YOU WEREN'T SUPPOSED TO GO.
IT WASN'T MY CRIME.
IT WAS KAYLEE'S AND LEONARD'S AND JAYNE'S.
AND HERE'S SOME OF THEIR BLOOD TO PROVE IT.
FWOOOOOOSH
SO NOW YOU'RE COVERING IT UP.
WOULD YOU LET YOUR FRIENDS GET BUSTED FOR STEALING A FEW BOXES OF JUNK FROM A MULTI-TRILLION PLATINUM CORPORATION?
IF I WERE SHERIFF LIKE YOU...
...EH...
...MAYBE NOT.
THAT'S THE SPIRIT, MOON!
YOU'RE COMING AROUND!
THIS CAN'T LAST, REYNOLDS.

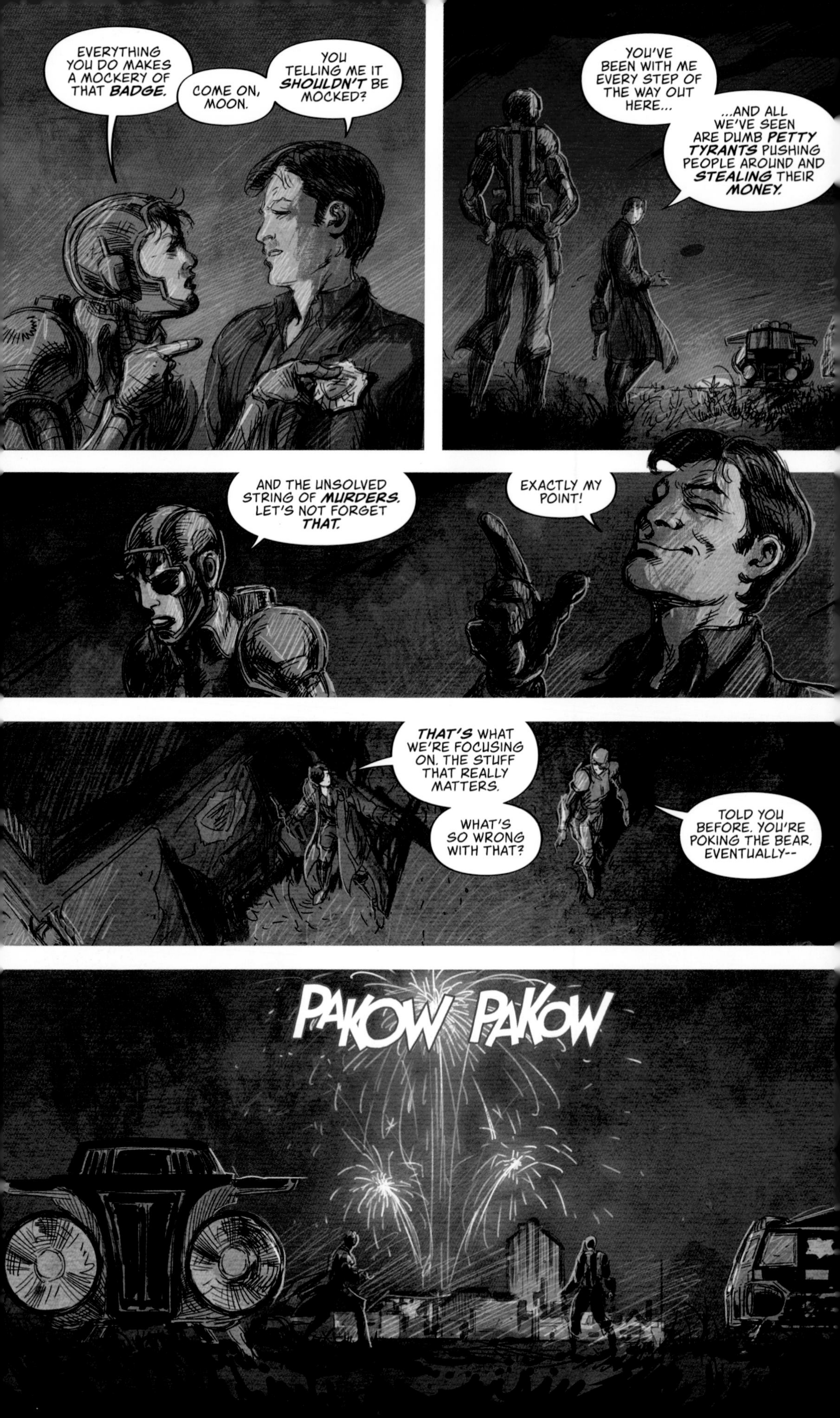
EVERYTHING YOU DO MAKES A MOCKERY OF THAT BADGE.
COME ON, MOON.
YOU TELLING ME IT SHOULDN'T BE MOCKED?
YOU'VE BEEN WITH ME EVERY STEP OF THE WAY OUT HERE...
...AND ALL WE'VE SEEN ARE DUMB PETTY TYRANTS PUSHING PEOPLE AROUND AND STEALING THEIR MONEY.
AND THE UNSOLVED STRING OF MURDERS. LET'S NOT FORGET THAT.
EXACTLY MY POINT!
THAT'S WHAT WE'RE FOCUSING ON. THE STUFF THAT REALLY MATTERS.
WHAT'S SO WRONG WITH THAT?
TOLD YOU BEFORE. YOU'RE POKING THE BEAR. EVENTUALLY--
PAKOW PAKOW

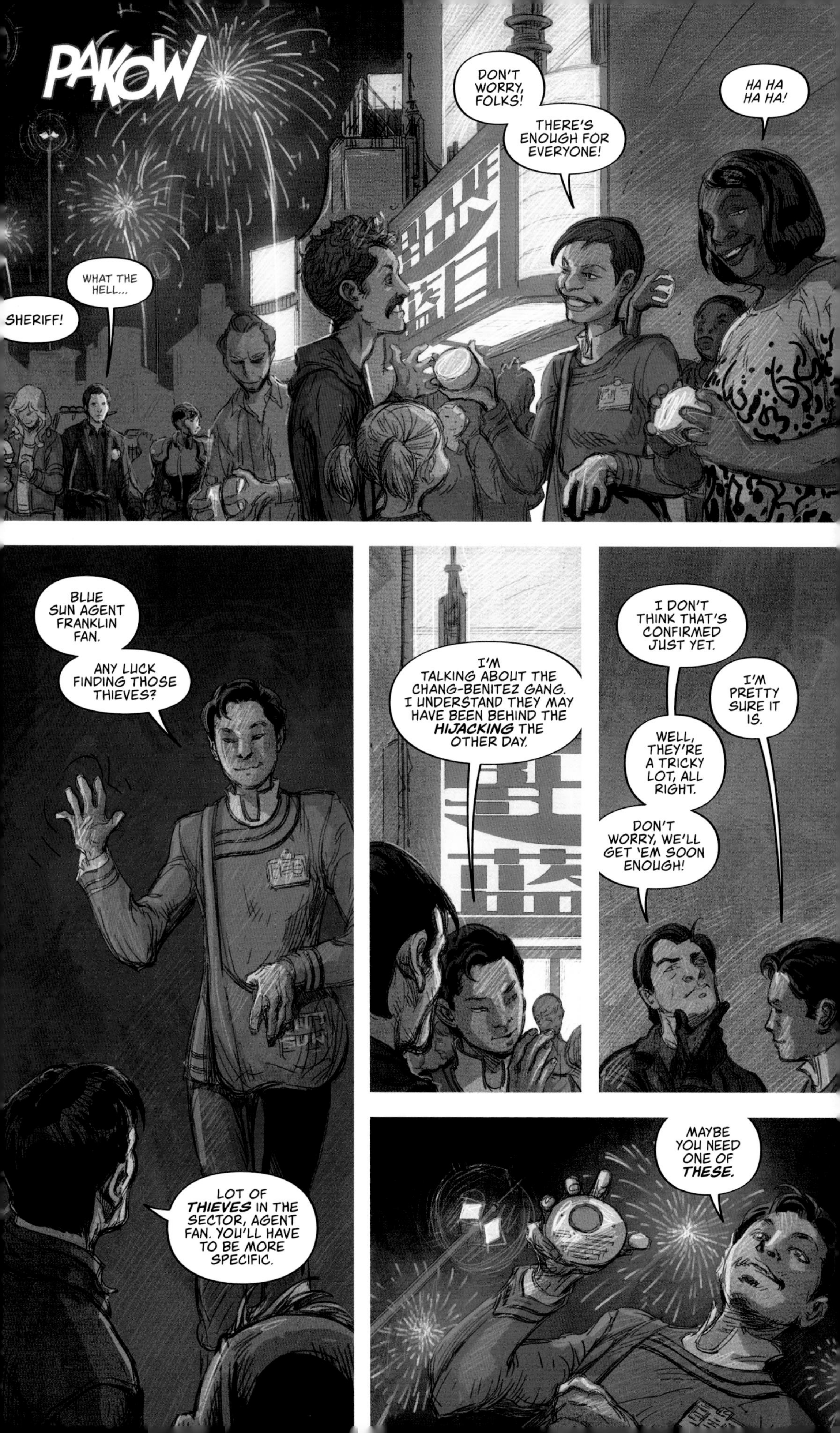
PAKOW
DON'T WORRY, FOLKS!
THERE'S ENOUGH FOR EVERYONE!
HA HA HA HA!
SHERIFF!
WHAT THE HELL...
BLUE SUN AGENT FRANKLIN FAN.
ANY LUCK FINDING THOSE THIEVES?
LOT OF *THIEVES* IN THE SECTOR, AGENT FAN. YOU'LL HAVE TO BE MORE SPECIFIC.
I'M TALKING ABOUT THE CHANG-BENITEZ GANG. I UNDERSTAND THEY MAY HAVE BEEN BEHIND THE *HIJACKING* THE OTHER DAY.
I DON'T THINK THAT'S CONFIRMED JUST YET.
I'M PRETTY SURE IT IS.
WELL, THEY'RE A TRICKY LOT, ALL RIGHT.
DON'T WORRY, WE'LL GET 'EM SOON ENOUGH!
MAYBE YOU NEED ONE OF *THESE.*

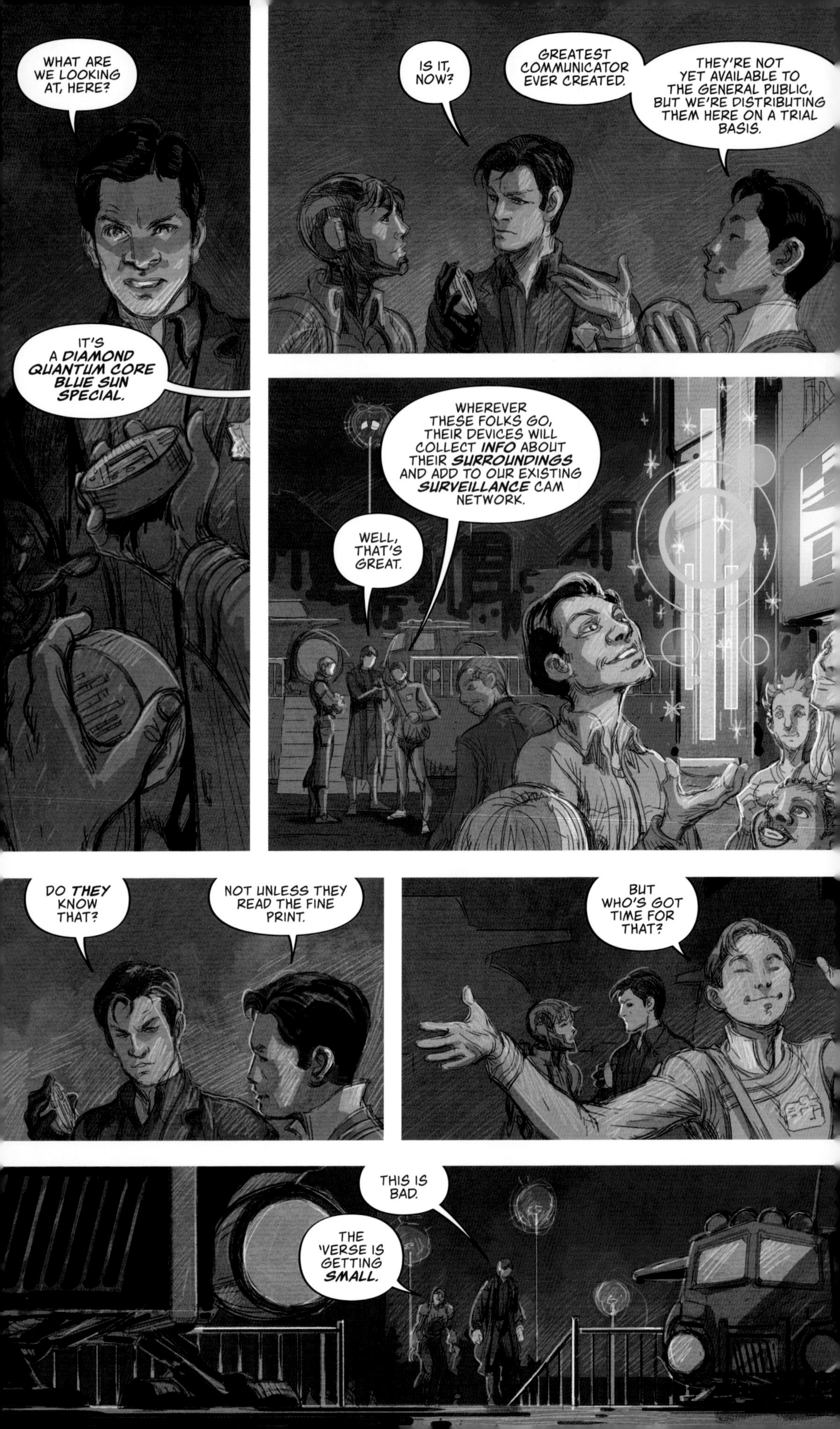
WHAT ARE WE LOOKING AT, HERE?
IS IT, NOW?
GREATEST COMMUNICATOR EVER CREATED.
THEY'RE NOT YET AVAILABLE TO THE GENERAL PUBLIC, BUT WE'RE DISTRIBUTING THEM HERE ON A TRIAL BASIS.
IT'S A *DIAMOND QUANTUM CORE BLUE SUN SPECIAL.*
WHEREVER THESE FOLKS GO, THEIR DEVICES WILL COLLECT *INFO* ABOUT THEIR *SURROUNDINGS* AND ADD TO OUR EXISTING *SURVEILLANCE* CAM NETWORK.
WELL, THAT'S GREAT.
DO *THEY* KNOW THAT?
NOT UNLESS THEY READ THE FINE PRINT.
BUT WHO'S GOT TIME FOR THAT?
THIS IS BAD.
THE 'VERSE IS GETTING *SMALL.*

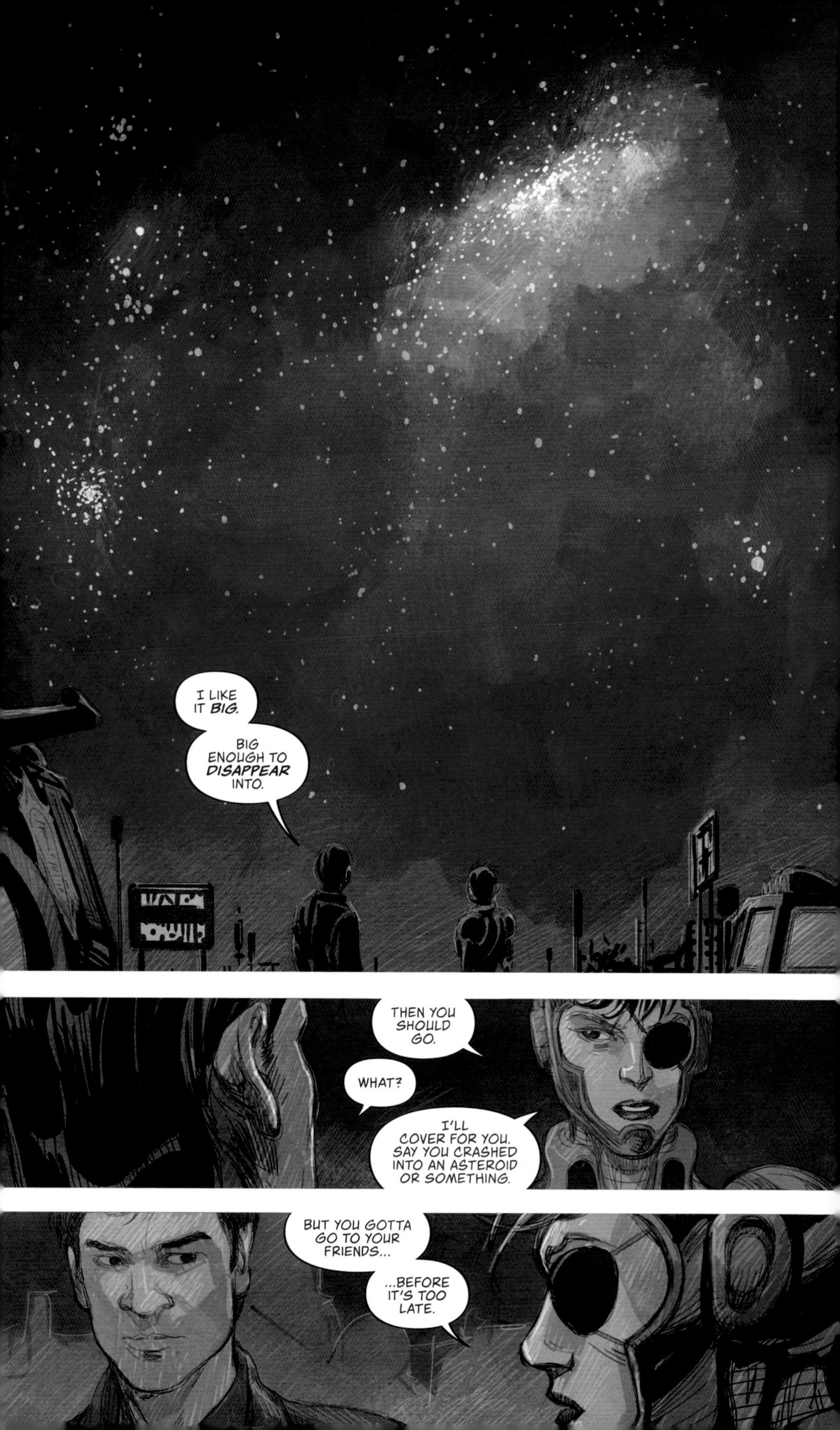
I LIKE IT BIG.
BIG ENOUGH TO DISAPPEAR INTO.
THEN YOU SHOULD GO.
WHAT?
I'LL COVER FOR YOU. SAY YOU CRASHED INTO AN ASTEROID OR SOMETHING.
BUT YOU GOTTA GO TO YOUR FRIENDS...
...BEFORE IT'S TOO LATE.

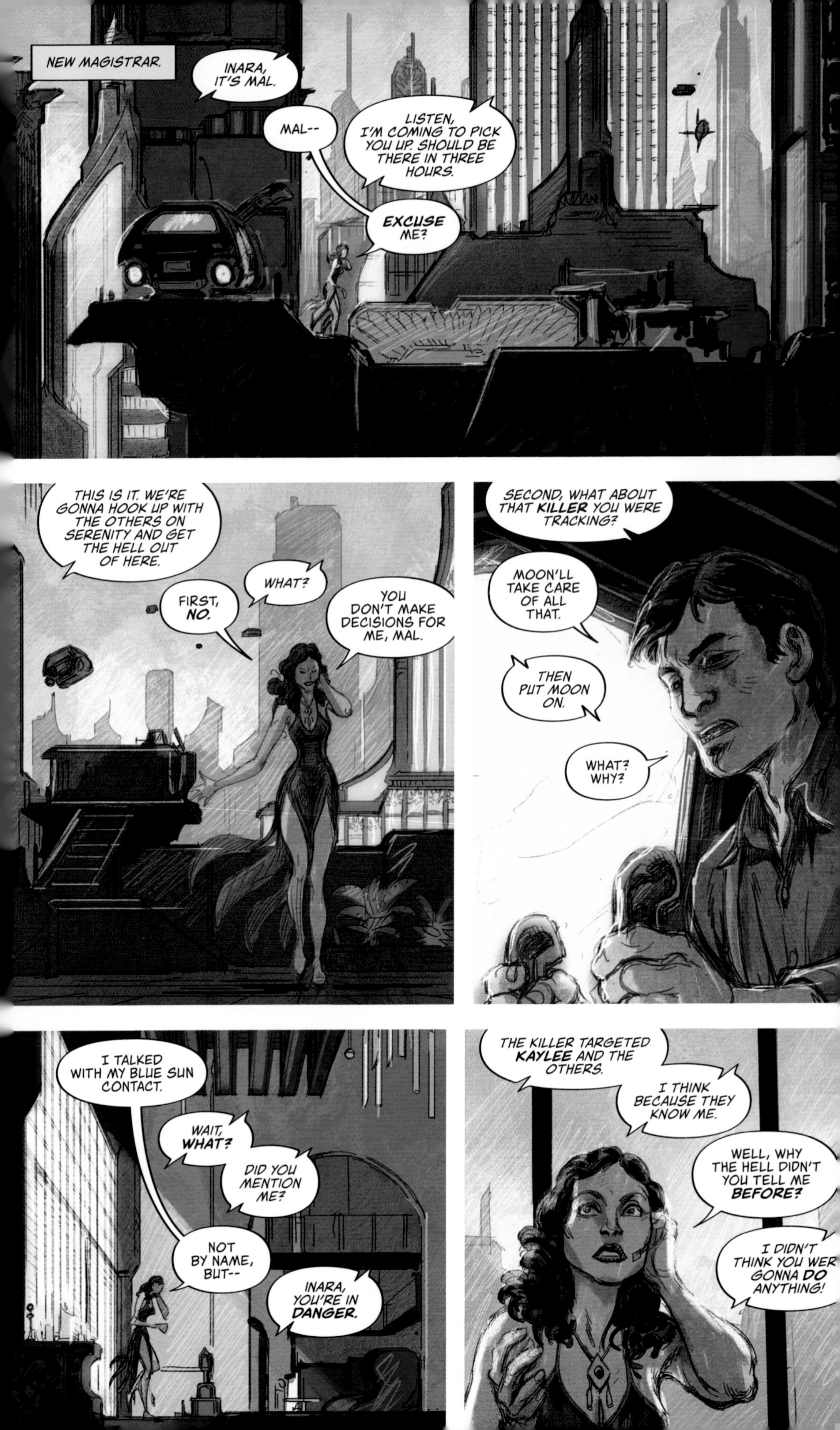
NEW MAGISTRAR.
INARA, IT'S MAL.
MAL--
LISTEN, I'M COMING TO PICK YOU UP. SHOULD BE THERE IN THREE HOURS.
EXCUSE ME?
THIS IS IT. WE'RE GONNA HOOK UP WITH THE OTHERS ON SERENITY AND GET THE HELL OUT OF HERE.
FIRST, NO.
WHAT?
YOU DON'T MAKE DECISIONS FOR ME, MAL.
SECOND, WHAT ABOUT THAT KILLER YOU WERE TRACKING?
MOON'LL TAKE CARE OF ALL THAT.
THEN PUT MOON ON.
WHAT? WHY?
I TALKED WITH MY BLUE SUN CONTACT.
WAIT, WHAT?
DID YOU MENTION ME?
NOT BY NAME, BUT--
INARA, YOU'RE IN DANGER.
THE KILLER TARGETED KAYLEE AND THE OTHERS.
I THINK BECAUSE THEY KNOW ME.
WELL, WHY THE HELL DIDN'T YOU TELL ME BEFORE?
I DIDN'T THINK YOU WER GONNA DO ANYTHING!

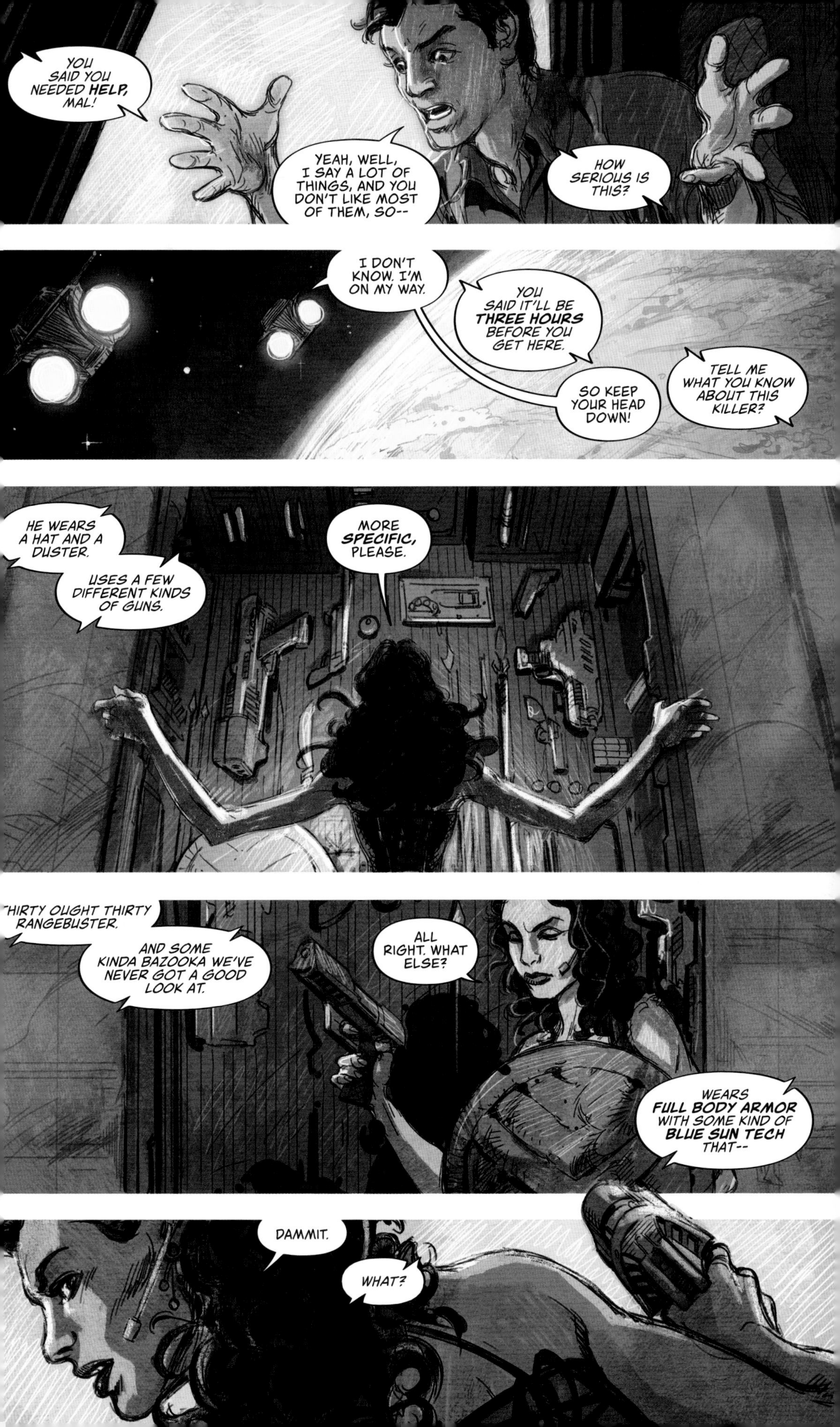
YOU SAID YOU NEEDED HELP, MAL!
YEAH, WELL, I SAY A LOT OF THINGS, AND YOU DON'T LIKE MOST OF THEM, SO--
HOW SERIOUS IS THIS?
I DON'T KNOW. I'M ON MY WAY.
YOU SAID IT'LL BE THREE HOURS BEFORE YOU GET HERE.
SO KEEP YOUR HEAD DOWN!
TELL ME WHAT YOU KNOW ABOUT THIS KILLER?
HE WEARS A HAT AND A DUSTER.
USES A FEW DIFFERENT KINDS OF GUNS.
MORE SPECIFIC, PLEASE.
THIRTY OUGHT THIRTY RANGEBUSTER.
AND SOME KINDA BAZOOKA WE'VE NEVER GOT A GOOD LOOK AT.
ALL RIGHT. WHAT ELSE?
WEARS FULL BODY ARMOR WITH SOME KIND OF BLUE SUN TECH THAT--
DAMMIT.
WHAT?

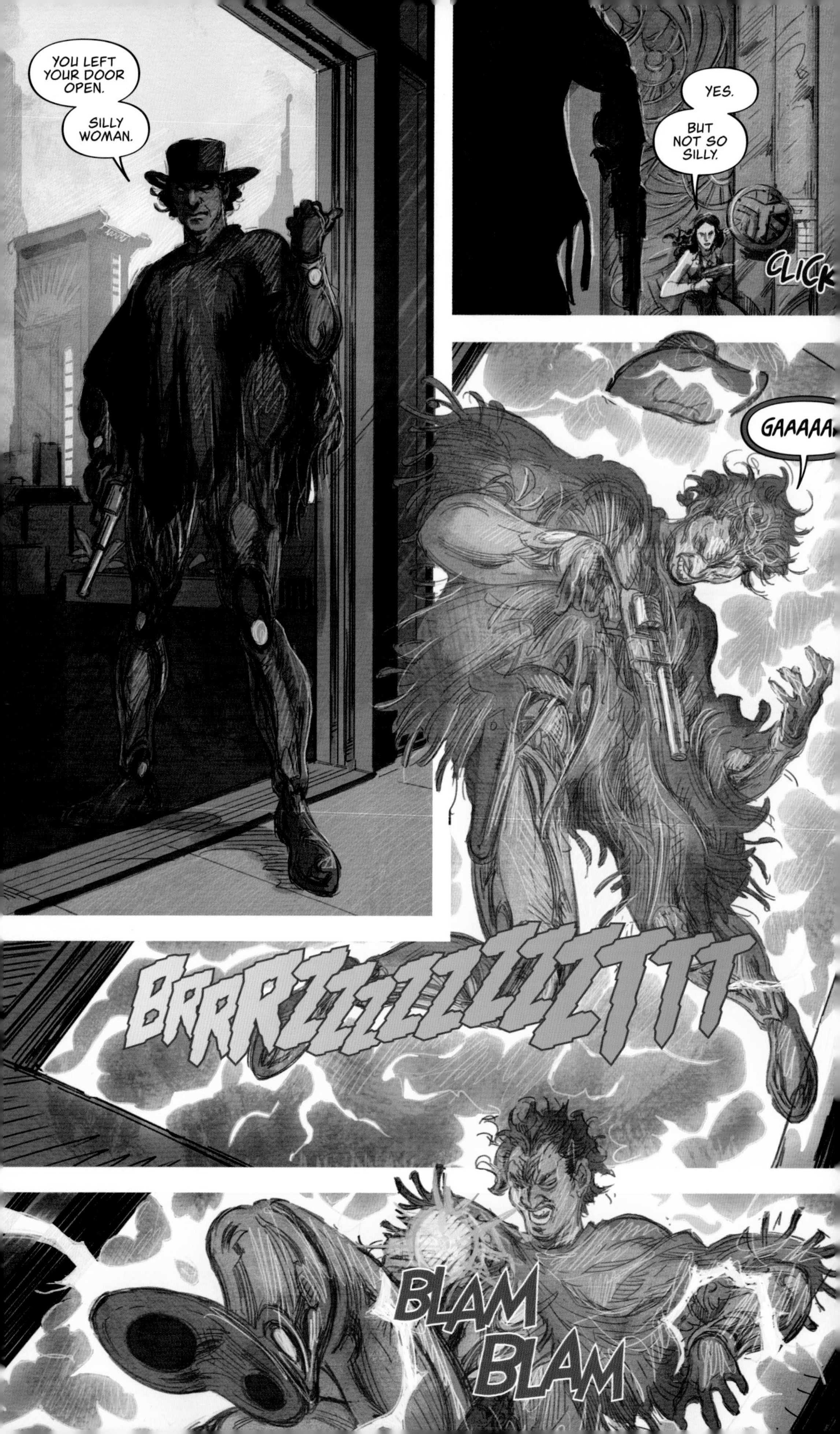
YOU LEFT YOUR DOOR OPEN.
SILLY WOMAN.
YES.
BUT NOT SO SILLY.
CLICK
GAAAAA
BRRRZZZZZZZZTTT
BLAM
BLAM

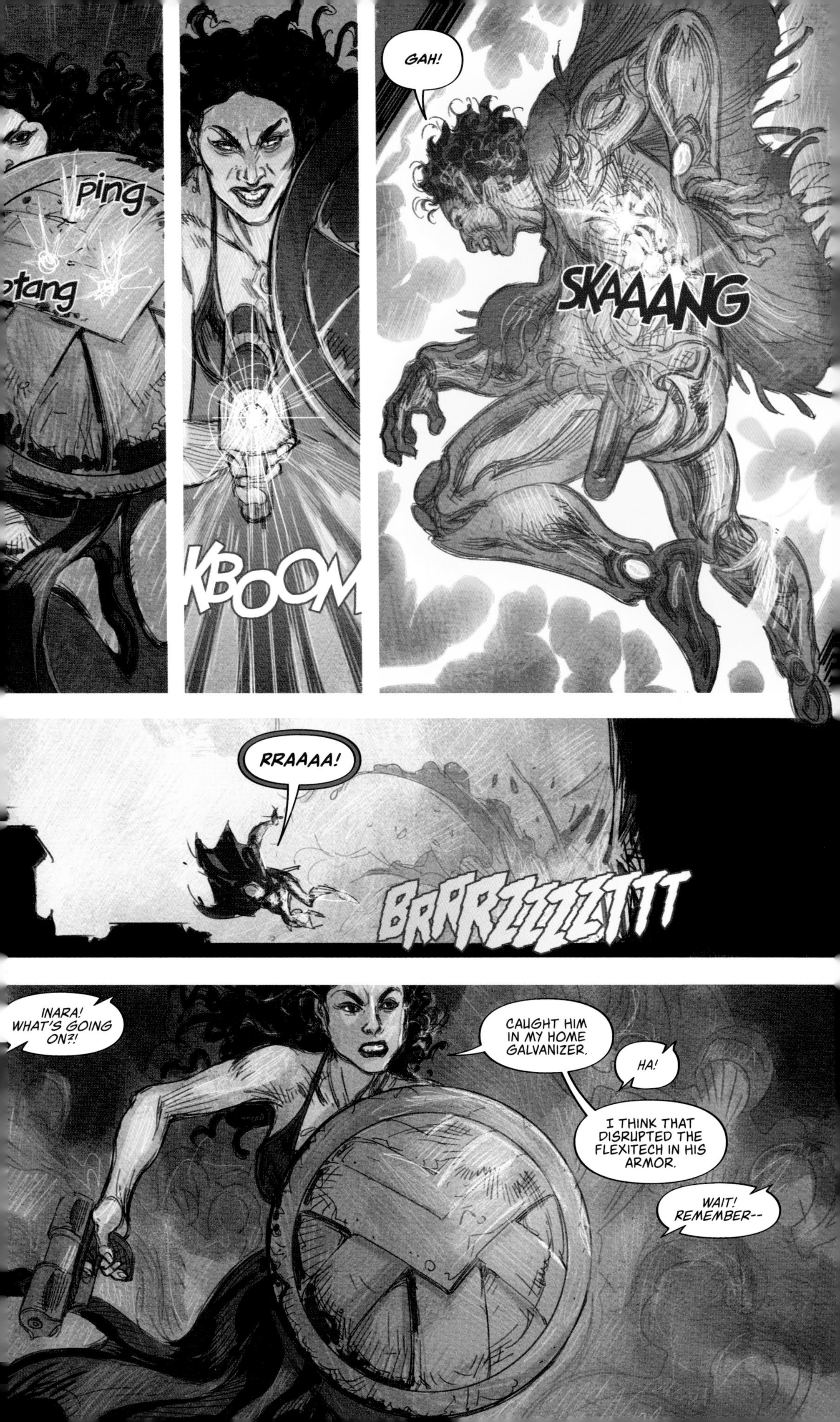
ping
tang
KBOOM
GAH!
SKAAANG
RRAAAA!
BRRRZZZZTTT
INARA! WHAT'S GOING ON?!
CAUGHT HIM IN MY HOME GALVANIZER.
HA!
I THINK THAT DISRUPTED THE FLEXITECH IN HIS ARMOR.
WAIT! REMEMBER--

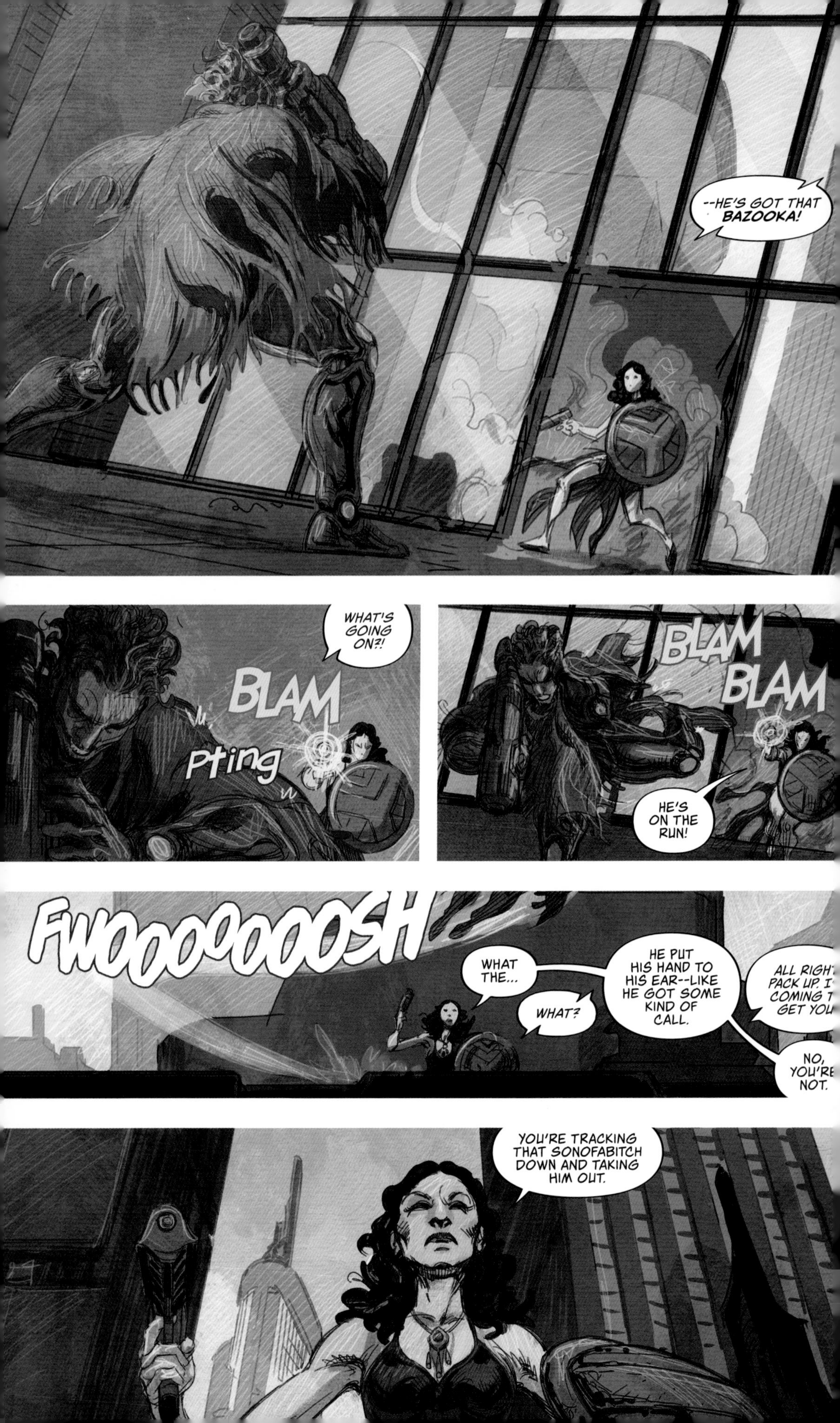
--HE'S GOT THAT BAZOOKA!
WHAT'S GOING ON?!
BLAM
Pting
BLAM
BLAM
HE'S ON THE RUN!
FWOOOOOOOOSH
WHAT THE...
WHAT?
HE PUT HIS HAND TO HIS EAR--LIKE HE GOT SOME KIND OF CALL.
NO, YOU'RE NOT.
YOU'RE TRACKING THAT SONOFABITCH DOWN AND TAKING HIM OUT.

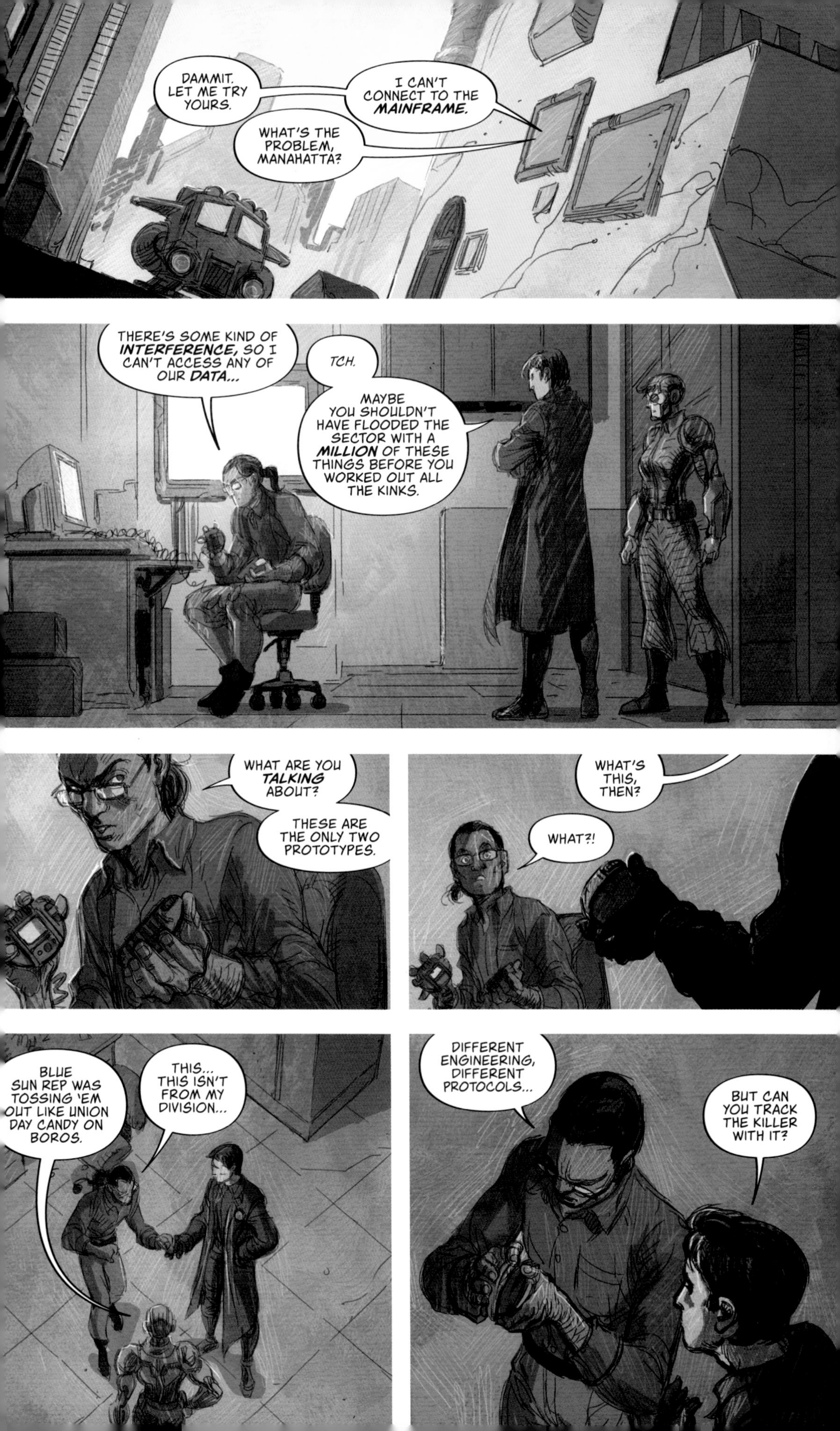
I CAN'T CONNECT TO THE ***MAINFRAME.***
DAMMIT. LET ME TRY YOURS.
WHAT'S THE PROBLEM, MANAHATTA?
THERE'S SOME KIND OF ***INTERFERENCE,*** SO I CAN'T ACCESS ANY OF OUR ***DATA...***
TCH.
MAYBE YOU SHOULDN'T HAVE FLOODED THE SECTOR WITH A ***MILLION*** OF THESE THINGS BEFORE YOU WORKED OUT ALL THE KINKS.
WHAT ARE YOU ***TALKING*** ABOUT?
THESE ARE THE ONLY TWO PROTOTYPES.
WHAT'S THIS, THEN?
WHAT?!
THIS... THIS ISN'T FROM MY DIVISION...
BLUE SUN REP WAS TOSSING 'EM OUT LIKE UNION DAY CANDY ON BOROS.
DIFFERENT ENGINEERING, DIFFERENT PROTOCOLS...
BUT CAN YOU TRACK THE KILLER WITH IT?

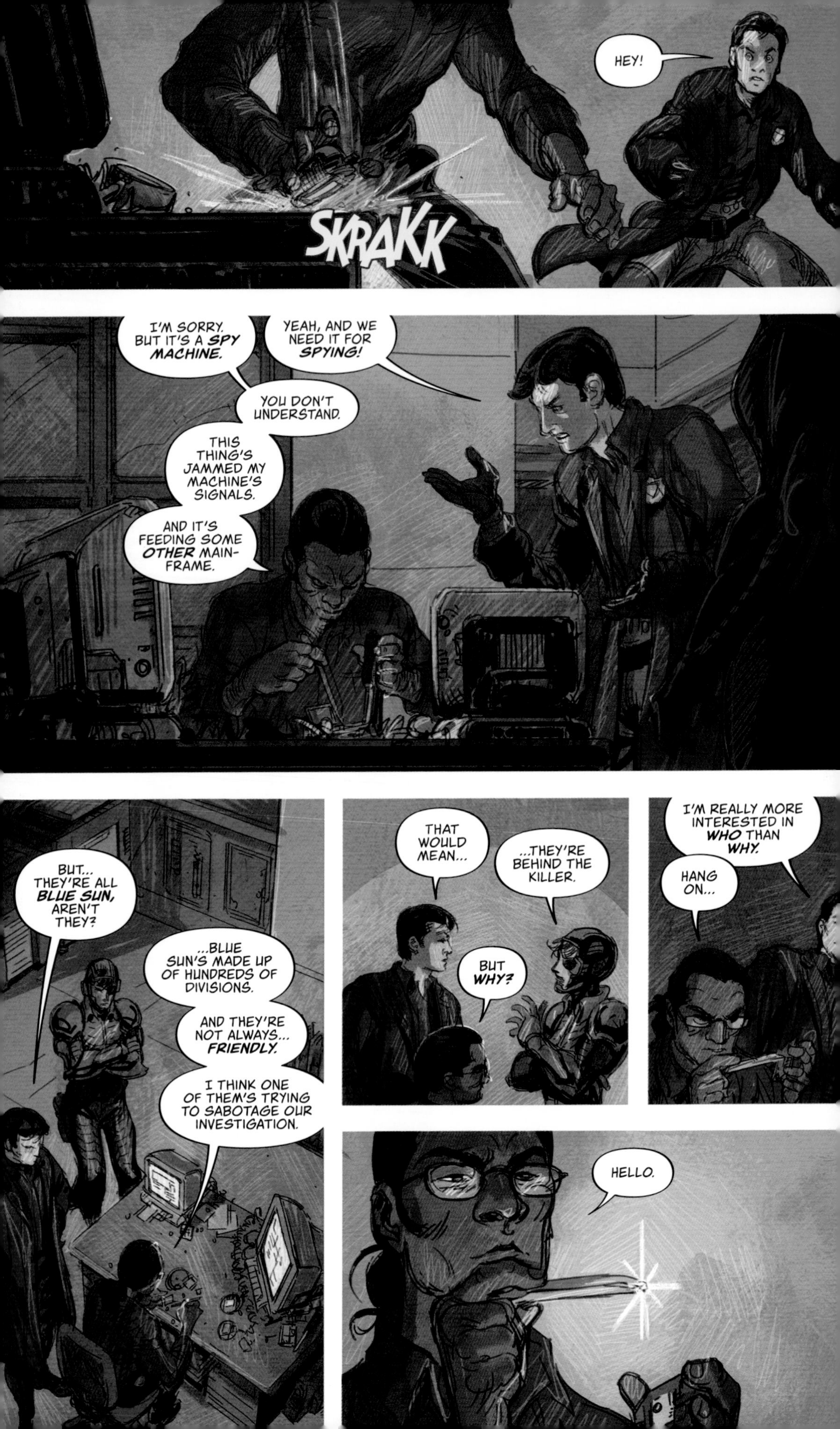
HEY!
SKRAKK
I'M SORRY. BUT IT'S A SPY MACHINE.
YEAH, AND WE NEED IT FOR SPYING!
YOU DON'T UNDERSTAND.
THIS THING'S JAMMED MY MACHINE'S SIGNALS.
AND IT'S FEEDING SOME OTHER MAIN-FRAME.
BUT... THEY'RE ALL BLUE SUN, AREN'T THEY?
...BLUE SUN'S MADE UP OF HUNDREDS OF DIVISIONS.
AND THEY'RE NOT ALWAYS... FRIENDLY.
I THINK ONE OF THEM'S TRYING TO SABOTAGE OUR INVESTIGATION.
THAT WOULD MEAN...
...THEY'RE BEHIND THE KILLER.
BUT WHY?
I'M REALLY MORE INTERESTED IN WHO THAN WHY.
HANG ON...
HELLO.

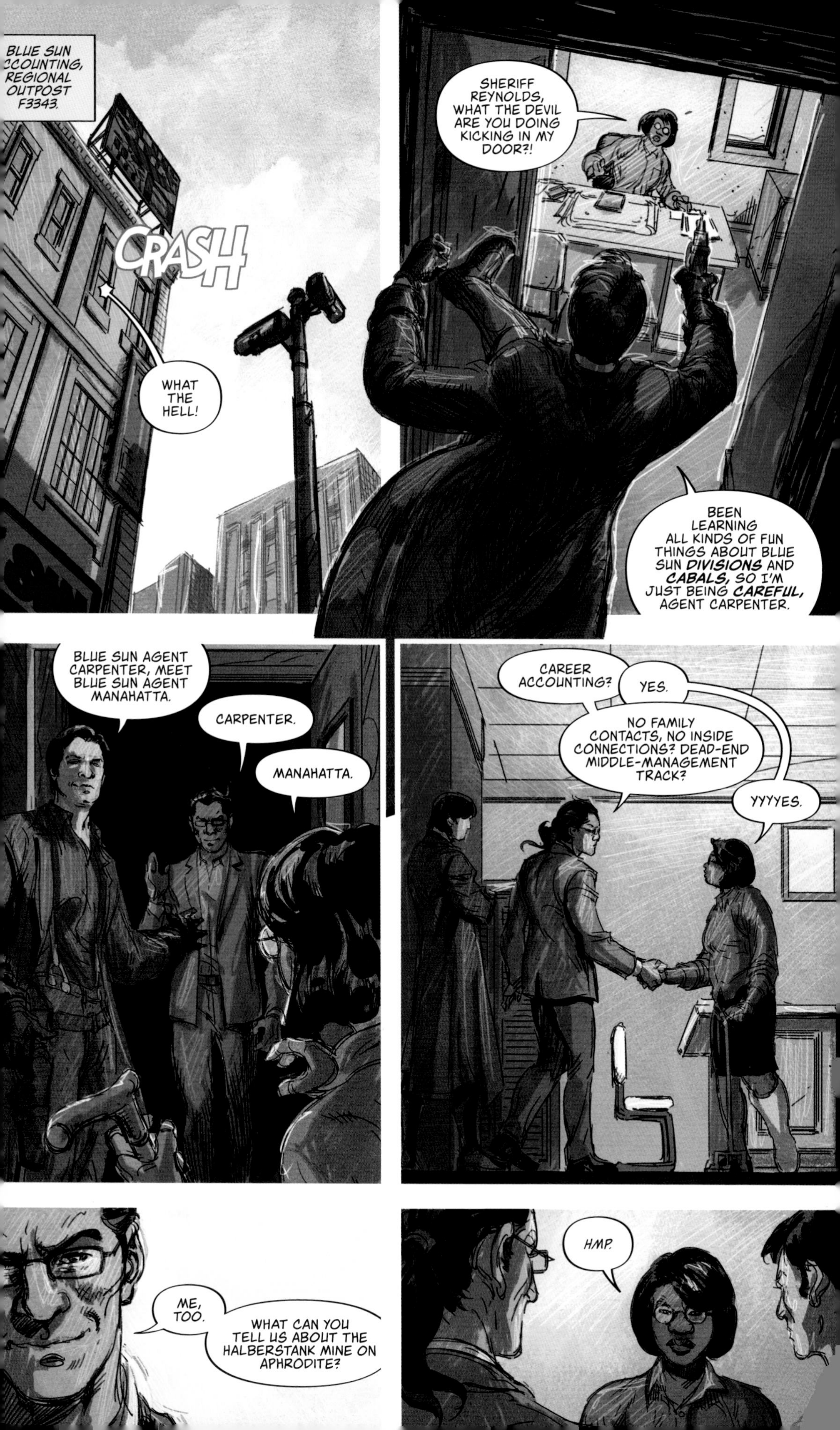
BLUE SUN
CCOUNTING,
REGIONAL
OUTPOST
F3343.
CRASH
WHAT THE HELL!
SHERIFF REYNOLDS, WHAT THE DEVIL ARE YOU DOING KICKING IN MY DOOR?!
BEEN LEARNING ALL KINDS OF FUN THINGS ABOUT BLUE SUN *DIVISIONS* AND *CABALS,* SO I'M JUST BEING *CAREFUL,* AGENT CARPENTER.
BLUE SUN AGENT CARPENTER, MEET BLUE SUN AGENT MANAHATTA.
CARPENTER.
MANAHATTA.
CAREER ACCOUNTING?
YES.
NO FAMILY CONTACTS, NO INSIDE CONNECTIONS? DEAD-END MIDDLE-MANAGEMENT TRACK?
YYYYES.
ME, TOO.
WHAT CAN YOU TELL US ABOUT THE HALBERSTANK MINE ON APHRODITE?
HMP.

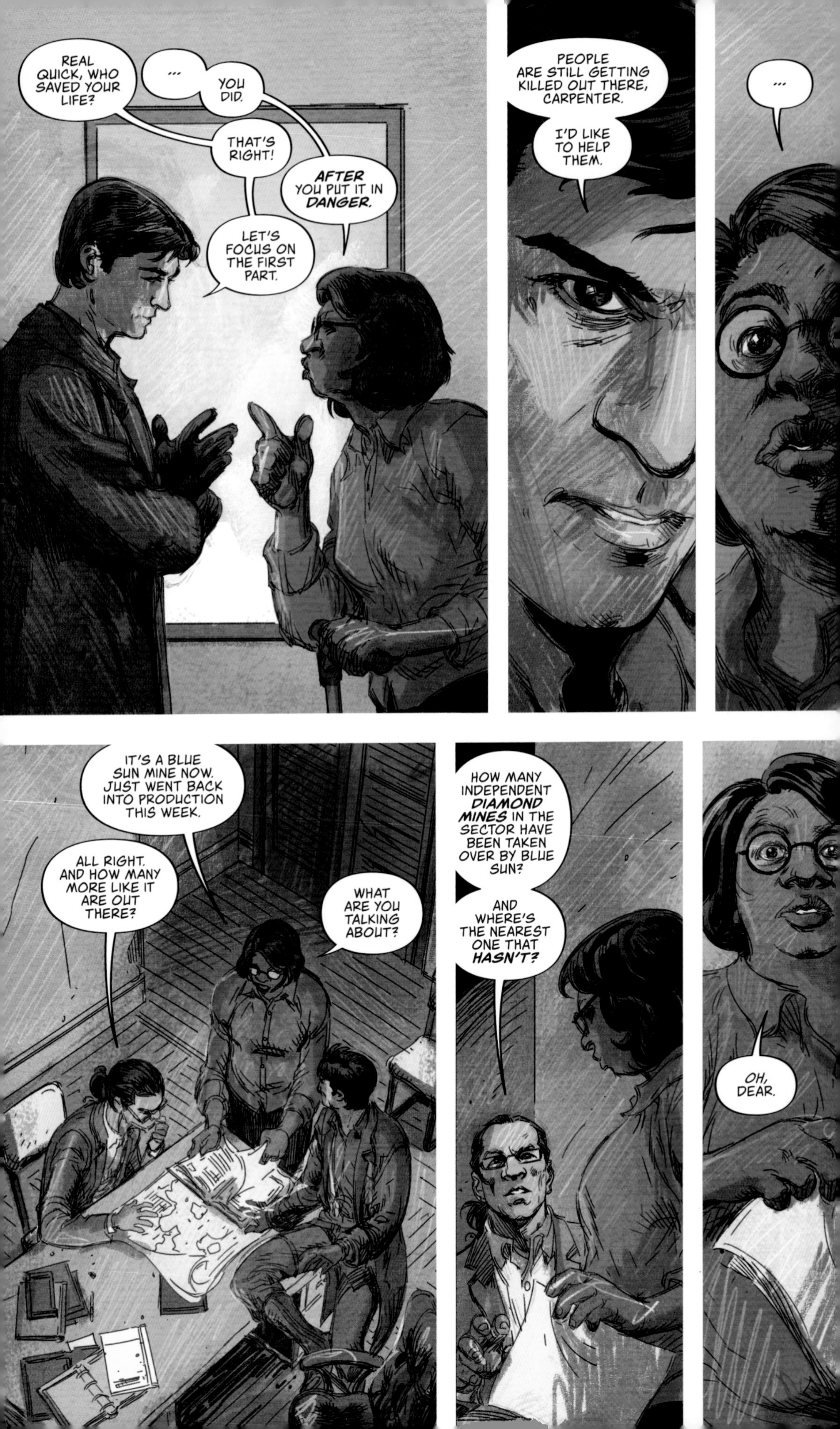
REAL QUICK, WHO SAVED YOUR LIFE?
...
YOU DID.
THAT'S RIGHT!
AFTER YOU PUT IT IN DANGER.
LET'S FOCUS ON THE FIRST PART.
PEOPLE ARE STILL GETTING KILLED OUT THERE, CARPENTER.
I'D LIKE TO HELP THEM.
...
IT'S A BLUE SUN MINE NOW. JUST WENT BACK INTO PRODUCTION THIS WEEK.
ALL RIGHT. AND HOW MANY MORE LIKE IT ARE OUT THERE?
WHAT ARE YOU TALKING ABOUT?
HOW MANY INDEPENDENT DIAMOND MINES IN THE SECTOR HAVE BEEN TAKEN OVER BY BLUE SUN?
AND WHERE'S THE NEAREST ONE THAT HASN'T?
OH, DEAR.

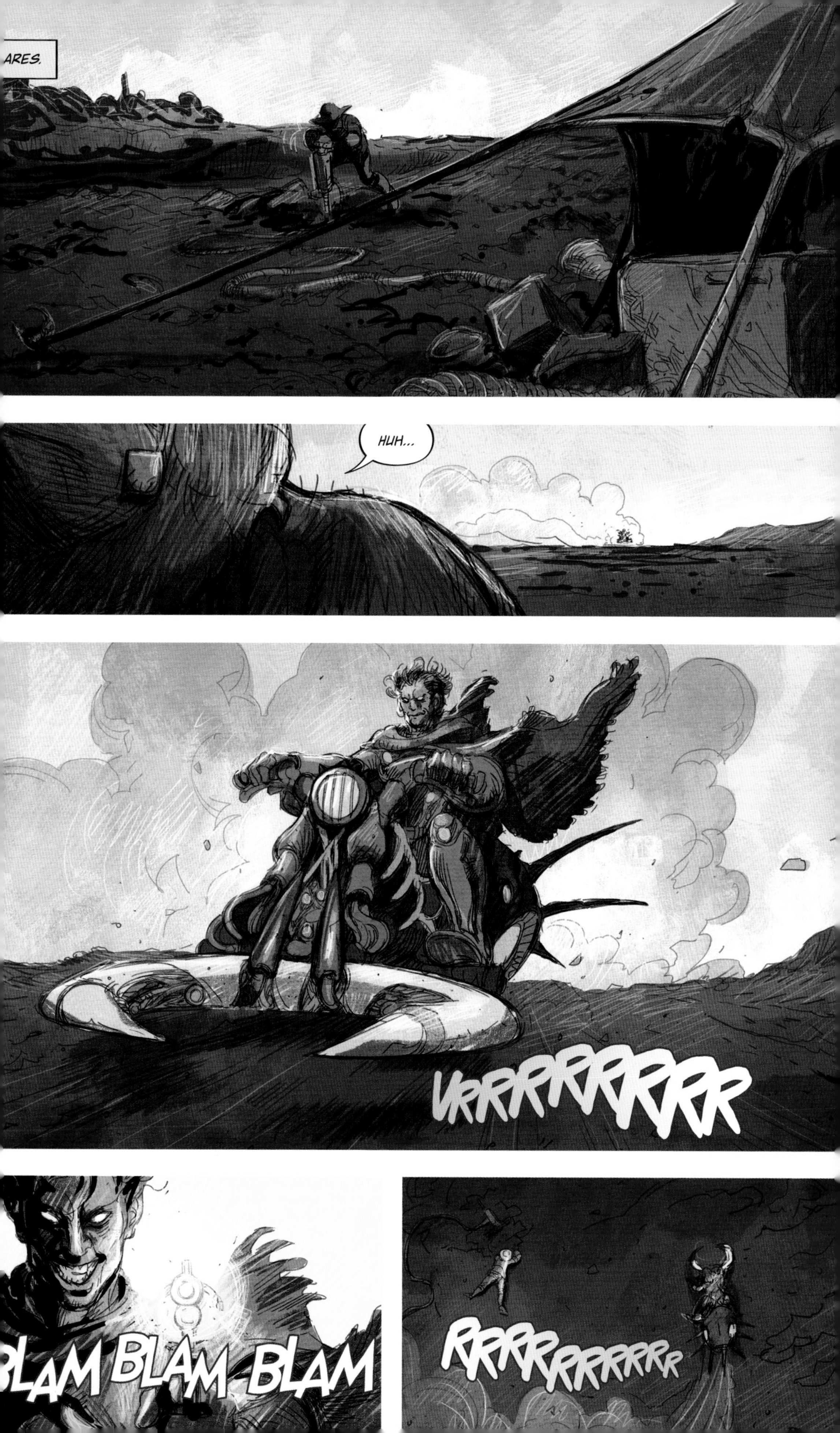
ARES.
HUH...
URRRRRRRRRR
BLAM BLAM BLAM
RRRRRRRRRRR

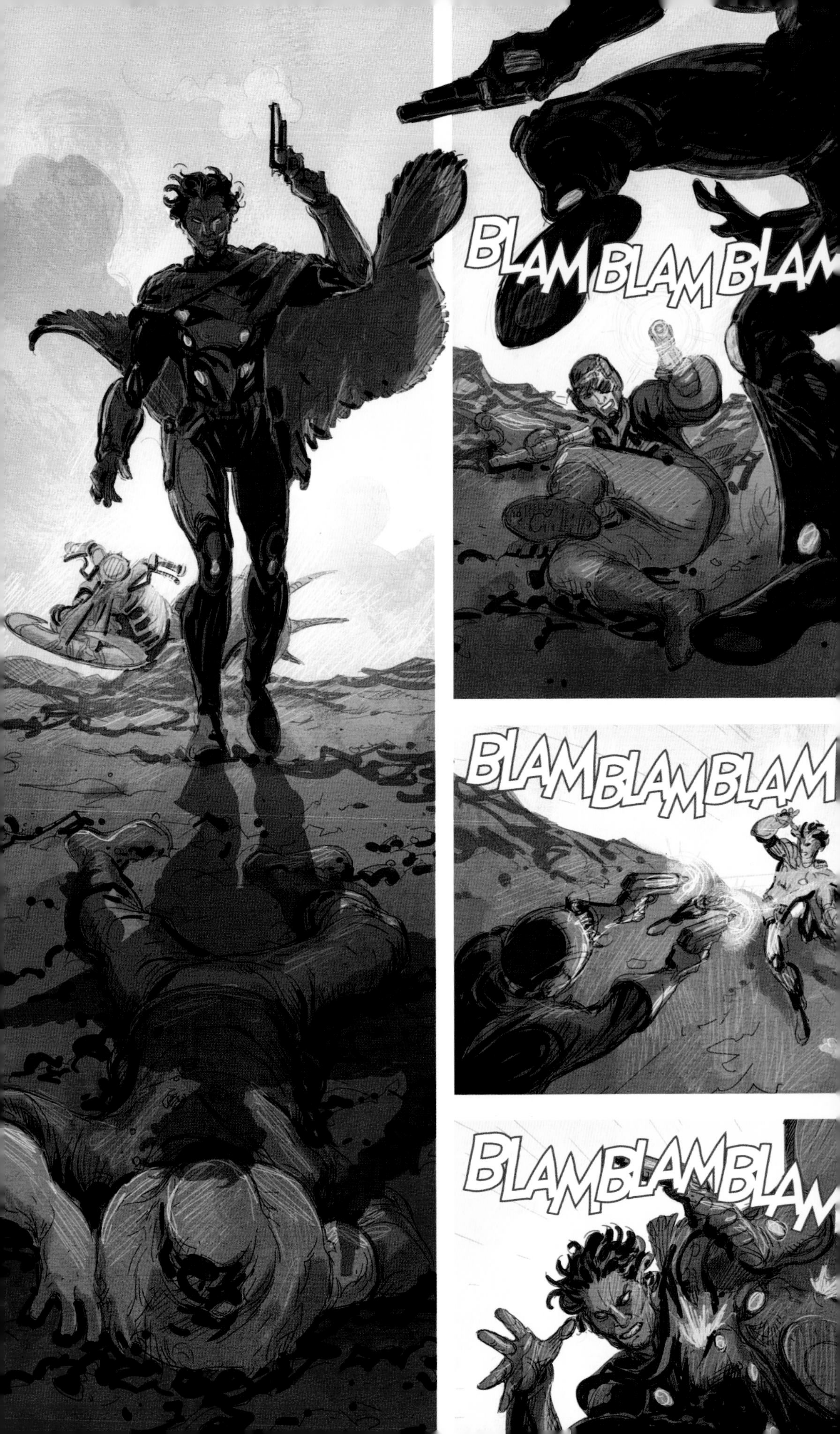
BLAM BLAM BLAM
BLAM BLAM BLAM
BLAM BLAM BLAM

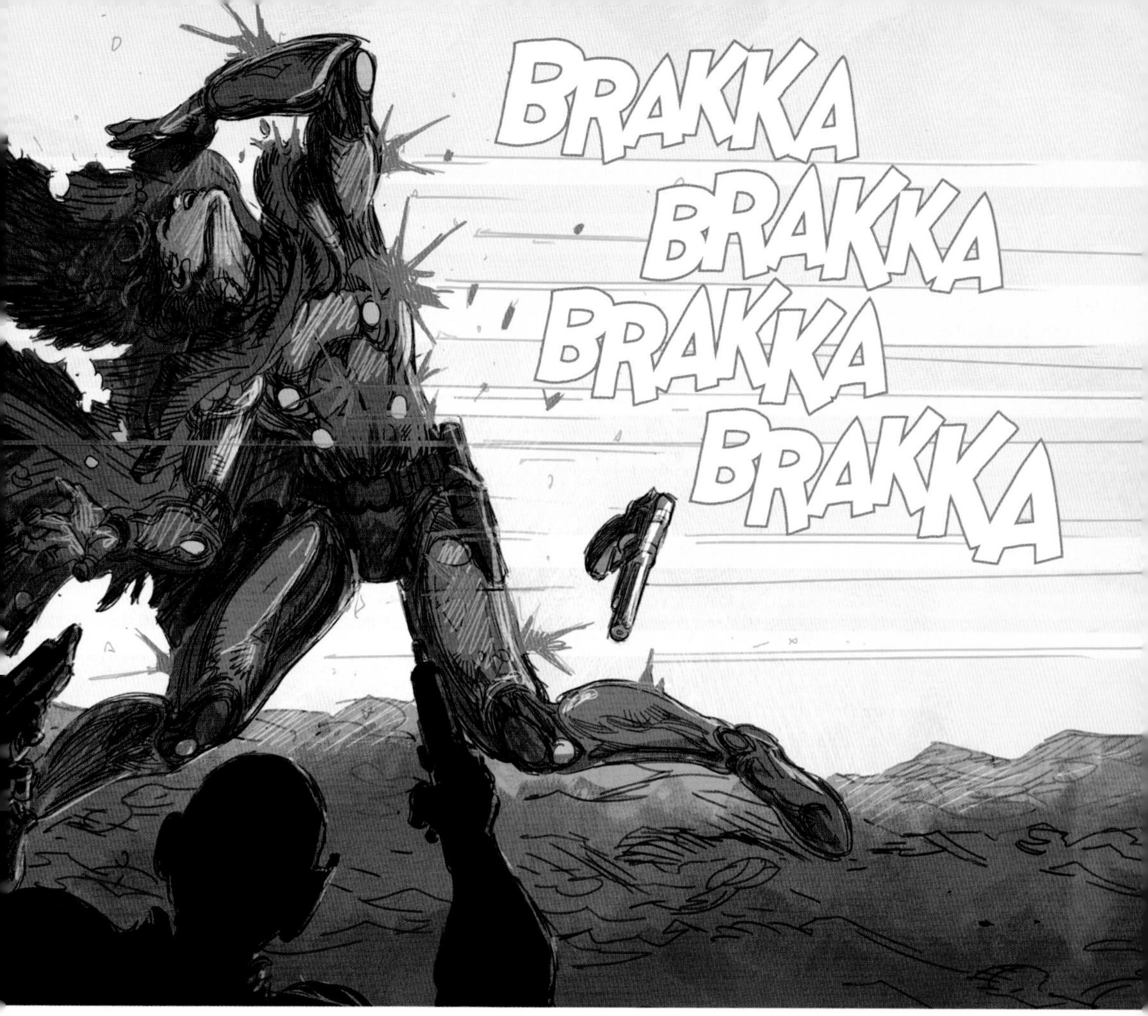
BRAKKA
BRAKKA
BRAKKA
BRAKKA

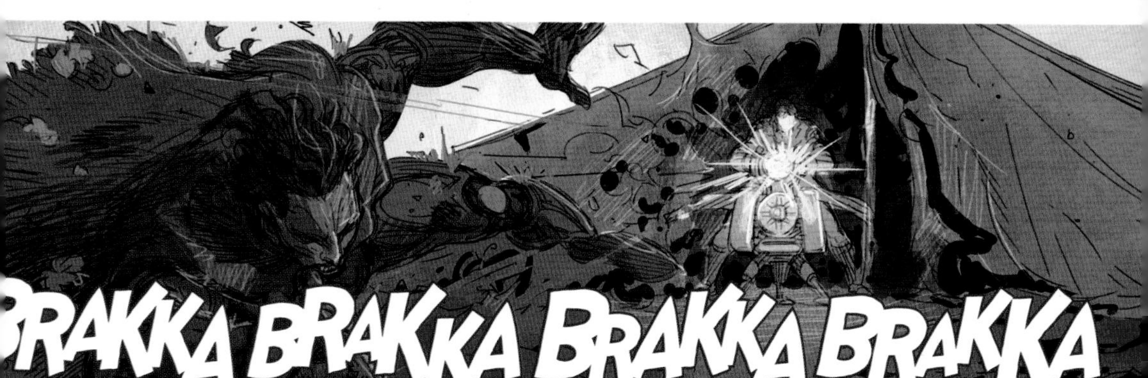
RAKKA BRAKKA BRAKKA BRAKKA

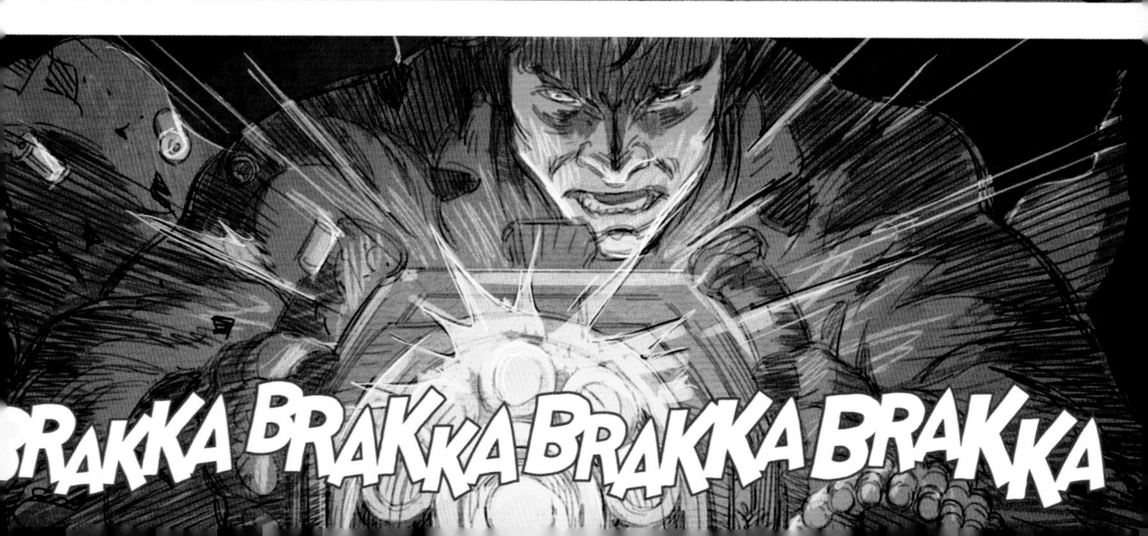
RAKKA BRAKKA BRAKKA BRAKKA

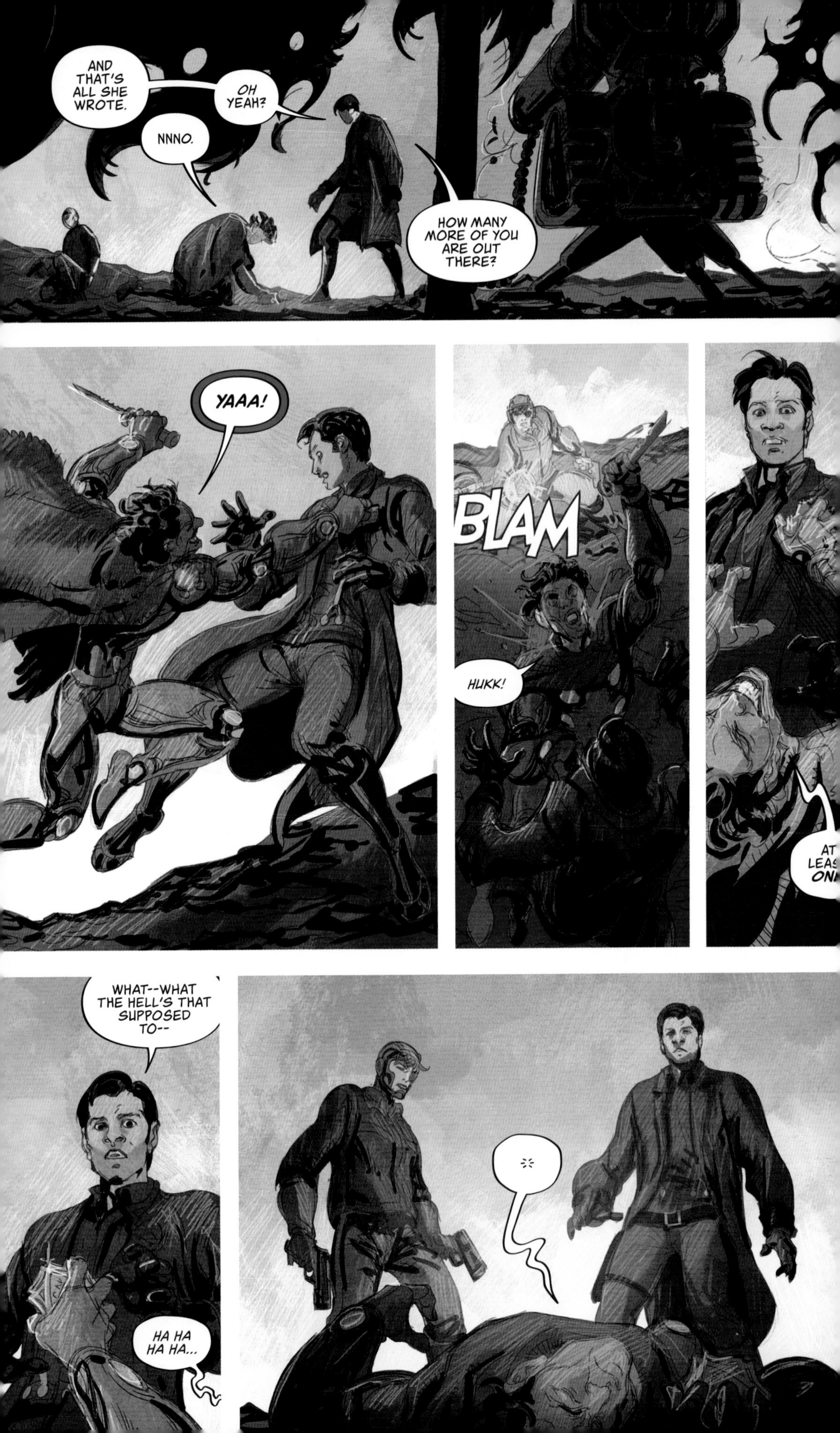
AND THAT'S ALL SHE WROTE.
OH YEAH?
NNNO.
HOW MANY MORE OF YOU ARE OUT THERE?
YAAA!
BLAM
HUKK!
AT LEAS ON
WHAT--WHAT THE HELL'S THAT SUPPOSED TO--
HA HA HA HA...

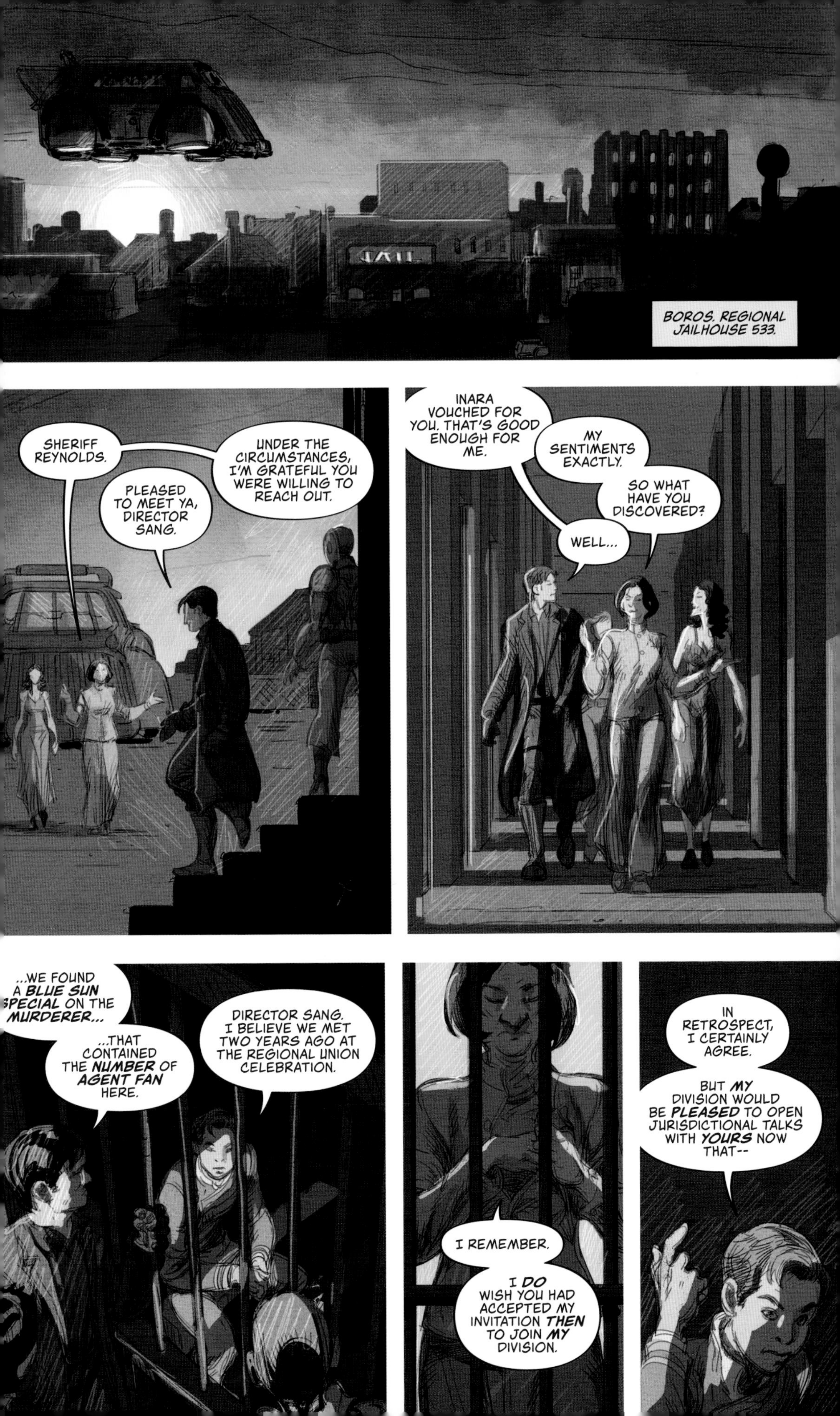
JAIL
BOROS. REGIONAL JAILHOUSE 533.
SHERIFF REYNOLDS.
UNDER THE CIRCUMSTANCES, I'M GRATEFUL YOU WERE WILLING TO REACH OUT.
PLEASED TO MEET YA, DIRECTOR SANG.
INARA VOUCHED FOR YOU. THAT'S GOOD ENOUGH FOR ME.
MY SENTIMENTS EXACTLY.
SO WHAT HAVE YOU DISCOVERED?
WELL...
...WE FOUND A **BLUE SUN** SPECIAL ON THE **MURDERER...**
...THAT CONTAINED THE **NUMBER** OF **AGENT FAN** HERE.
DIRECTOR SANG. I BELIEVE WE MET TWO YEARS AGO AT THE REGIONAL UNION CELEBRATION.
I REMEMBER.
I **DO** WISH YOU HAD ACCEPTED MY INVITATION **THEN** TO JOIN **MY** DIVISION.
IN RETROSPECT, I CERTAINLY AGREE.
BUT **MY** DIVISION WOULD BE **PLEASED** TO OPEN JURISDICTIONAL TALKS WITH **YOURS** NOW THAT--

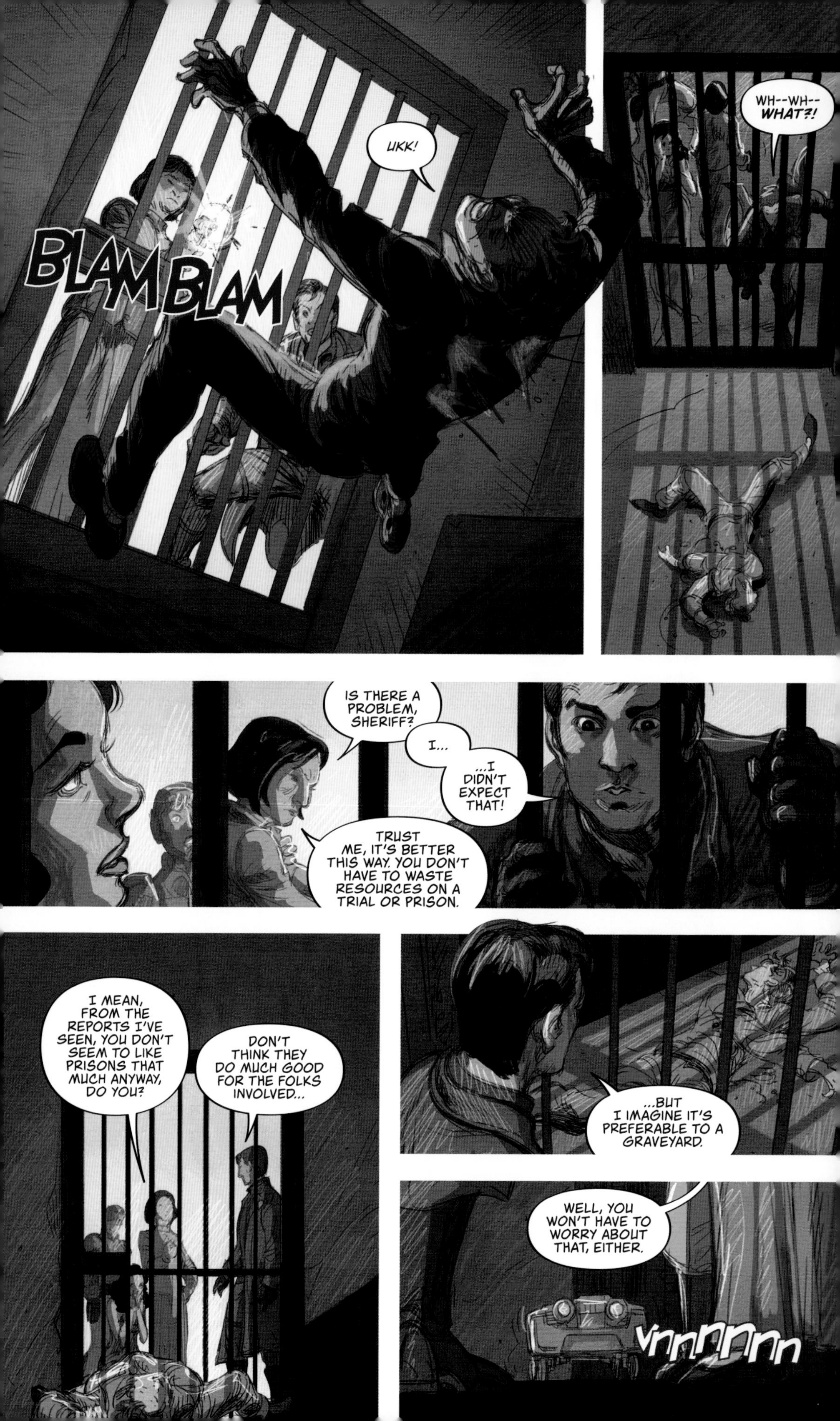
BLAM BLAM
UKK!
WH--WH--
WHAT?!
IS THERE A PROBLEM, SHERIFF?
I...
...I DIDN'T EXPECT THAT!
TRUST ME, IT'S BETTER THIS WAY. YOU DON'T HAVE TO WASTE RESOURCES ON A TRIAL OR PRISON.
I MEAN, FROM THE REPORTS I'VE SEEN, YOU DON'T SEEM TO LIKE PRISONS THAT MUCH ANYWAY, DO YOU?
DON'T THINK THEY DO MUCH GOOD FOR THE FOLKS INVOLVED...
...BUT I IMAGINE IT'S PREFERABLE TO A GRAVEYARD.
WELL, YOU WON'T HAVE TO WORRY ABOUT THAT, EITHER.
VNNNNNN

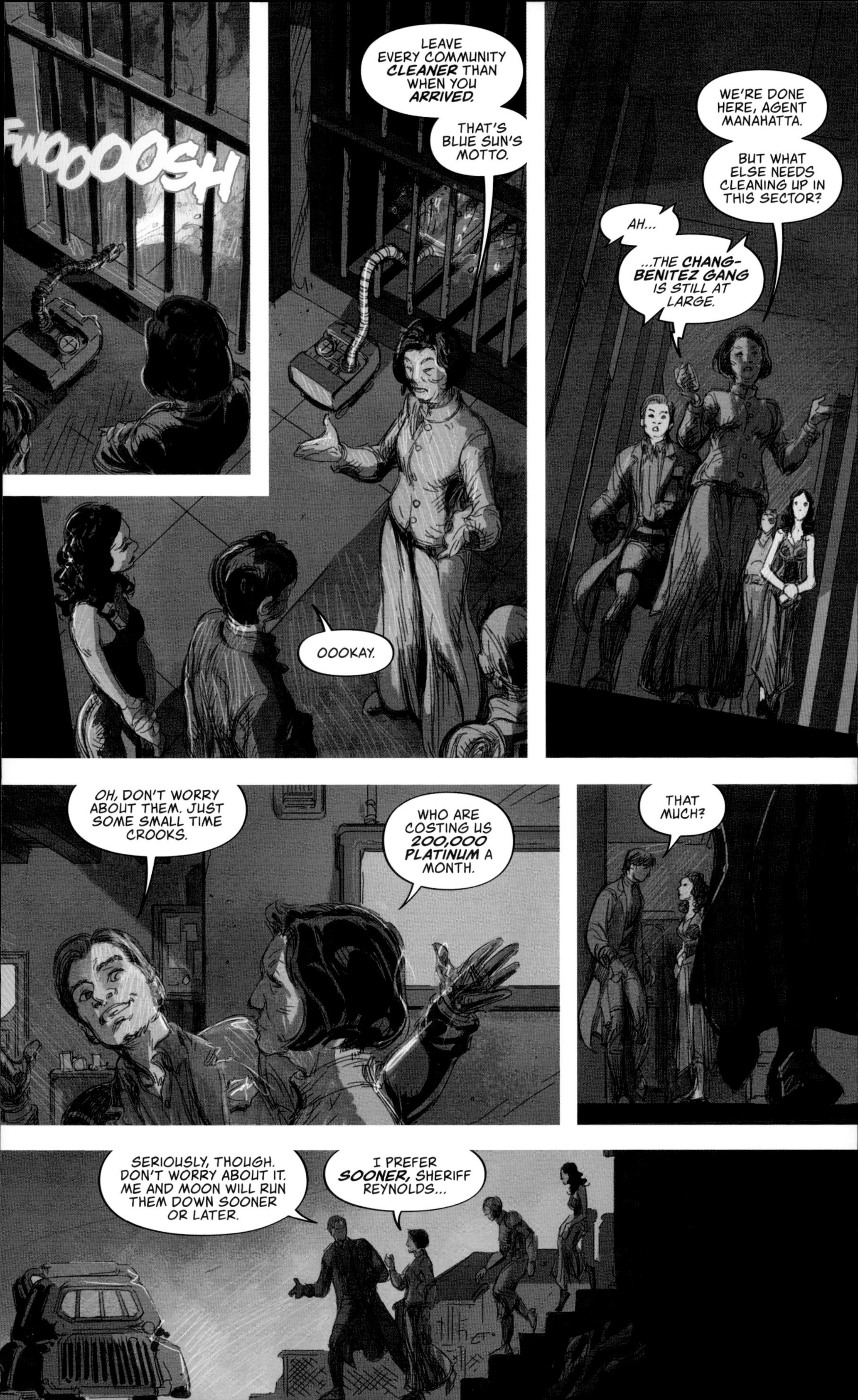
FWOOOOSH
LEAVE EVERY COMMUNITY CLEANER THAN WHEN YOU ARRIVED.
THAT'S BLUE SUN'S MOTTO.
OOOKAY.
WE'RE DONE HERE, AGENT MANAHATTA.
BUT WHAT ELSE NEEDS CLEANING UP IN THIS SECTOR?
AH...
...THE CHANG-BENITEZ GANG IS STILL AT LARGE.
OH, DON'T WORRY ABOUT THEM. JUST SOME SMALL TIME CROOKS.
WHO ARE COSTING US 200,000 PLATINUM A MONTH.
THAT MUCH?
SERIOUSLY, THOUGH. DON'T WORRY ABOUT IT. ME AND MOON WILL RUN THEM DOWN SOONER OR LATER.
I PREFER SOONER, SHERIFF REYNOLDS...

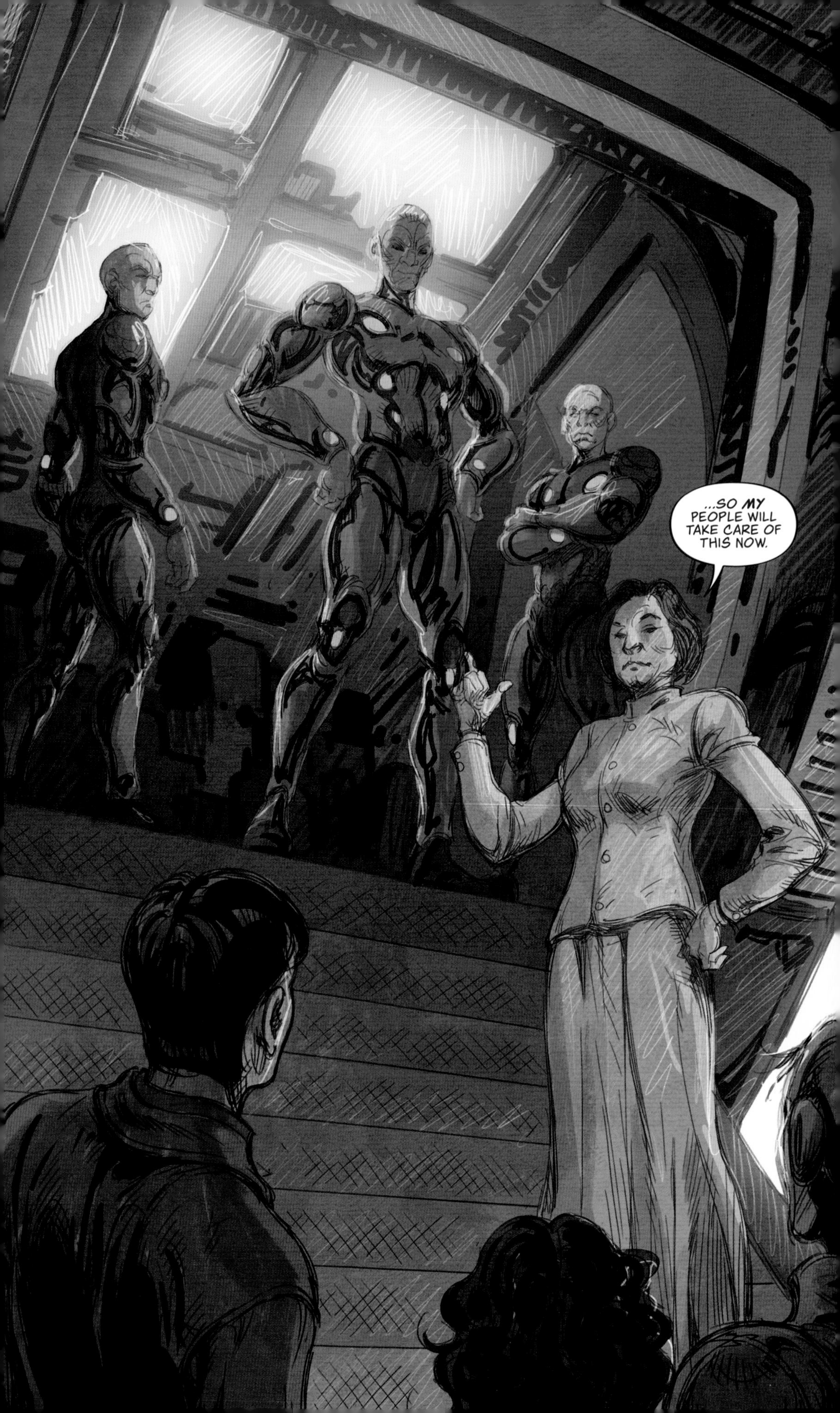
...SO MY PEOPLE WILL TAKE CARE OF THIS NOW.

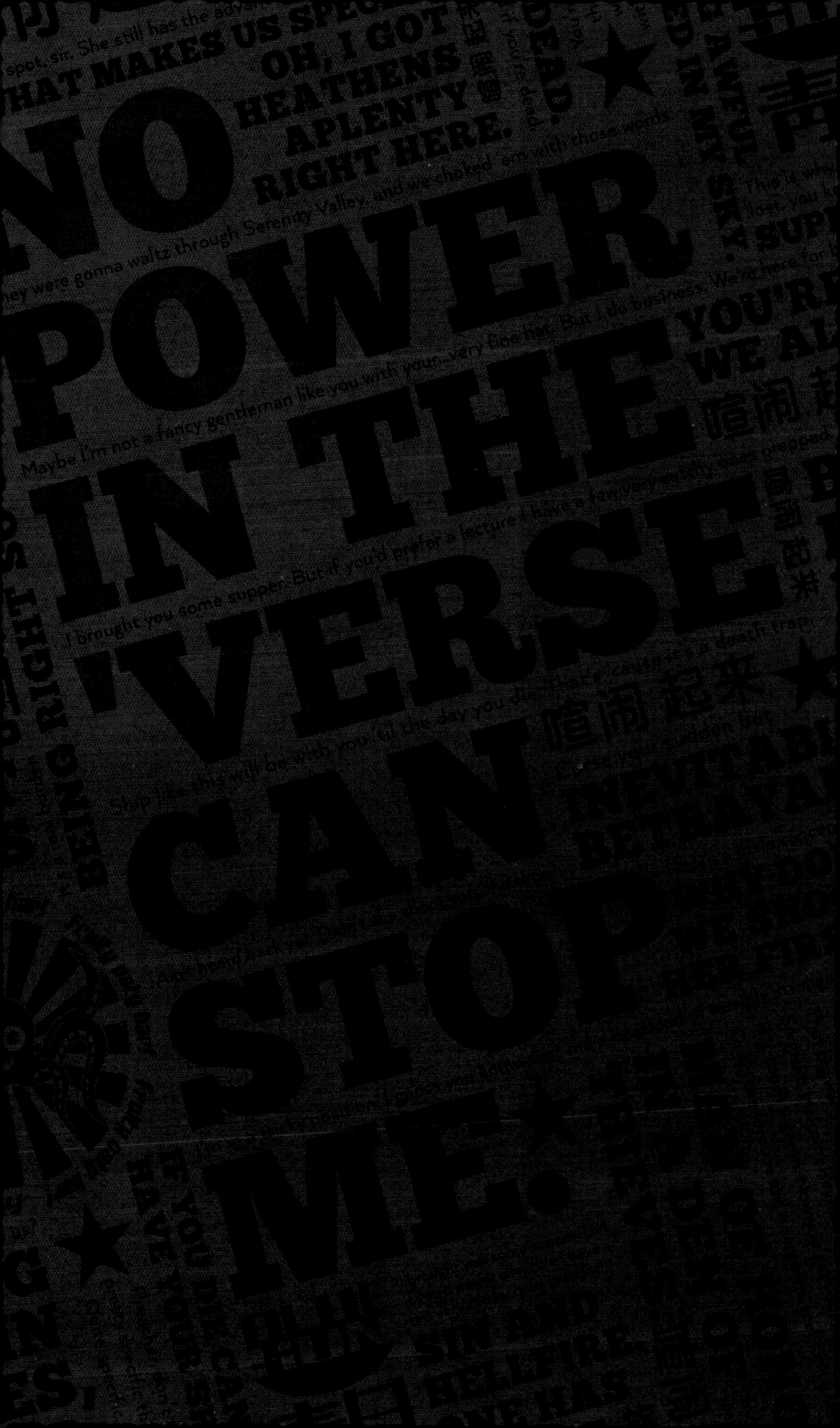

NO POWER IN THE 'VERSE CAN STOP ME.
OH, I GOT HEATHENS APLENTY RIGHT HERE.
I brought you some supper. But if you'd prefer a lecture I have a few very select ones prepped.
Maybe I'm not a fancy gentleman like you with your... very fine hat. But I do business.
They were gonna waltz through Serenity Valley, and we choked 'em with those words.

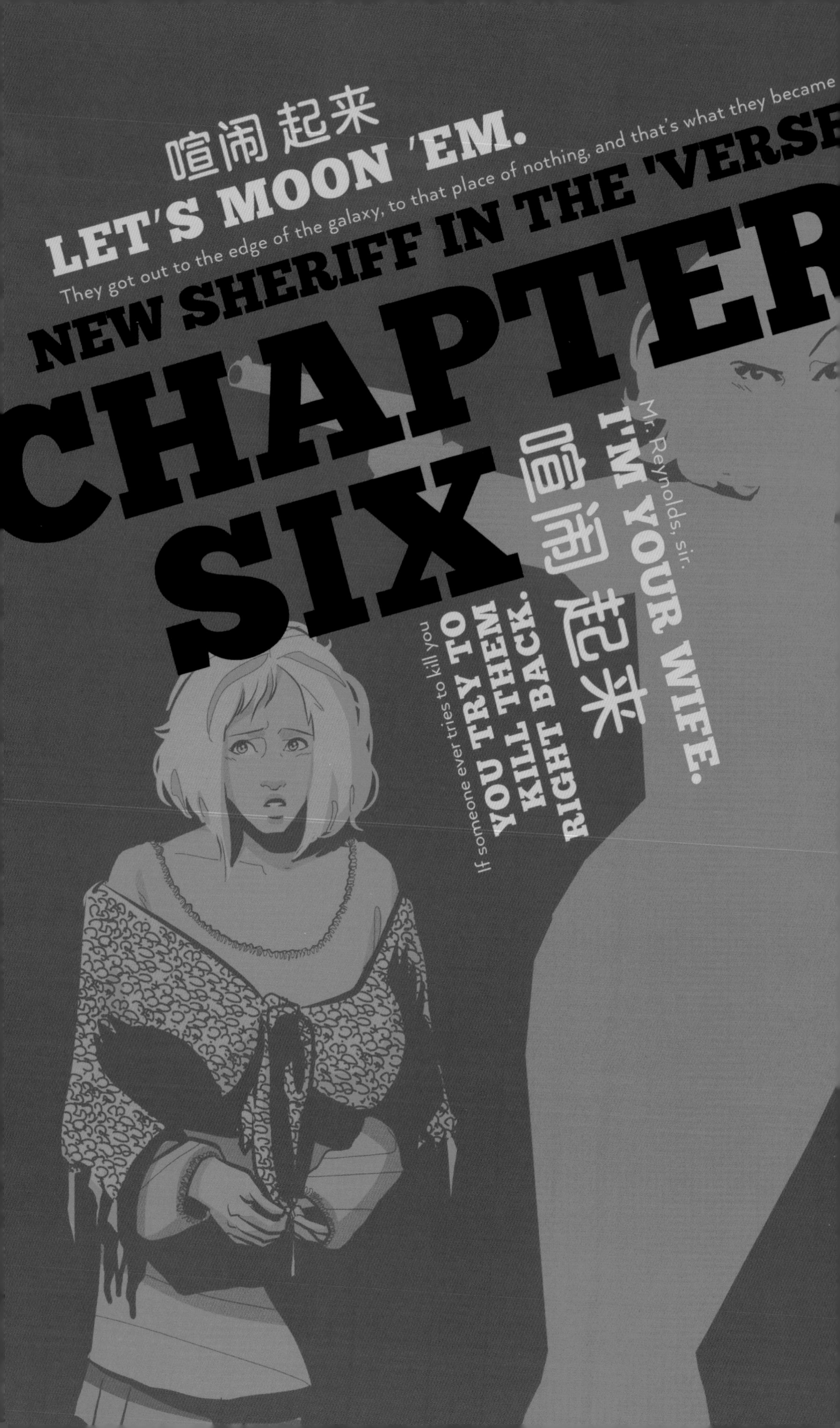
喧闹起来
LET'S MOON 'EM.
They got out to the edge of the galaxy, to that place of nothing, and that's what they became
NEW SHERIFF IN THE 'VERSE
CHAPTER SIX
Mr. Reynolds, sir.
I'M YOUR WIFE.
喧闹起来
If someone ever tries to kill you
YOU TRY TO KILL THEM RIGHT BACK.

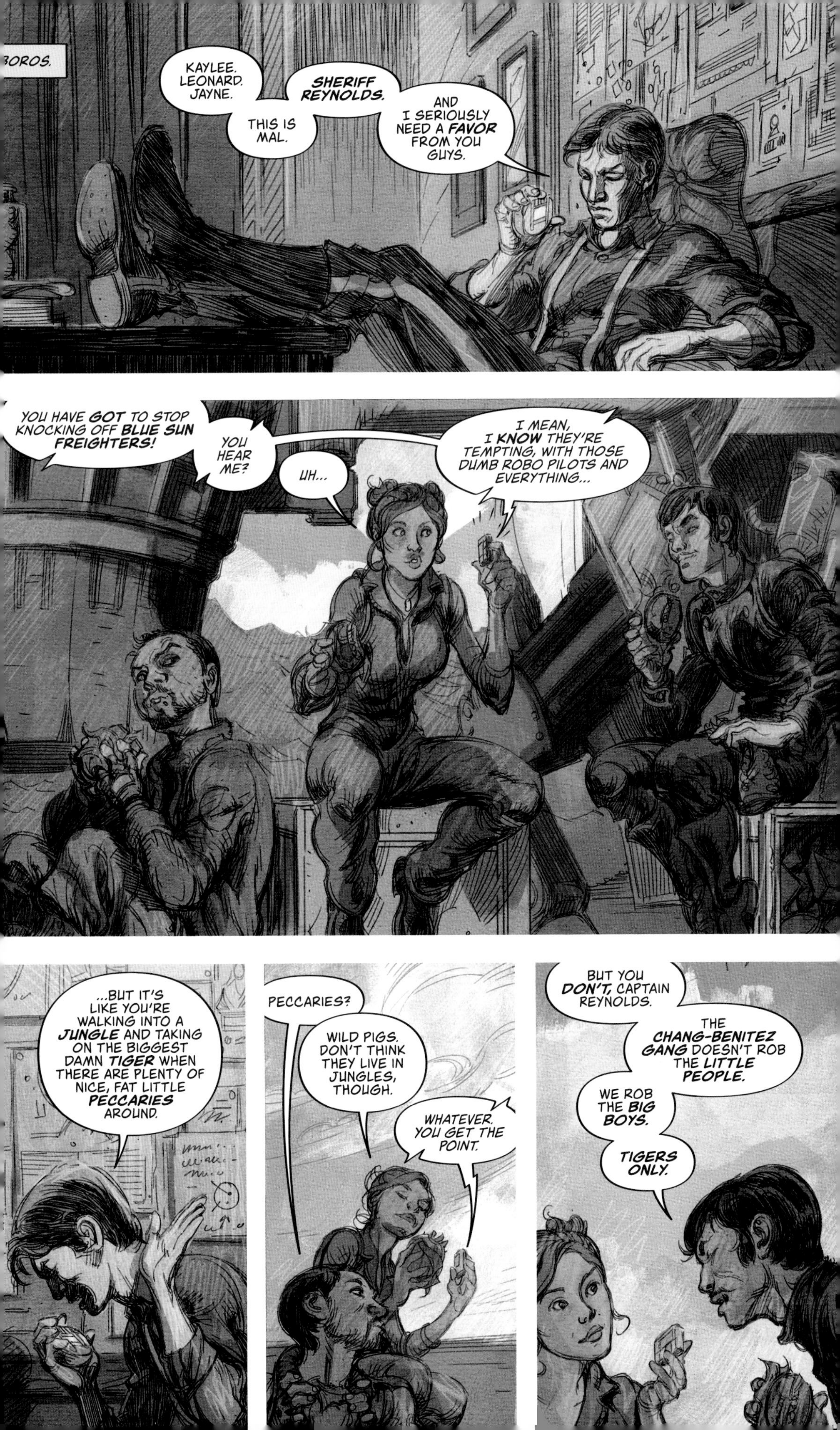

BOROS.
KAYLEE. LEONARD. JAYNE.
THIS IS MAL.
SHERIFF REYNOLDS.
AND I SERIOUSLY NEED A FAVOR FROM YOU GUYS.
YOU HAVE GOT TO STOP KNOCKING OFF BLUE SUN FREIGHTERS!
YOU HEAR ME?
UH...
I MEAN, I KNOW THEY'RE TEMPTING, WITH THOSE DUMB ROBO PILOTS AND EVERYTHING...
...BUT IT'S LIKE YOU'RE WALKING INTO A JUNGLE AND TAKING ON THE BIGGEST DAMN TIGER WHEN THERE ARE PLENTY OF NICE, FAT LITTLE PECCARIES AROUND.
PECCARIES?
WILD PIGS. DON'T THINK THEY LIVE IN JUNGLES, THOUGH.
WHATEVER. YOU GET THE POINT.
BUT YOU DON'T, CAPTAIN REYNOLDS.
THE CHANG-BENITEZ GANG DOESN'T ROB THE LITTLE PEOPLE.
WE ROB THE BIG BOYS.
TIGERS ONLY.

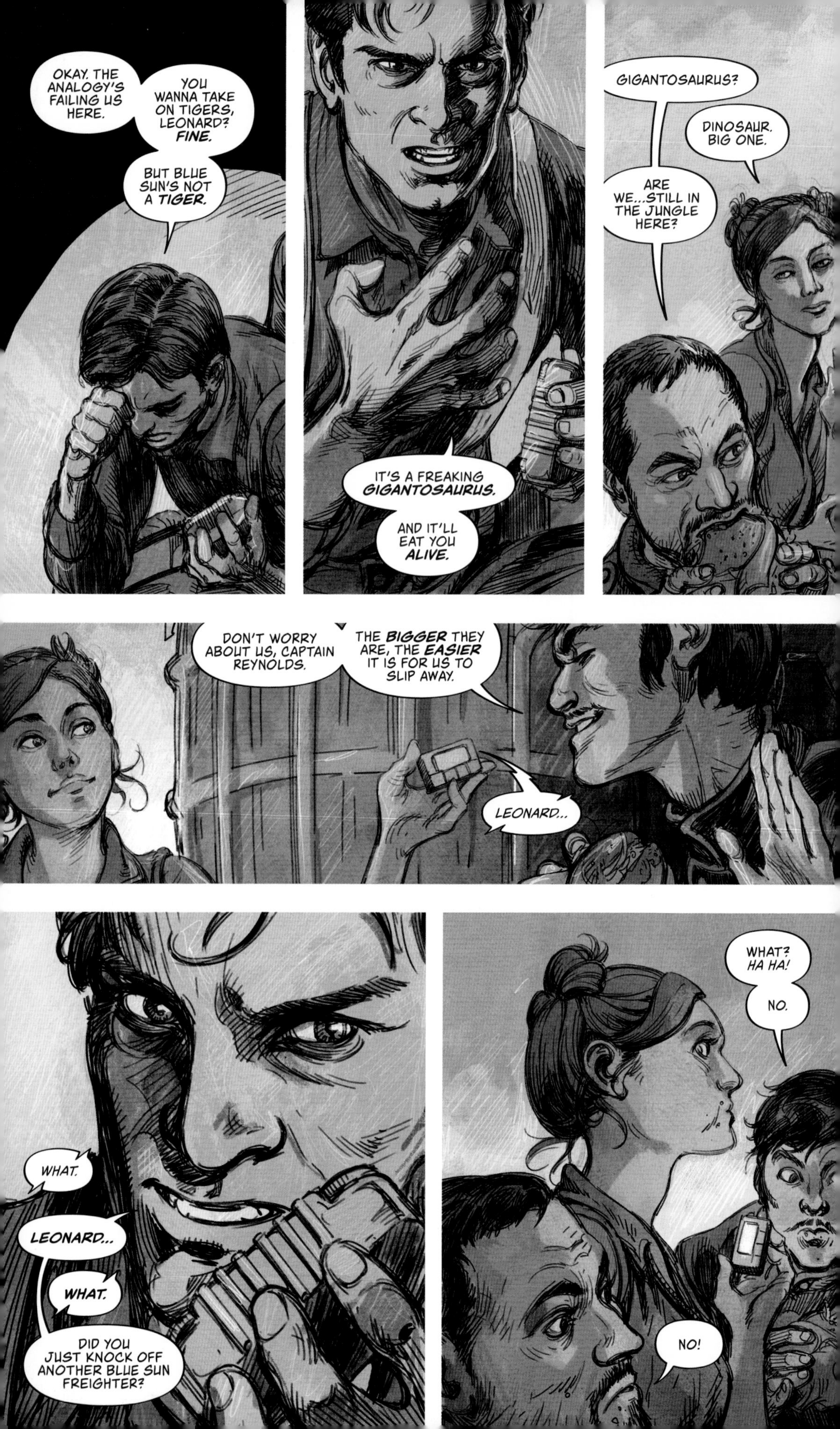
OKAY. THE ANALOGY'S FAILING US HERE.
YOU WANNA TAKE ON TIGERS, LEONARD? FINE.
BUT BLUE SUN'S NOT A TIGER.
IT'S A FREAKING GIGANTOSAURUS.
AND IT'LL EAT YOU ALIVE.
GIGANTOSAURUS?
DINOSAUR. BIG ONE.
ARE WE...STILL IN THE JUNGLE HERE?
DON'T WORRY ABOUT US, CAPTAIN REYNOLDS.
THE BIGGER THEY ARE, THE EASIER IT IS FOR US TO SLIP AWAY.
LEONARD...
WHAT.
LEONARD...
WHAT.
DID YOU JUST KNOCK OFF ANOTHER BLUE SUN FREIGHTER?
WHAT? HA HA!
NO.
NO!

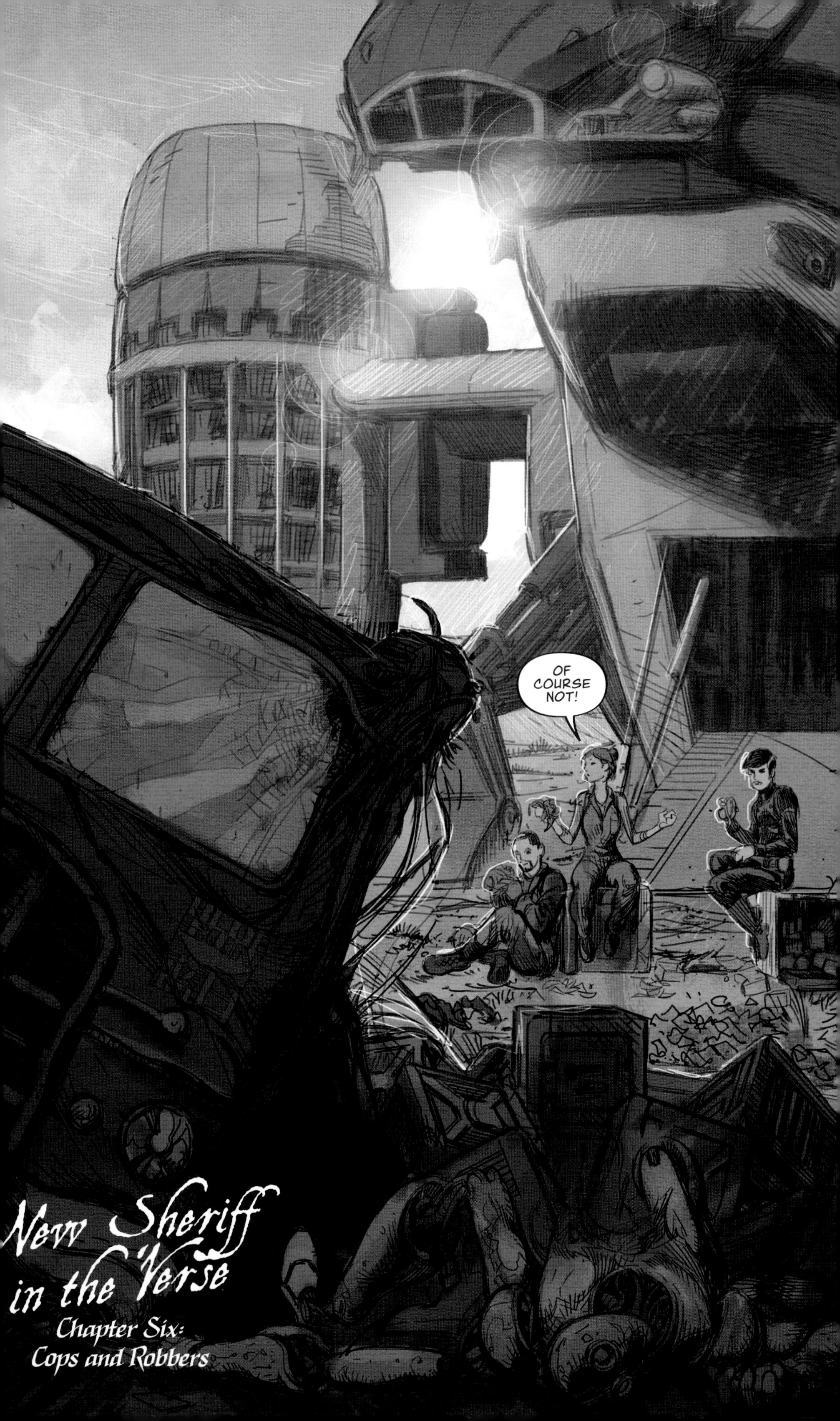
OF COURSE NOT!
New Sheriff in the 'Verse
Chapter Six:
Cops and Robbers

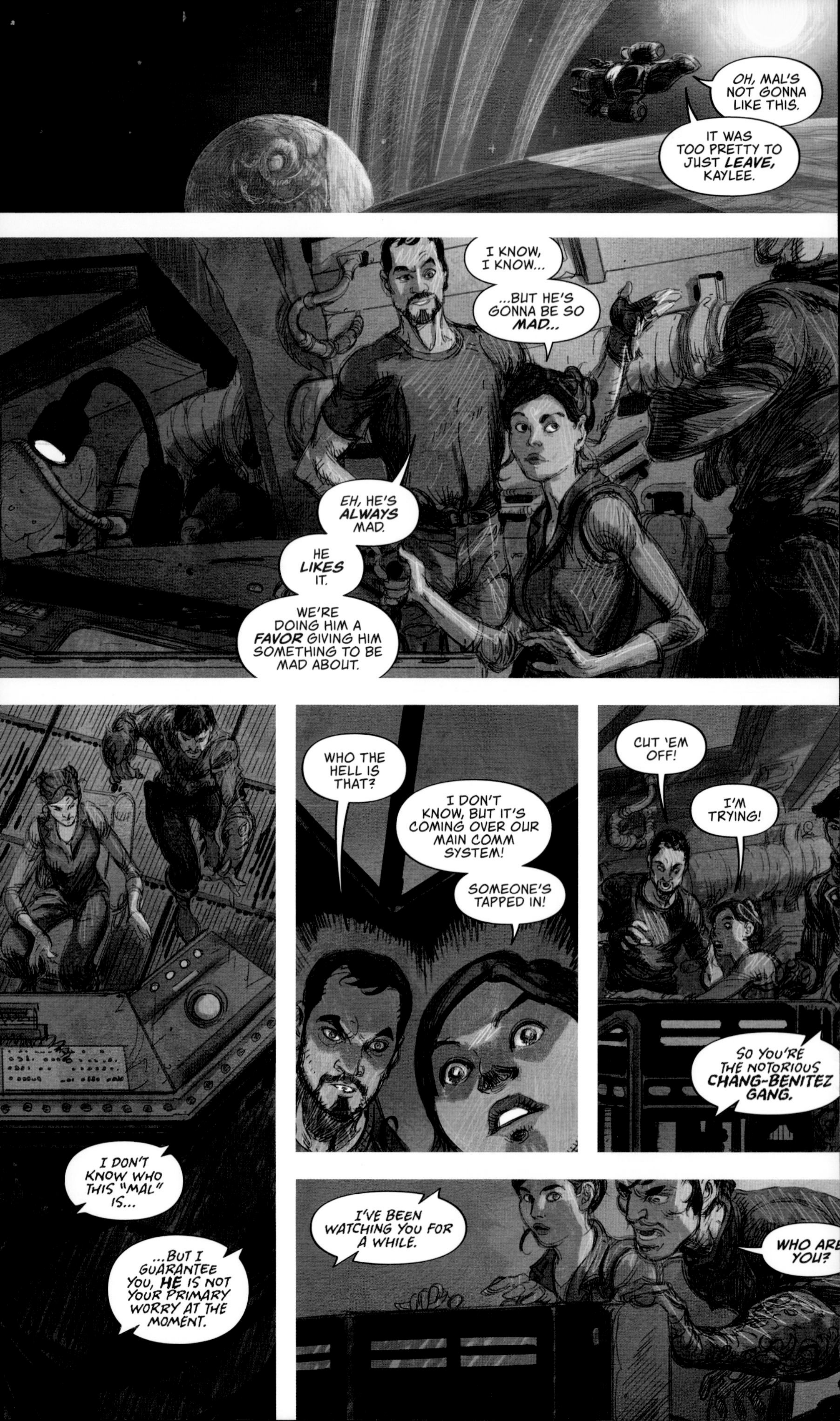
OH, MAL'S NOT GONNA LIKE THIS.
IT WAS TOO PRETTY TO JUST LEAVE, KAYLEE.
I KNOW, I KNOW...
...BUT HE'S GONNA BE SO MAD...
EH, HE'S ALWAYS MAD.
HE LIKES IT.
WE'RE DOING HIM A FAVOR GIVING HIM SOMETHING TO BE MAD ABOUT.
I DON'T KNOW WHO THIS "MAL" IS...
...BUT I GUARANTEE YOU, HE IS NOT YOUR PRIMARY WORRY AT THE MOMENT.
WHO THE HELL IS THAT?
I DON'T KNOW, BUT IT'S COMING OVER OUR MAIN COMM SYSTEM!
SOMEONE'S TAPPED IN!
CUT 'EM OFF!
I'M TRYING!
SO YOU'RE THE NOTORIOUS CHANG-BENITEZ GANG.
I'VE BEEN WATCHING YOU FOR A WHILE.
WHO ARE YOU?

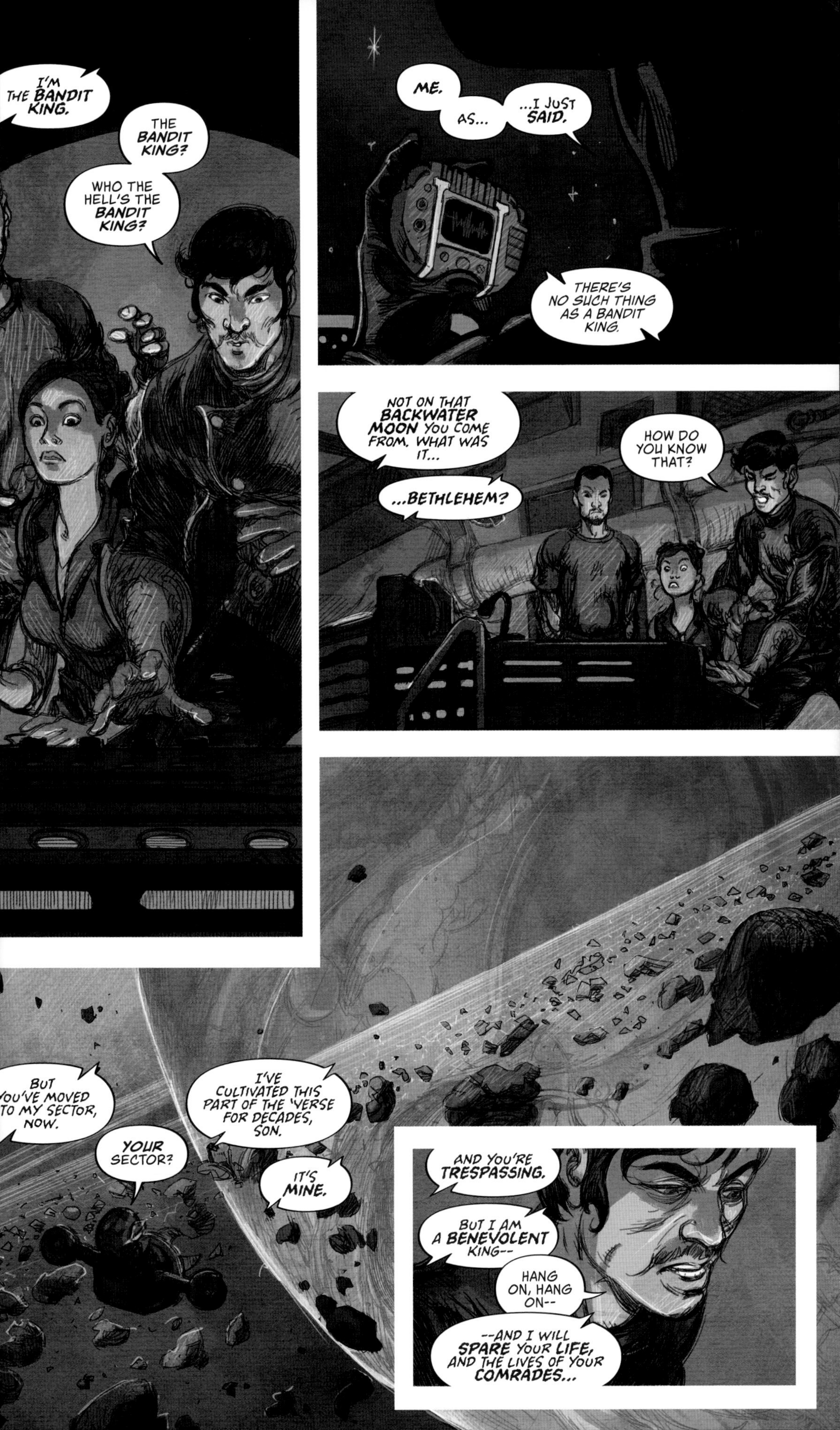
I'M THE BANDIT KING.
THE BANDIT KING?
WHO THE HELL'S THE BANDIT KING?
ME.
AS...
...I JUST SAID.
THERE'S NO SUCH THING AS A BANDIT KING.
NOT ON THAT BACKWATER MOON YOU COME FROM. WHAT WAS IT...
...BETHLEHEM?
HOW DO YOU KNOW THAT?
BUT YOU'VE MOVED TO MY SECTOR, NOW.
YOUR SECTOR?
I'VE CULTIVATED THIS PART OF THE 'VERSE FOR DECADES, SON.
IT'S MINE.
AND YOU'RE TRESPASSING.
BUT I AM A BENEVOLENT KING--
HANG ON, HANG ON--
--AND I WILL SPARE YOUR LIFE, AND THE LIVES OF YOUR COMRADES...

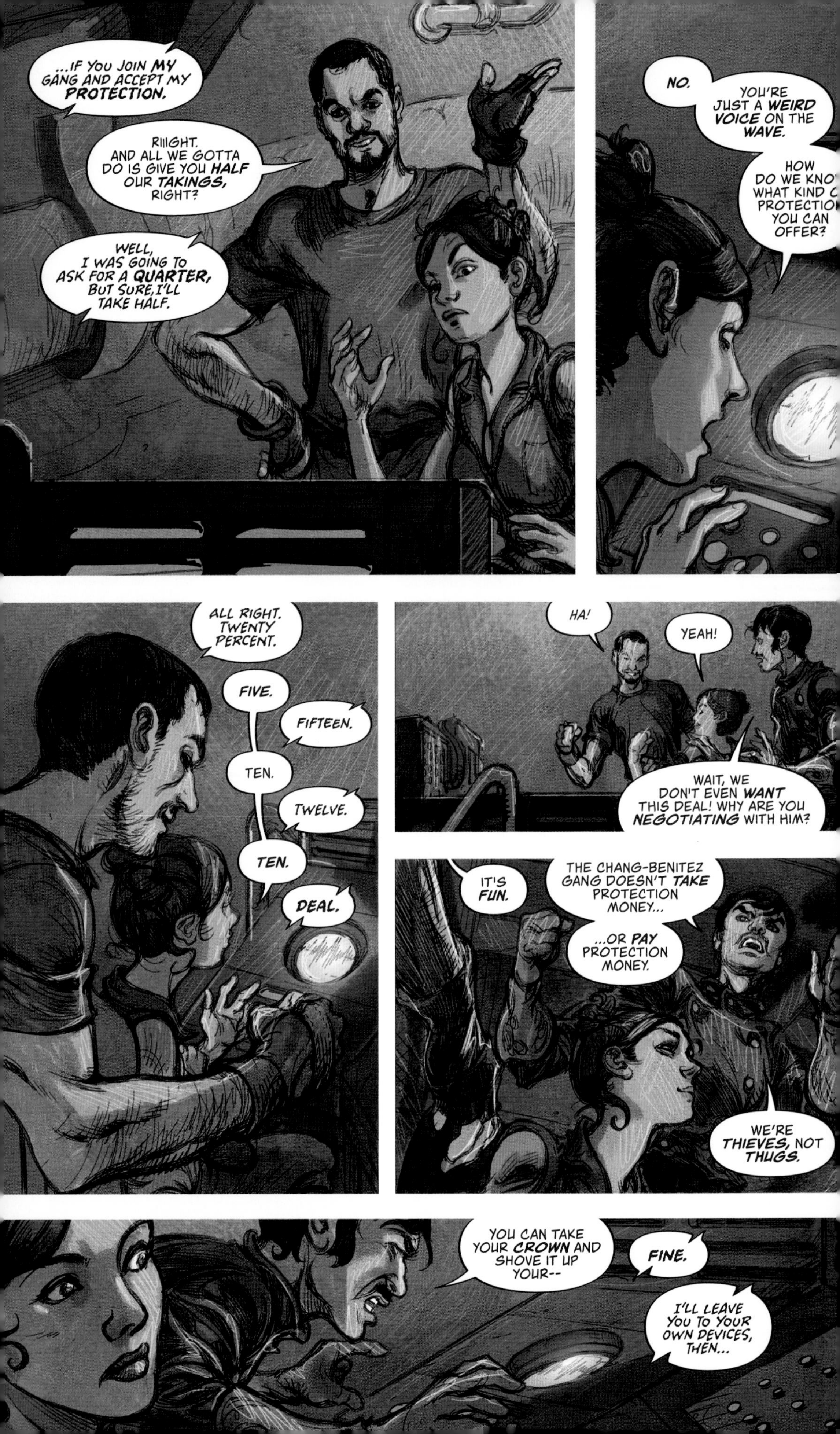
...IF YOU JOIN MY GANG AND ACCEPT MY PROTECTION.
RIIIGHT. AND ALL WE GOTTA DO IS GIVE YOU HALF OUR TAKINGS, RIGHT?
WELL, I WAS GOING TO ASK FOR A QUARTER, BUT SURE, I'LL TAKE HALF.
NO.
YOU'RE JUST A WEIRD VOICE ON THE WAVE.
HOW DO WE KNOW WHAT KIND OF PROTECTION YOU CAN OFFER?
ALL RIGHT. TWENTY PERCENT.
FIVE.
FIFTEEN.
TEN.
TWELVE.
TEN.
DEAL.
HA!
YEAH!
WAIT, WE DON'T EVEN WANT THIS DEAL! WHY ARE YOU NEGOTIATING WITH HIM?
IT'S FUN.
THE CHANG-BENITEZ GANG DOESN'T TAKE PROTECTION MONEY...
...OR PAY PROTECTION MONEY.
WE'RE THIEVES, NOT THUGS.
YOU CAN TAKE YOUR CROWN AND SHOVE IT UP YOUR--
FINE.
I'LL LEAVE YOU TO YOUR OWN DEVICES, THEN...

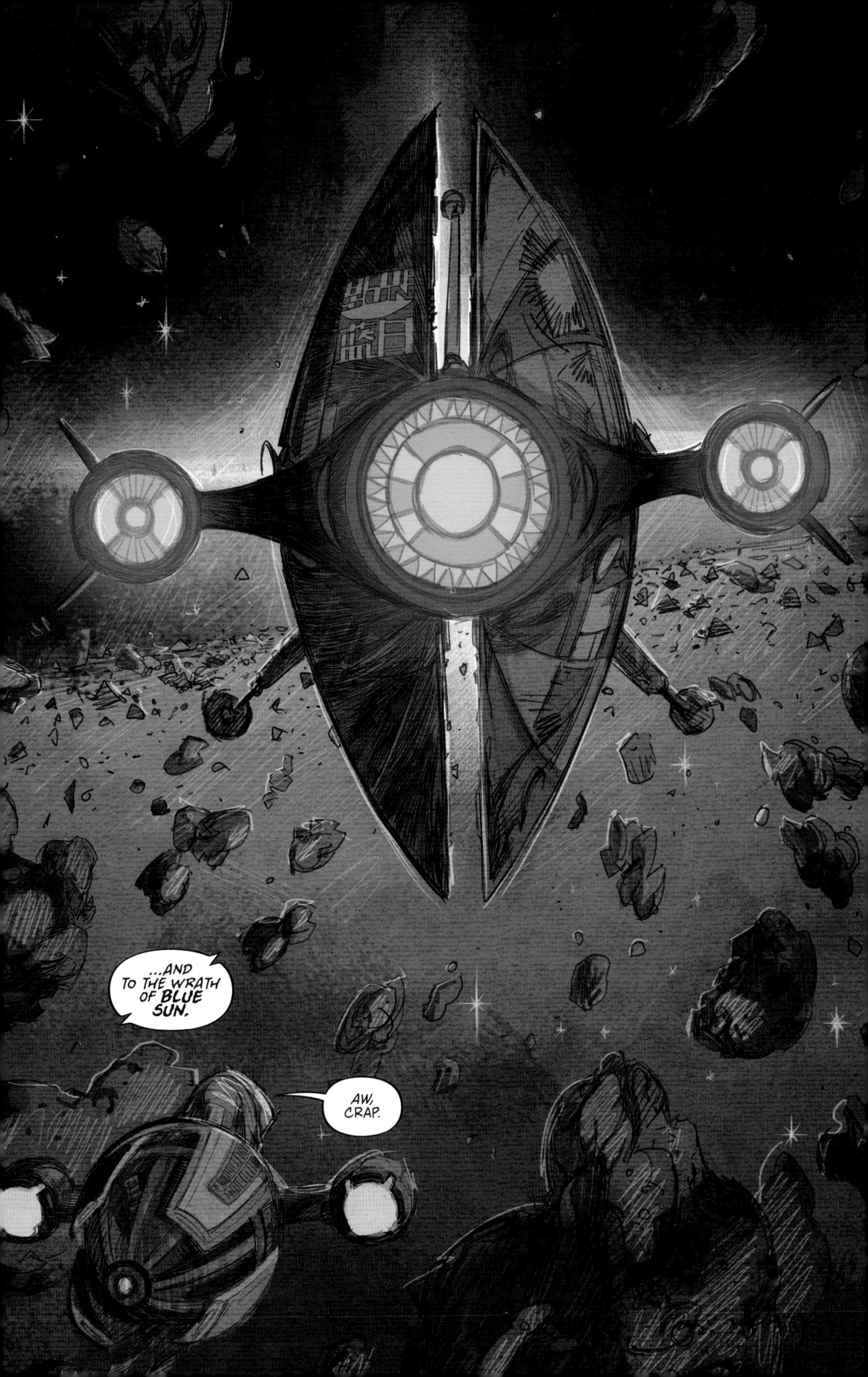
...AND TO THE WRATH OF **BLUE SUN.**
AW, CRAP.

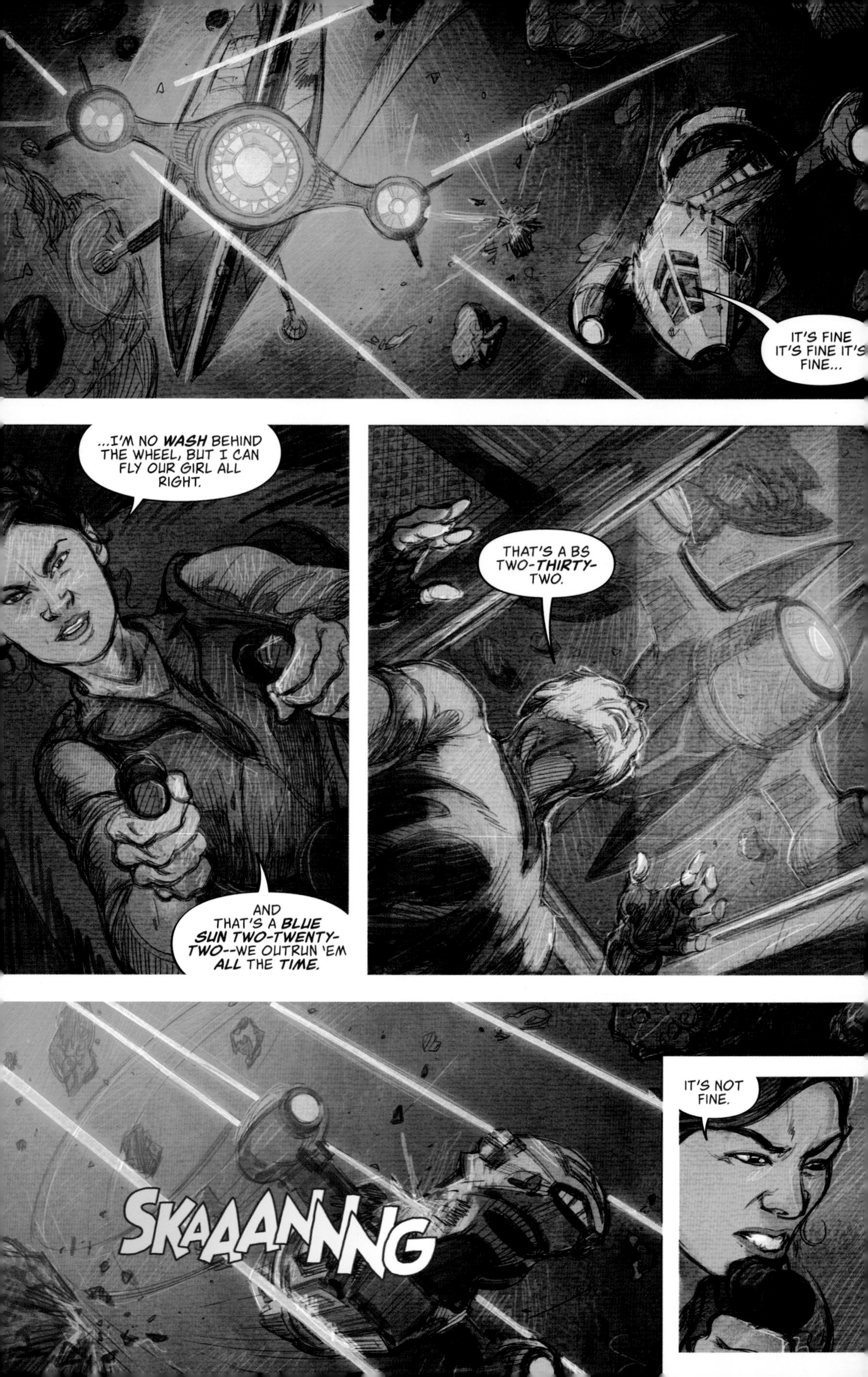
IT'S FINE IT'S FINE IT'S FINE...
...I'M NO WASH BEHIND THE WHEEL, BUT I CAN FLY OUR GIRL ALL RIGHT.
AND THAT'S A BLUE SUN TWO-TWENTY-TWO--WE OUTRUN 'EM ALL THE TIME.
THAT'S A BS TWO-THIRTY-TWO.
SKAAANNNG
IT'S NOT FINE.

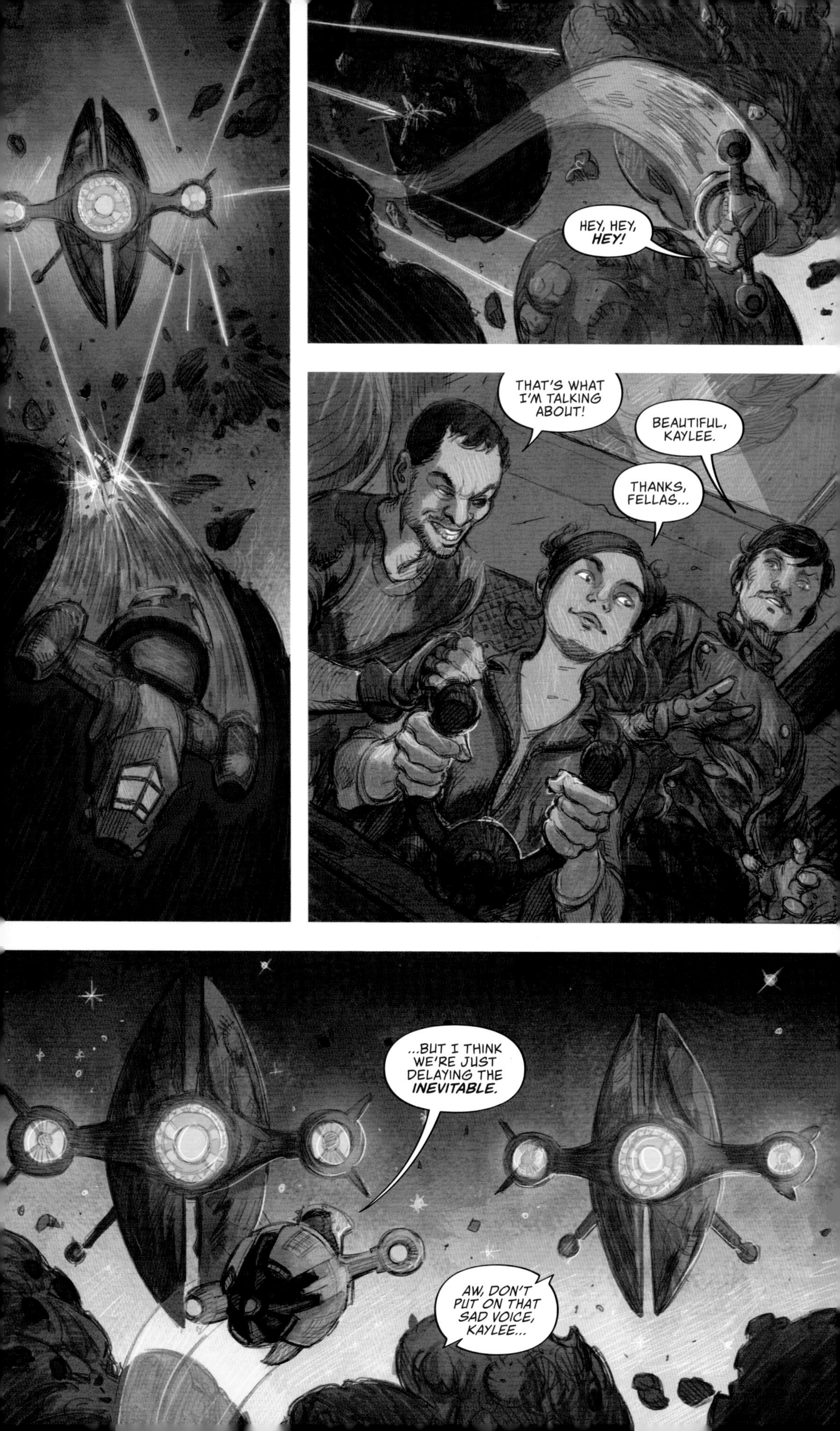
HEY, HEY, HEY!
THAT'S WHAT I'M TALKING ABOUT!
BEAUTIFUL, KAYLEE.
THANKS, FELLAS...
...BUT I THINK WE'RE JUST DELAYING THE INEVITABLE.
AW, DON'T PUT ON THAT SAD VOICE, KAYLEE...

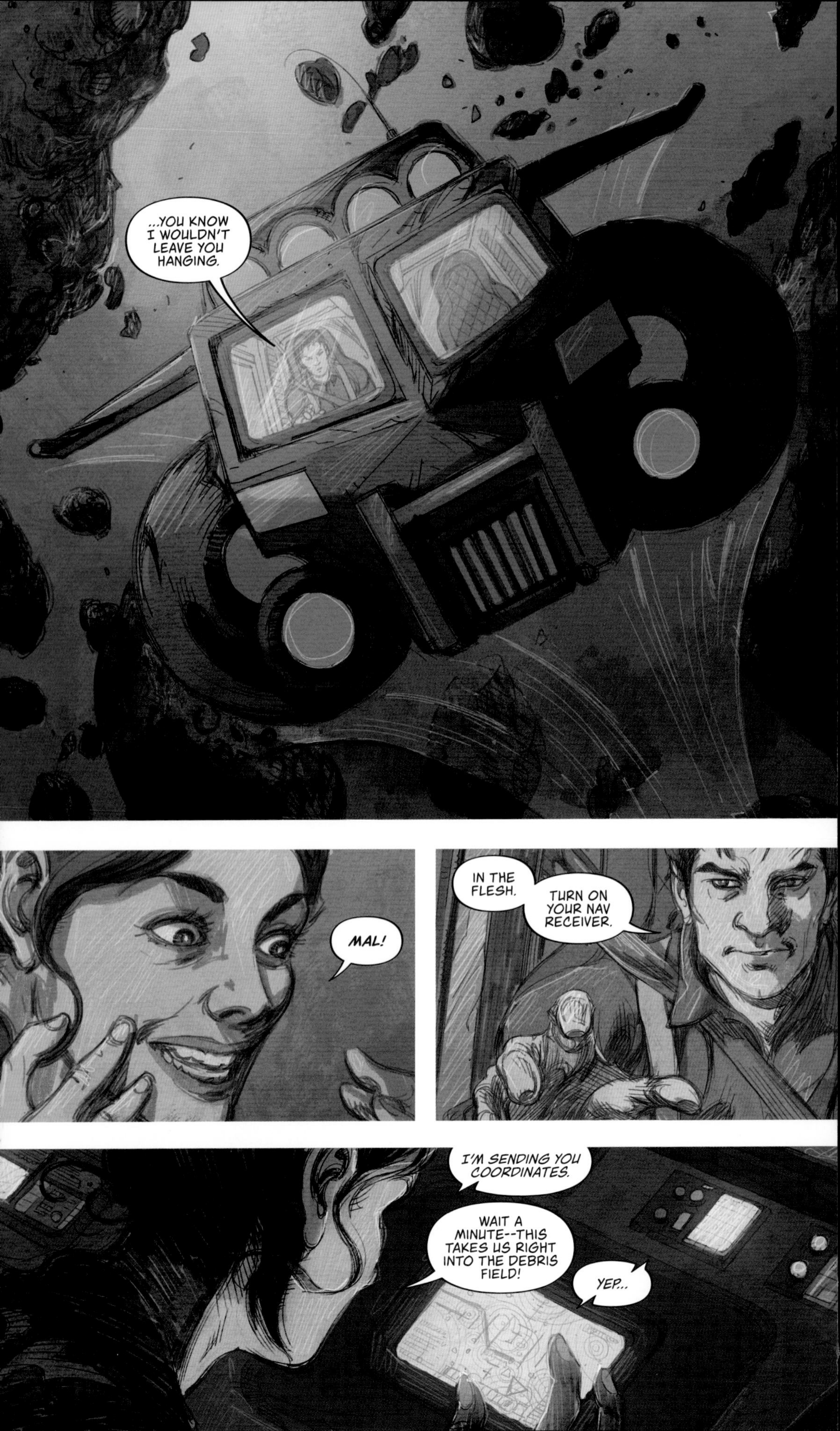
...YOU KNOW I WOULDN'T LEAVE YOU HANGING.
MAL!
IN THE FLESH.
TURN ON YOUR NAV RECEIVER.
I'M SENDING YOU COORDINATES.
WAIT A MINUTE--THIS TAKES US RIGHT INTO THE DEBRIS FIELD!
YEP...

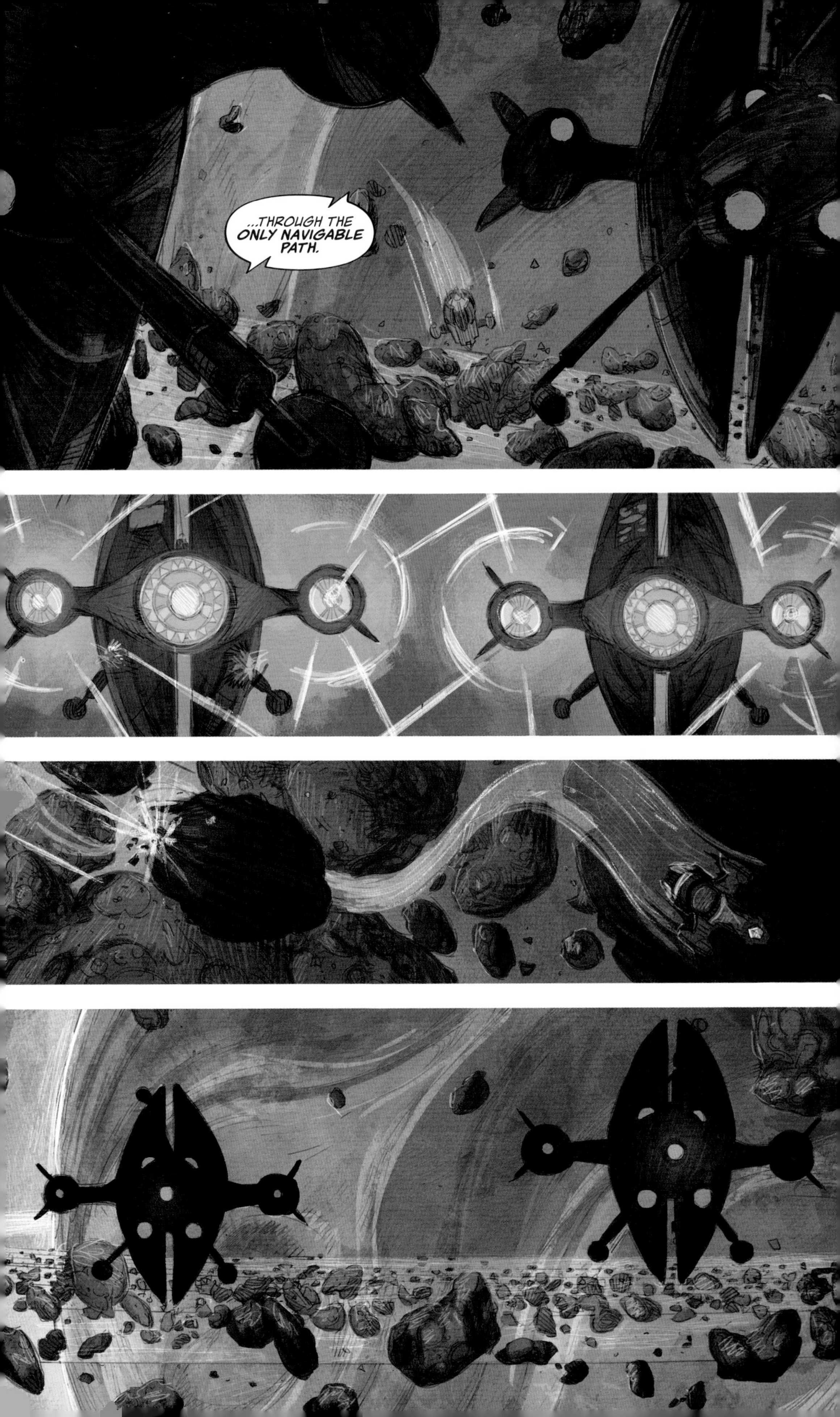
...THROUGH THE ONLY NAVIGABLE PATH.

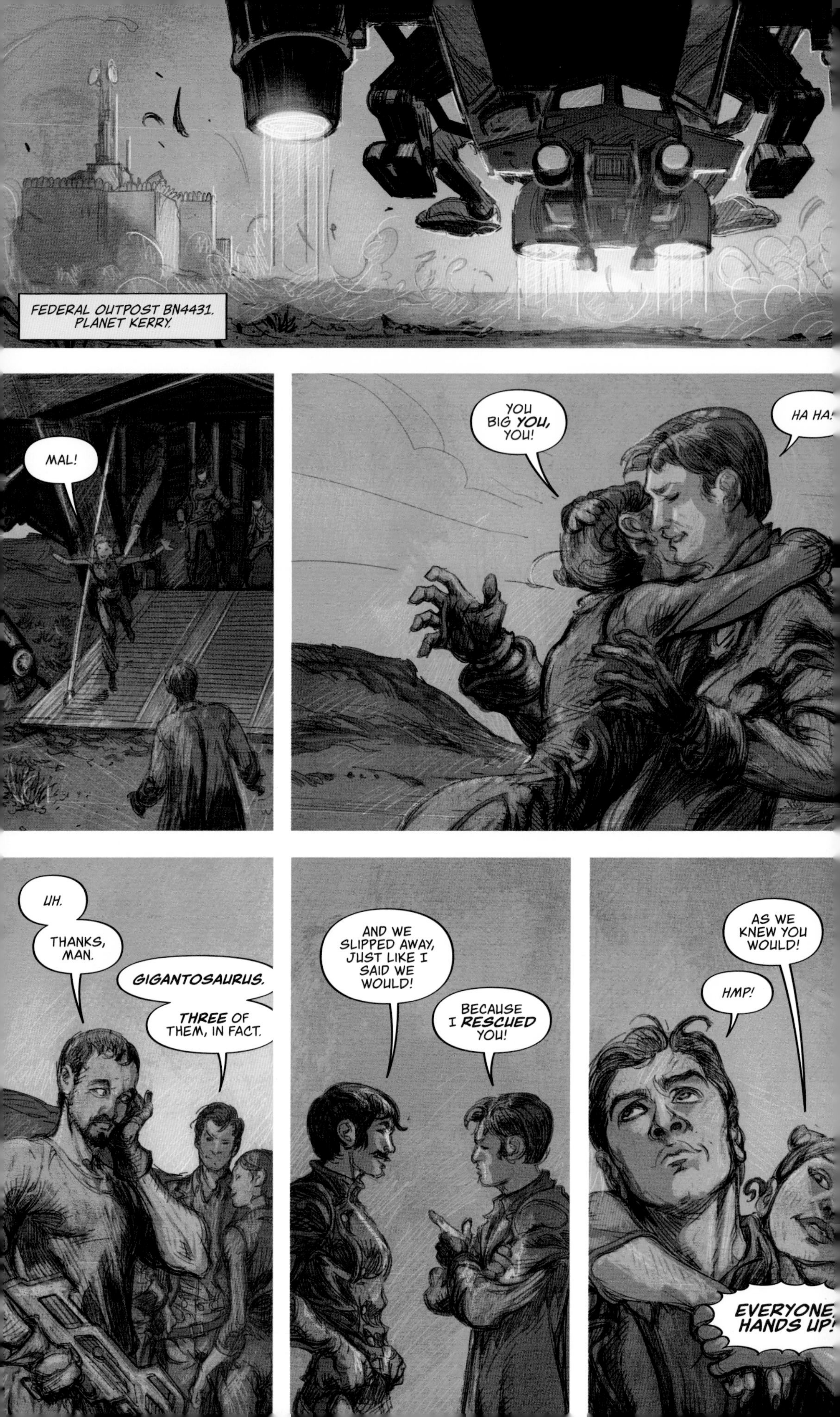
FEDERAL OUTPOST BN4431. PLANET KERRY.
MAL!
YOU BIG YOU, YOU!
HA HA!
UH.
THANKS, MAN.
GIGANTOSAURUS.
THREE OF THEM, IN FACT.
AND WE SLIPPED AWAY, JUST LIKE I SAID WE WOULD!
BECAUSE I RESCUED YOU!
AS WE KNEW YOU WOULD!
HMP!
EVERYONE, HANDS UP!

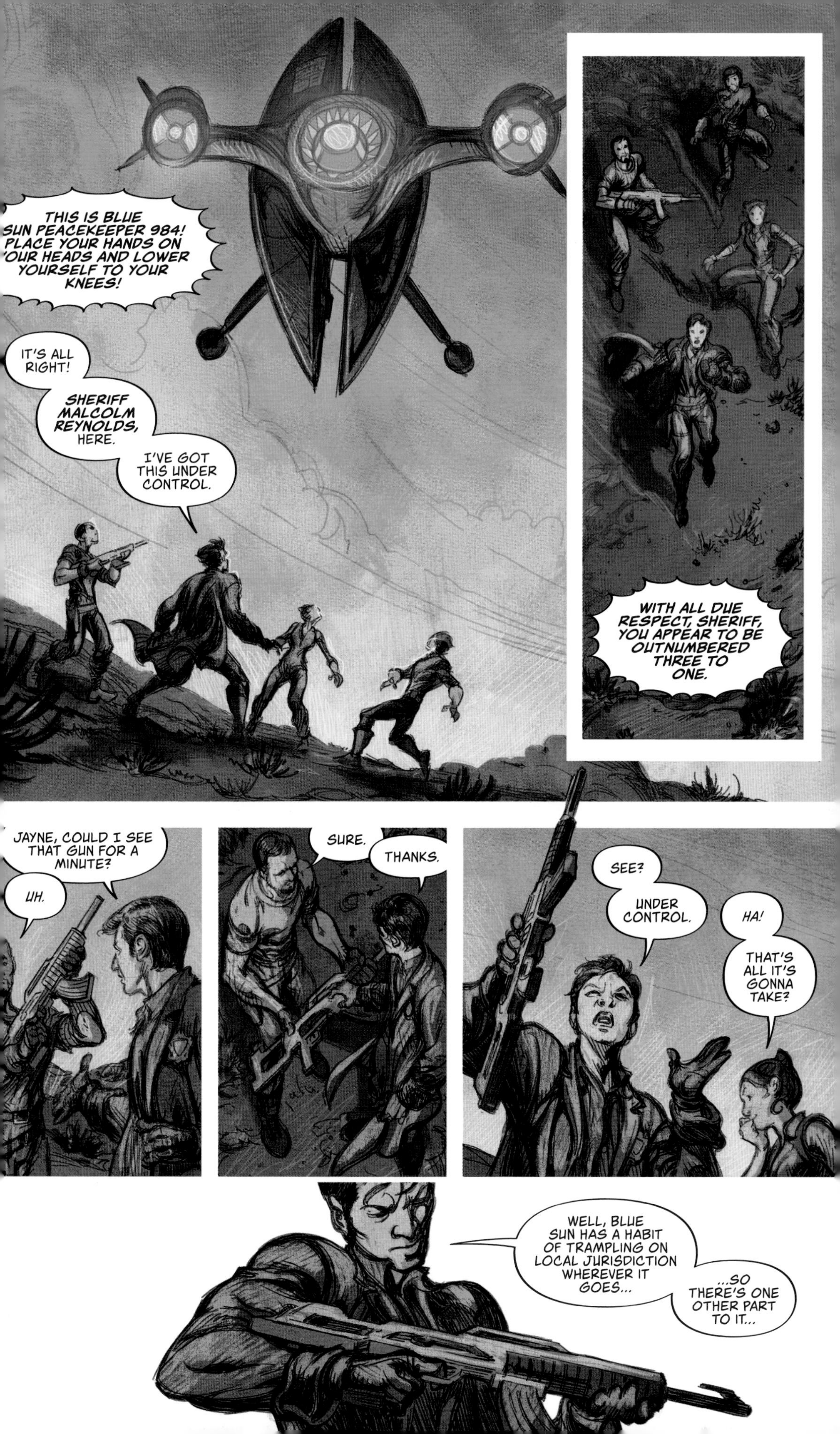
THIS IS BLUE SUN PEACEKEEPER 984! PLACE YOUR HANDS ON YOUR HEADS AND LOWER YOURSELF TO YOUR KNEES!
IT'S ALL RIGHT!
SHERIFF MALCOLM REYNOLDS, HERE.
I'VE GOT THIS UNDER CONTROL.
WITH ALL DUE RESPECT, SHERIFF, YOU APPEAR TO BE OUTNUMBERED THREE TO ONE.
JAYNE, COULD I SEE THAT GUN FOR A MINUTE?
UH.
SURE.
THANKS.
SEE?
UNDER CONTROL.
HA!
THAT'S ALL IT'S GONNA TAKE?
WELL, BLUE SUN HAS A HABIT OF TRAMPLING ON LOCAL JURISDICTION WHEREVER IT GOES...
...SO THERE'S ONE OTHER PART TO IT...

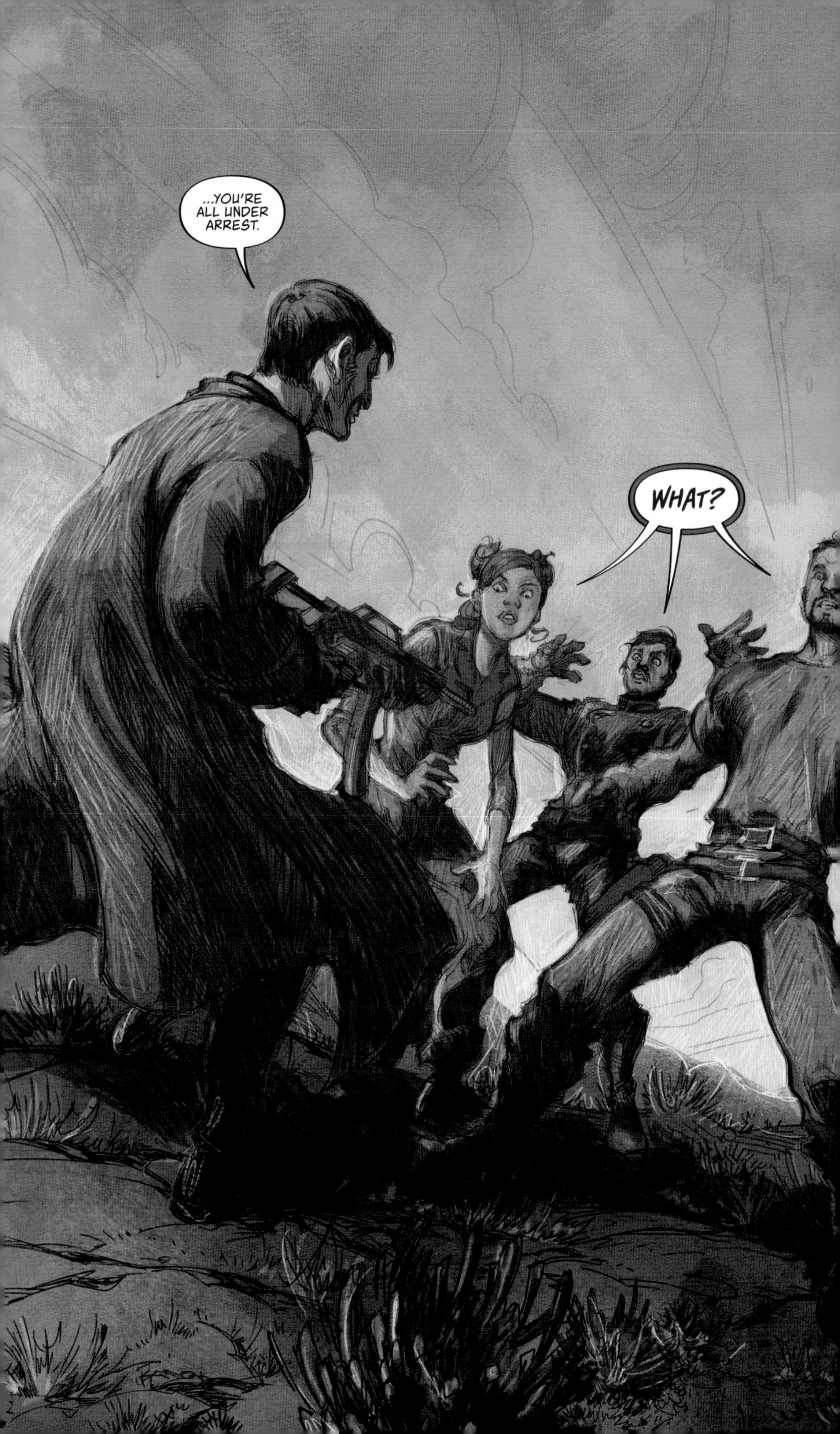
...YOU'RE ALL UNDER ARREST.
WHAT?

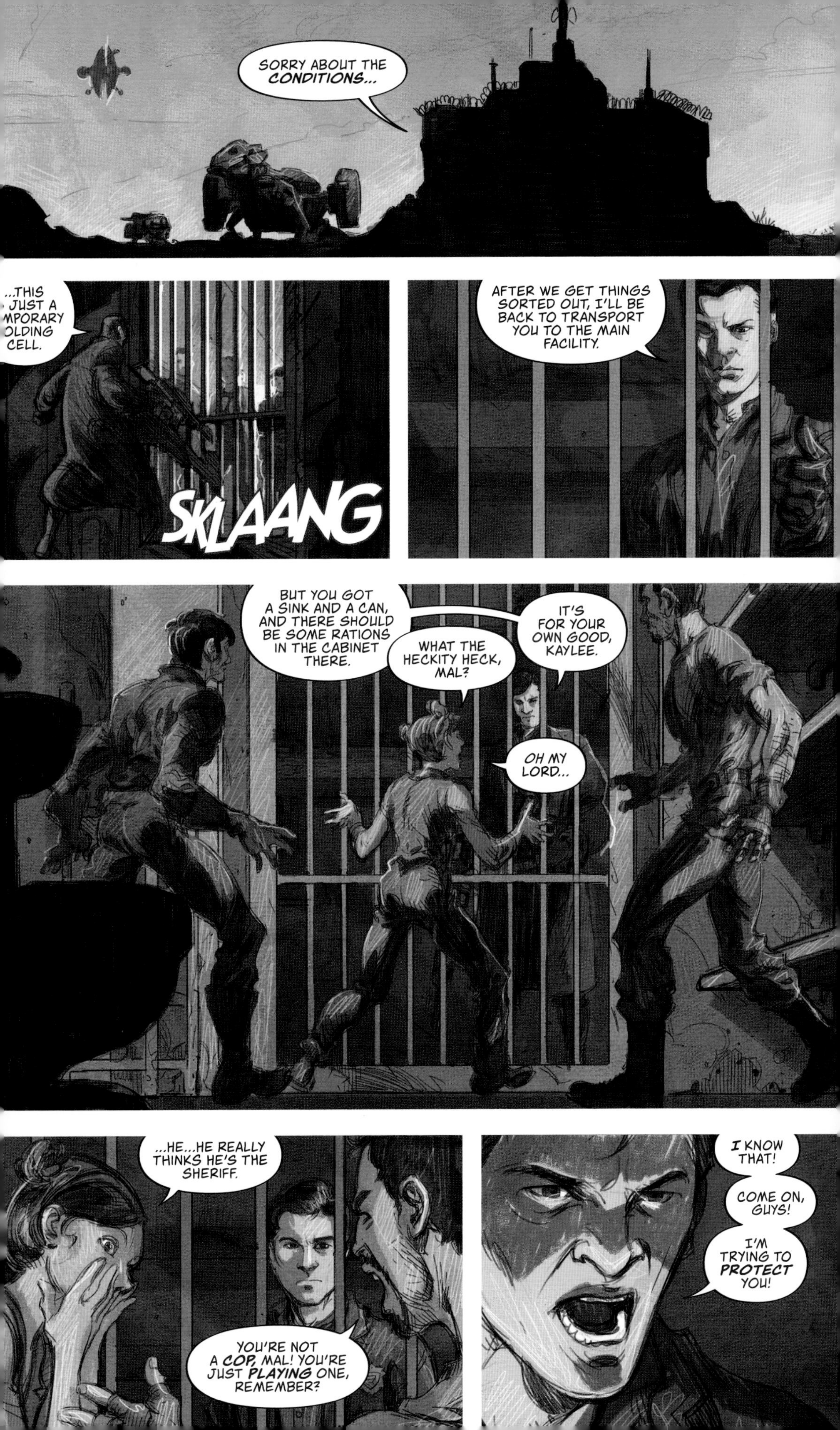
SORRY ABOUT THE CONDITIONS...
...THIS JUST A MPORARY OLDING CELL.
SKLAANG
AFTER WE GET THINGS SORTED OUT, I'LL BE BACK TO TRANSPORT YOU TO THE MAIN FACILITY.
BUT YOU GOT A SINK AND A CAN, AND THERE SHOULD BE SOME RATIONS IN THE CABINET THERE.
IT'S FOR YOUR OWN GOOD, KAYLEE.
WHAT THE HECKITY HECK, MAL?
OH MY LORD...
...HE...HE REALLY THINKS HE'S THE SHERIFF.
YOU'RE NOT A COP, MAL! YOU'RE JUST PLAYING ONE, REMEMBER?
I KNOW THAT!
COME ON, GUYS!
I'M TRYING TO PROTECT YOU!

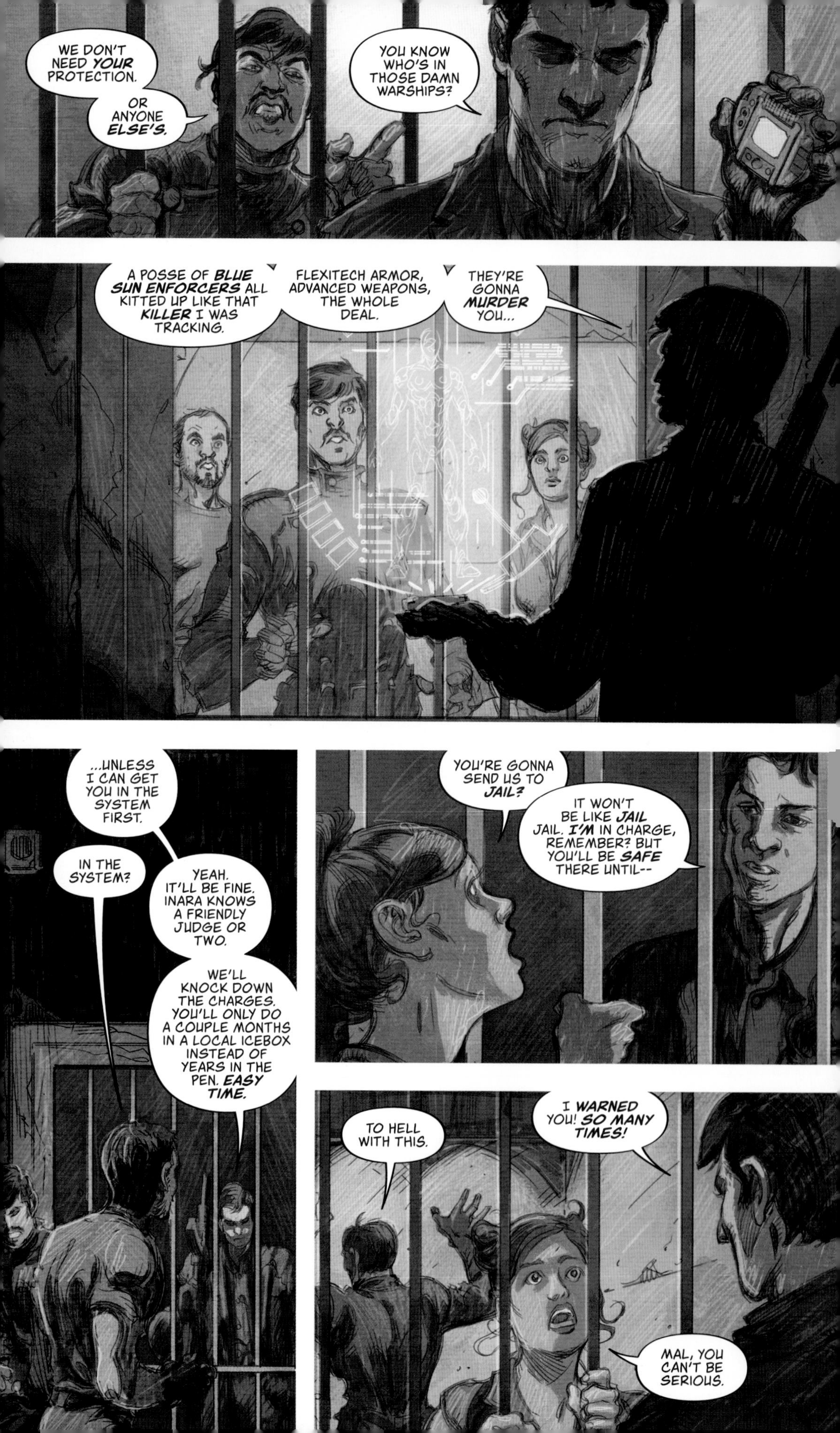
WE DON'T NEED YOUR PROTECTION.
OR ANYONE ELSE'S.
YOU KNOW WHO'S IN THOSE DAMN WARSHIPS?
A POSSE OF BLUE SUN ENFORCERS ALL KITTED UP LIKE THAT KILLER I WAS TRACKING.
FLEXITECH ARMOR, ADVANCED WEAPONS, THE WHOLE DEAL.
THEY'RE GONNA MURDER YOU...
...UNLESS I CAN GET YOU IN THE SYSTEM FIRST.
IN THE SYSTEM?
YEAH. IT'LL BE FINE. INARA KNOWS A FRIENDLY JUDGE OR TWO.
WE'LL KNOCK DOWN THE CHARGES. YOU'LL ONLY DO A COUPLE MONTHS IN A LOCAL ICEBOX INSTEAD OF YEARS IN THE PEN. EASY TIME.
YOU'RE GONNA SEND US TO JAIL?
IT WON'T BE LIKE JAIL JAIL. I'M IN CHARGE, REMEMBER? BUT YOU'LL BE SAFE THERE UNTIL--
TO HELL WITH THIS.
I WARNED YOU! SO MANY TIMES!
MAL, YOU CAN'T BE SERIOUS.

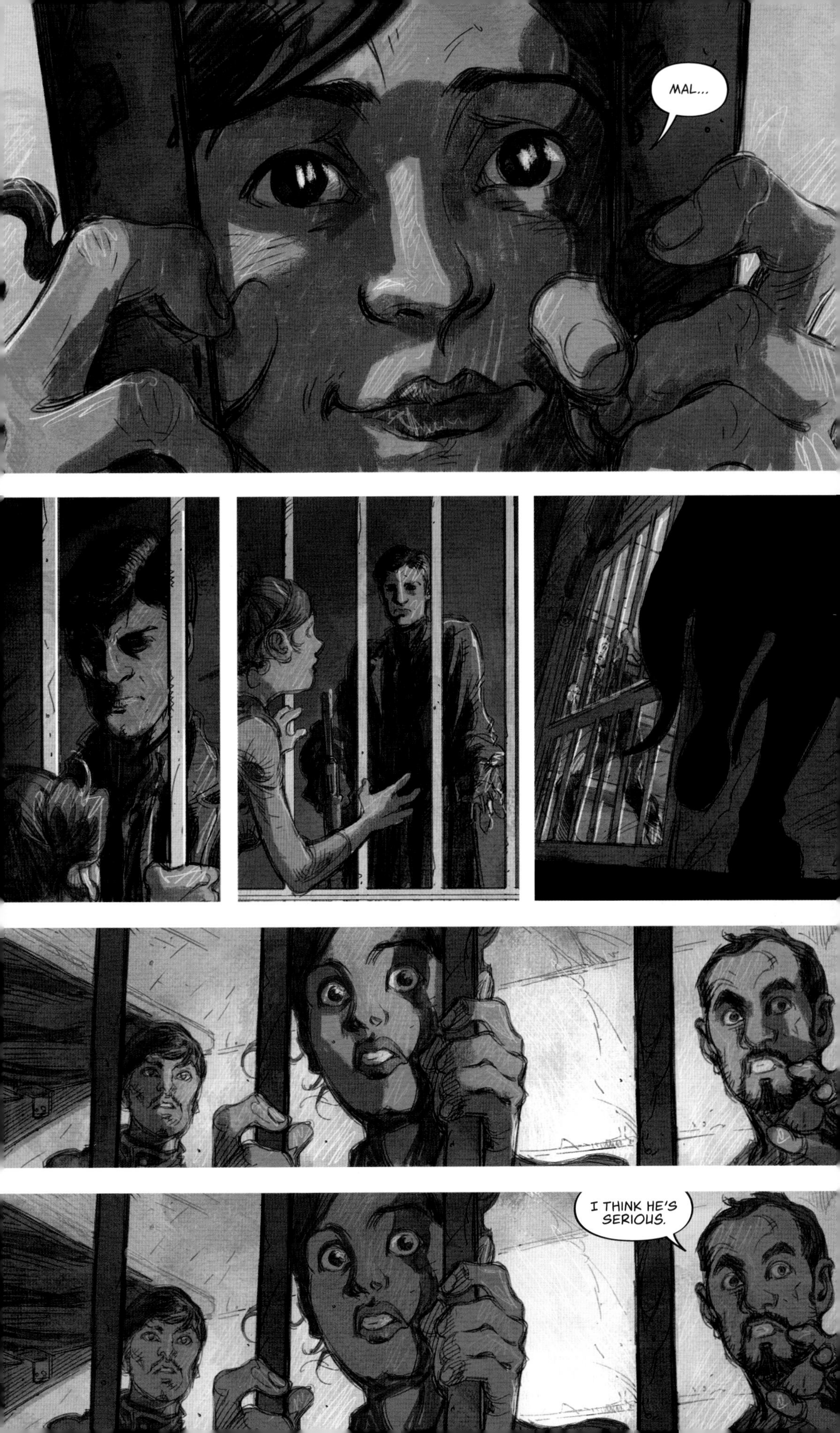
MAL...
I THINK HE'S SERIOUS.

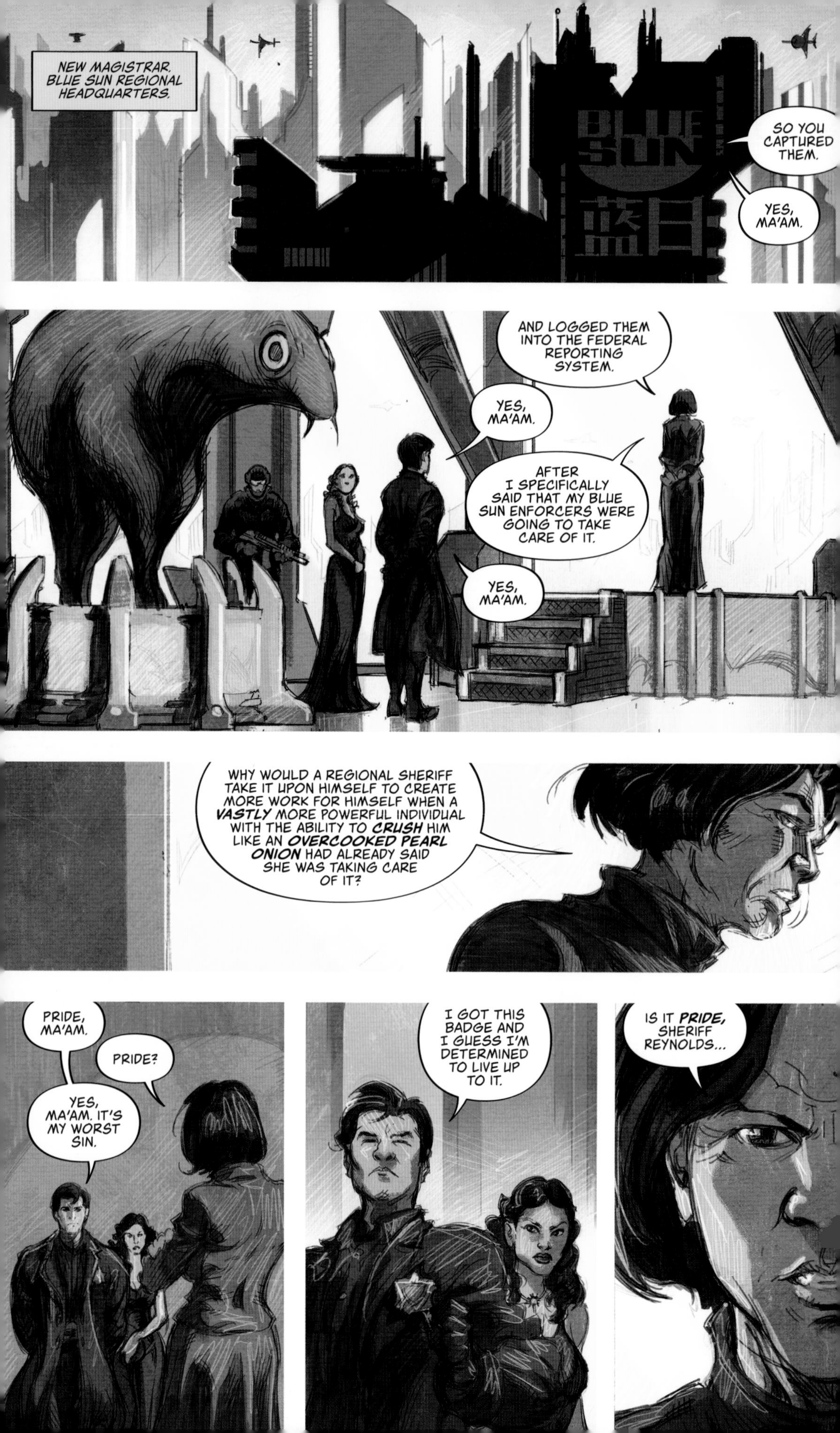
NEW MAGISTRAR. BLUE SUN REGIONAL HEADQUARTERS.
BLUE SUN
蓝日
SO YOU CAPTURED THEM.
YES, MA'AM.
AND LOGGED THEM INTO THE FEDERAL REPORTING SYSTEM.
YES, MA'AM.
AFTER I SPECIFICALLY SAID THAT MY BLUE SUN ENFORCERS WERE GOING TO TAKE CARE OF IT.
YES, MA'AM.
WHY WOULD A REGIONAL SHERIFF TAKE IT UPON HIMSELF TO CREATE MORE WORK FOR HIMSELF WHEN A *VASTLY* MORE POWERFUL INDIVIDUAL WITH THE ABILITY TO *CRUSH* HIM LIKE AN *OVERCOOKED PEARL ONION* HAD ALREADY SAID SHE WAS TAKING CARE OF IT?
PRIDE, MA'AM.
PRIDE?
YES, MA'AM. IT'S MY WORST SIN.
I GOT THIS BADGE AND I GUESS I'M DETERMINED TO LIVE UP TO IT.
IS IT *PRIDE*, SHERIFF REYNOLDS...

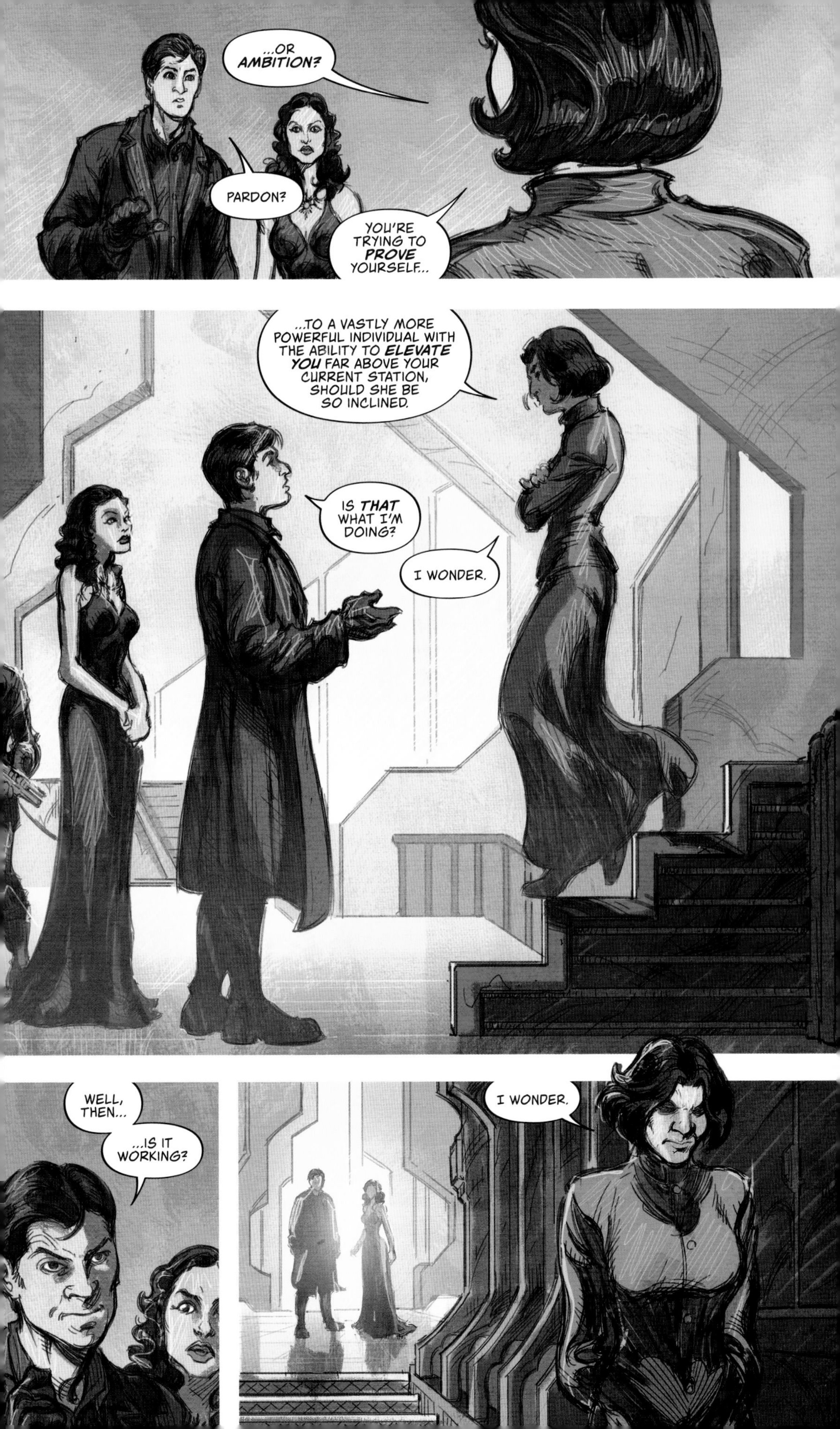
...OR AMBITION?
PARDON?
YOU'RE TRYING TO PROVE YOURSELF...
...TO A VASTLY MORE POWERFUL INDIVIDUAL WITH THE ABILITY TO ELEVATE YOU FAR ABOVE YOUR CURRENT STATION, SHOULD SHE BE SO INCLINED.
IS THAT WHAT I'M DOING?
I WONDER.
WELL, THEN...
...IS IT WORKING?
I WONDER.

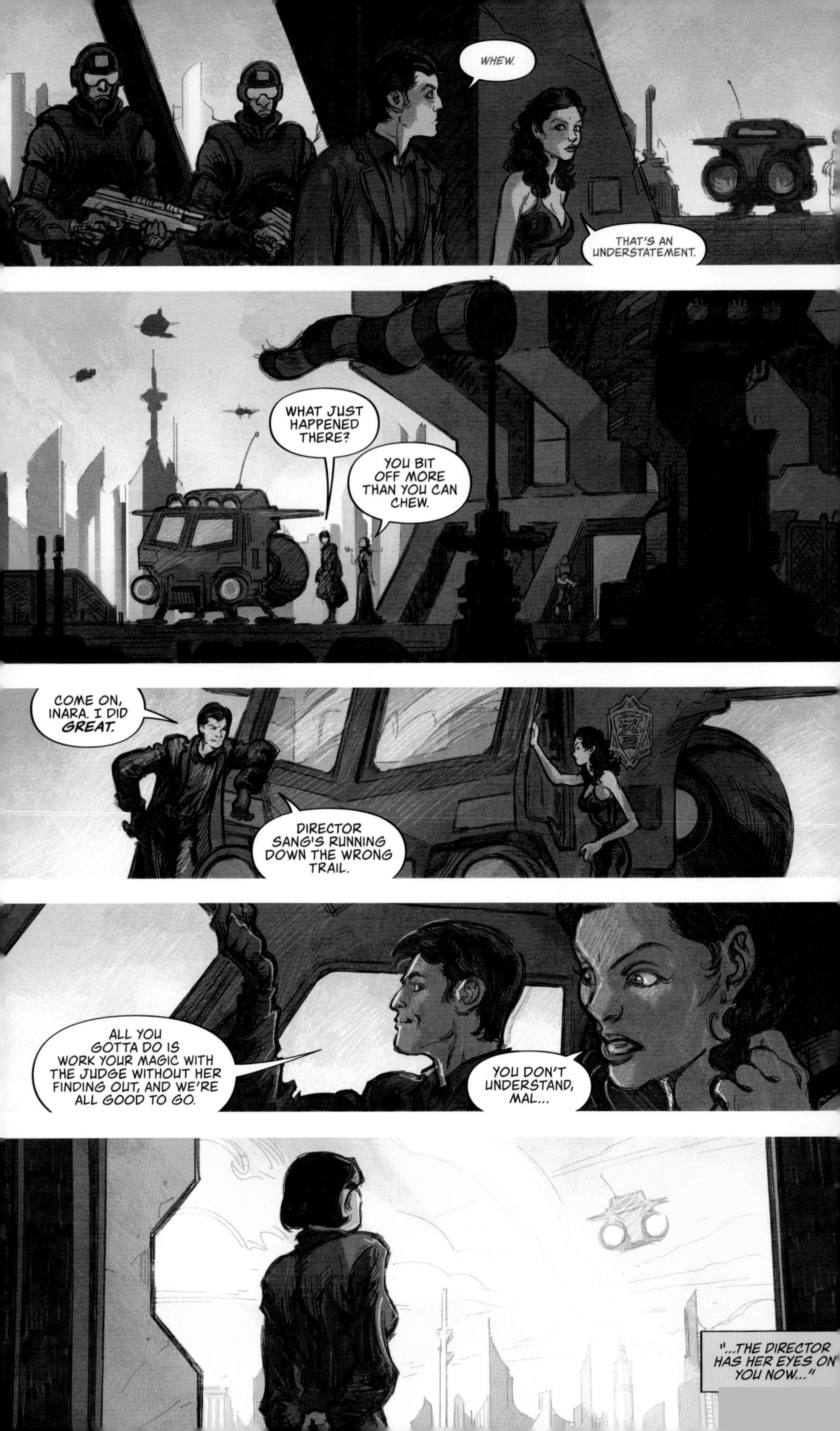
WHEW.
THAT'S AN UNDERSTATEMENT.
WHAT JUST HAPPENED THERE?
YOU BIT OFF MORE THAN YOU CAN CHEW.
COME ON, INARA. I DID GREAT.
DIRECTOR SANG'S RUNNING DOWN THE WRONG TRAIL.
ALL YOU GOTTA DO IS WORK YOUR MAGIC WITH THE JUDGE WITHOUT HER FINDING OUT, AND WE'RE ALL GOOD TO GO.
YOU DON'T UNDERSTAND, MAL...
"...THE DIRECTOR HAS HER EYES ON YOU NOW..."

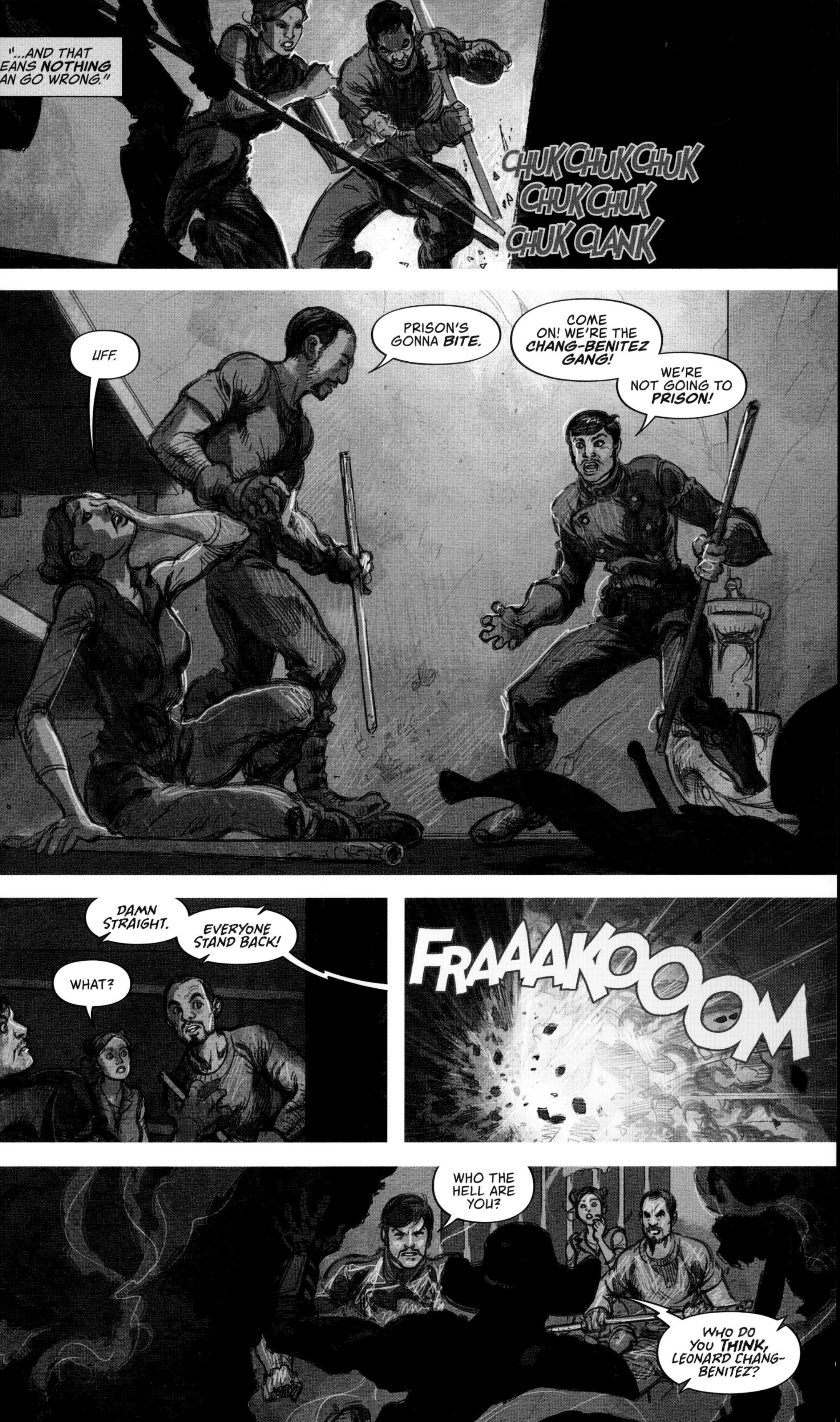
"...AND THAT
EANS NOTHING
AN GO WRONG."
CHUK CHUK CHUK
CHUK CHUK
CHUK CLANK
UFF.
PRISON'S GONNA BITE.
COME ON! WE'RE THE CHANG-BENITEZ GANG!
WE'RE NOT GOING TO PRISON!
DAMN STRAIGHT.
EVERYONE STAND BACK!
WHAT?
FRAAAKOOOM
WHO THE HELL ARE YOU?
WHO DO YOU THINK, LEONARD CHANG-BENITEZ?

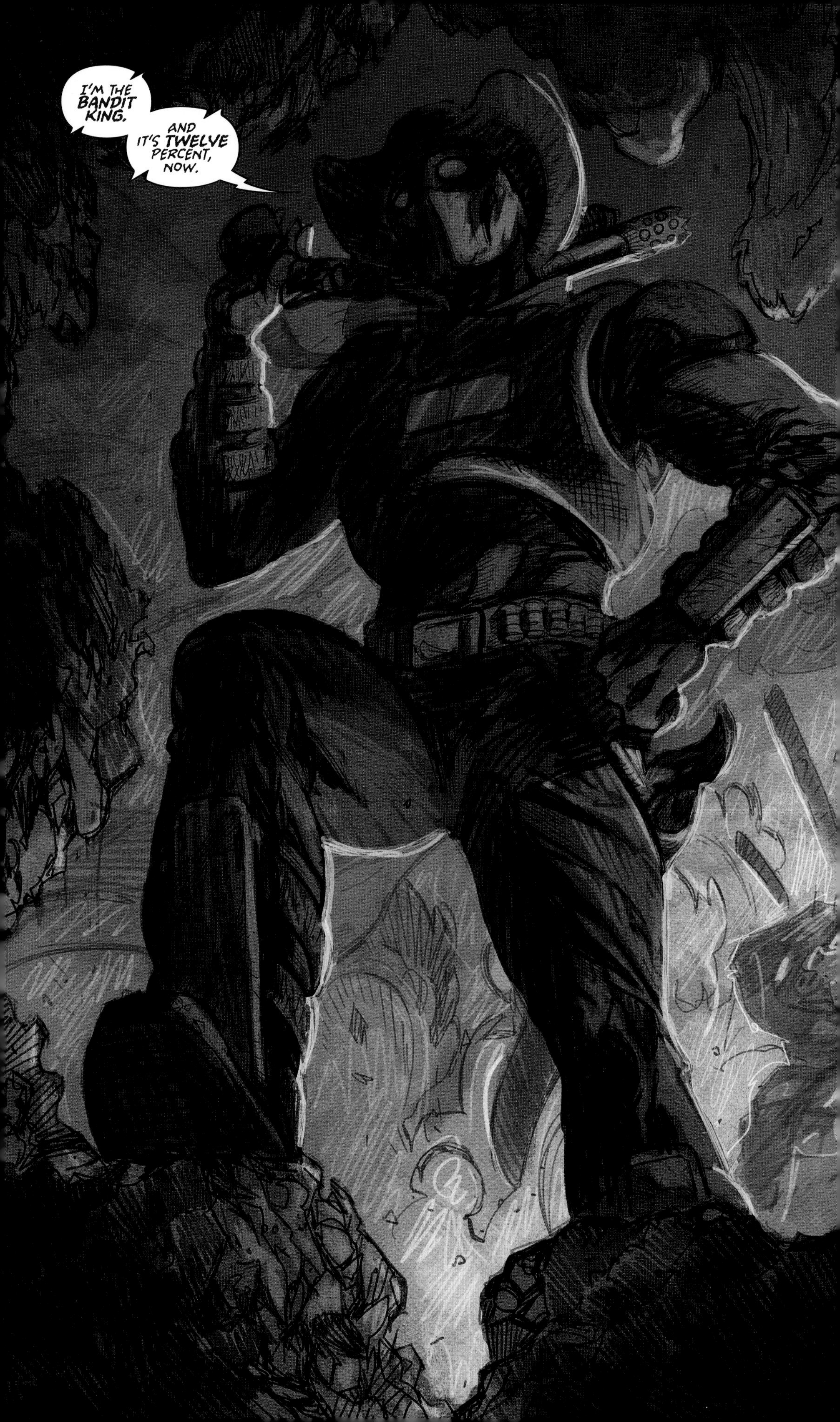
I'M THE BANDIT KING.
AND IT'S TWELVE PERCENT, NOW.

NO POWER IN THE 'VERSE CAN STOP ME.

THAT MAKES US SPE...

OH, I GOT HEATHENS APLENTY RIGHT HERE.

...if you're dead.

DEAD.

...D IN MY AWFUL MY SKY.

...spot, sir. She still has the...

...ey were gonna waltz through Serenity Valley, and we choked 'em with those words.

This is why... lost, you k...

SUP...

YOU'R... WE AL...

Maybe I'm not a fancy gentleman like you with your...very fine hat. But I do business. We're here for...

喧闹起...

I brought you some supper. But if you'd prefer a lecture I have a few very catchy ones prepped.

喧闹起来

Ship like this will be with you 'til the day you die. That's 'cause it's a death trap.

喧闹起来

Curse your sudden but INEVITABLE BETRAYAL.

Ain't heard back yet. Didn't she shoot you one time?

WHY DO... WE SHO... HER FIRS...

BEING RIGHT...

It's a real burden...

I'm in a tricky position. I guess you know. Got me a boatload of...

THIEVES. IN A DEN OF THIEVES.

A MAN OF HONO...

IF YOU DIE... HAVE YOUR... CAN...

Preacher, don't t...

pretty specific...

Quite specific.

I brought you some supper. But if you'd prefer a lecture I have a few very catchy ones prepped.

SIN AND HELLFIRE. ONE HAS...

喧闹

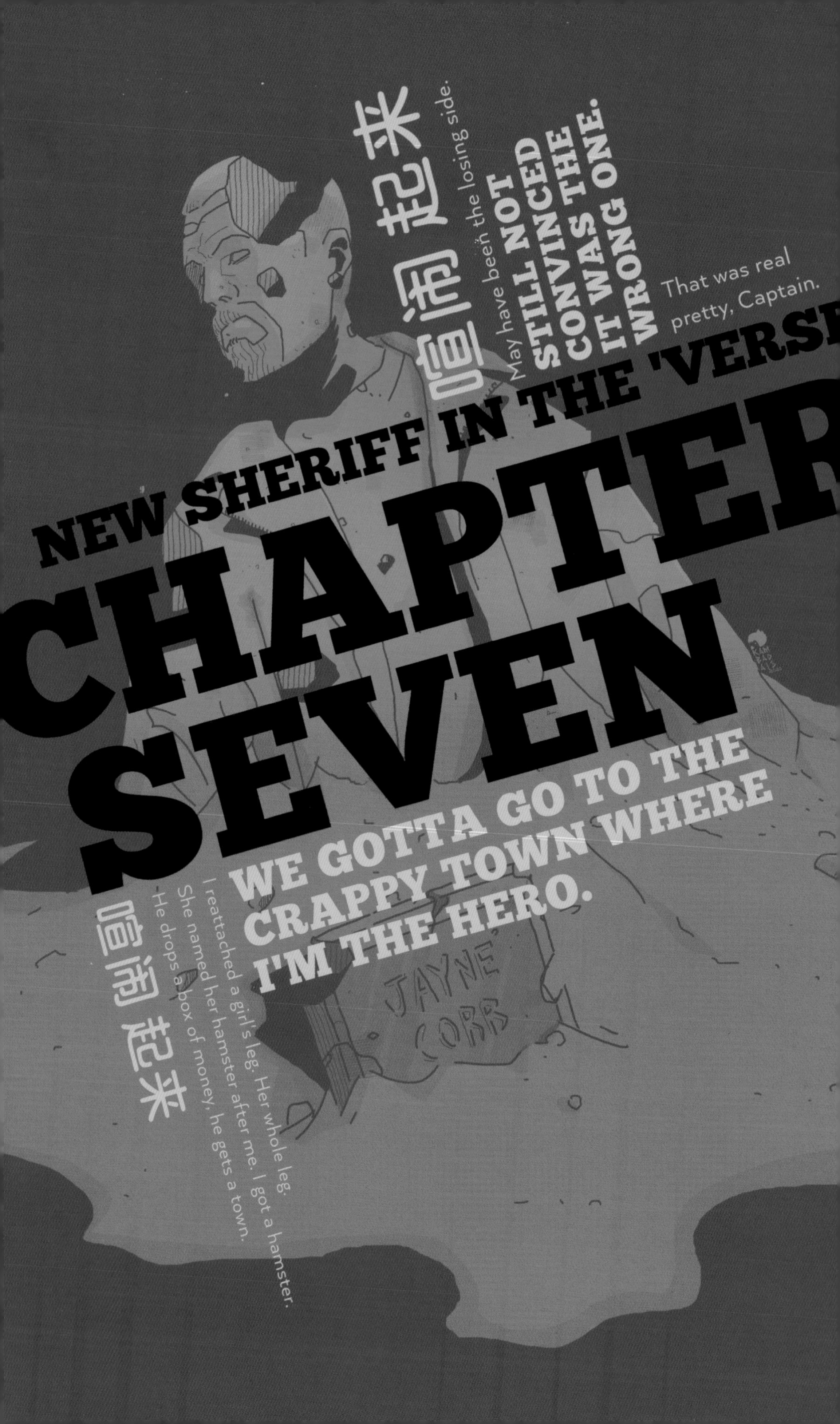
喧闹起来
May have been the losing side.
STILL NOT CONVINCED IT WAS THE WRONG ONE.
That was real pretty, Captain.
NEW SHERIFF IN THE 'VERSE
CHAPTER SEVEN
WE GOTTA GO TO THE CRAPPY TOWN WHERE I'M THE HERO.
喧闹起来
I reattached a girl's leg. Her whole leg.
She named her hamster after me. I got a hamster.
He drops a box of money, he gets a town.
JAYNE COBB

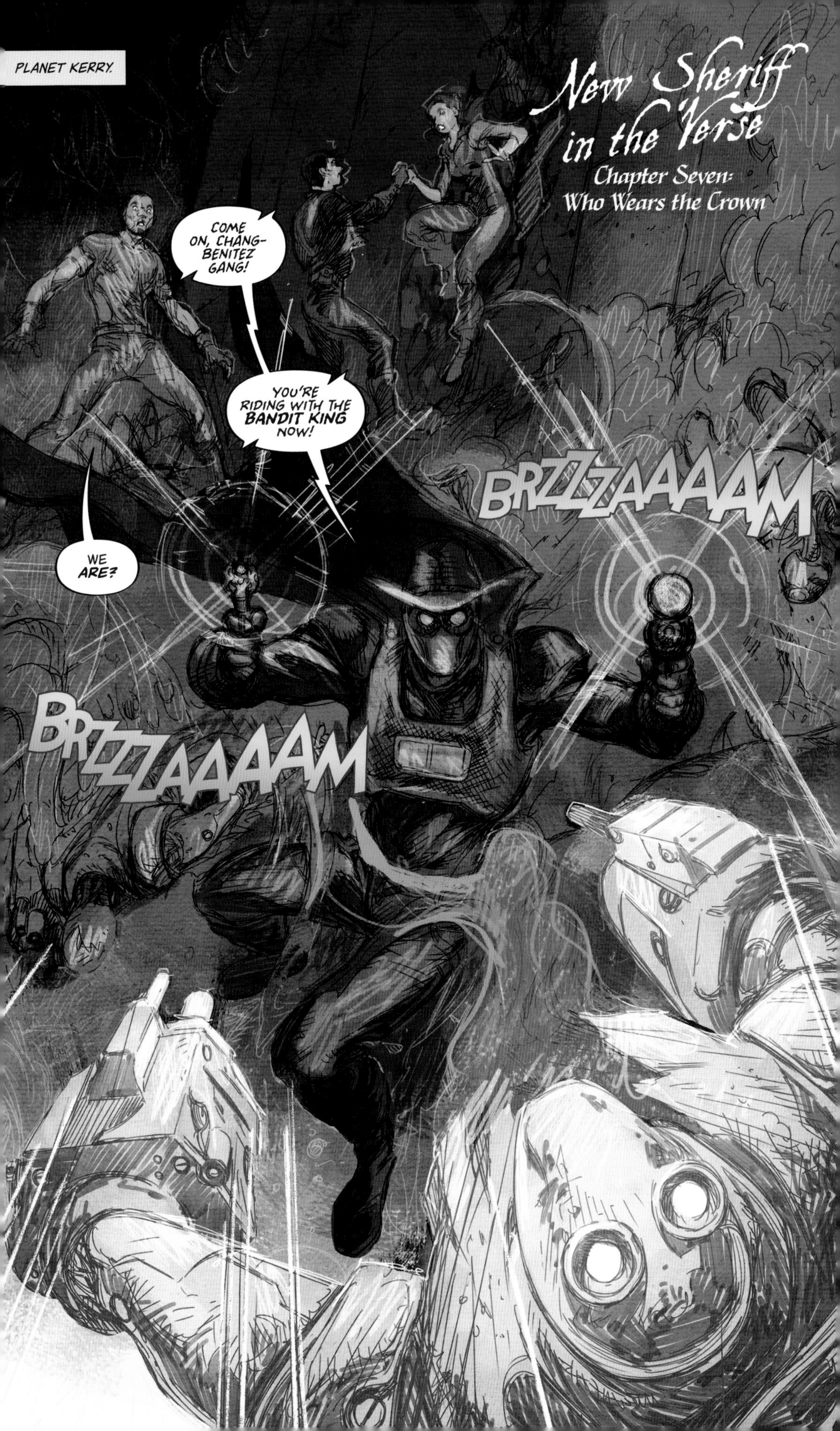
PLANET KERRY.
New Sheriff in the 'Verse
Chapter Seven: Who Wears the Crown
COME ON, CHANG-BENITEZ GANG!
YOU'RE RIDING WITH THE BANDIT KING NOW!
WE ARE?
BRZZZAAAAAM
BRZZZAAAAAM

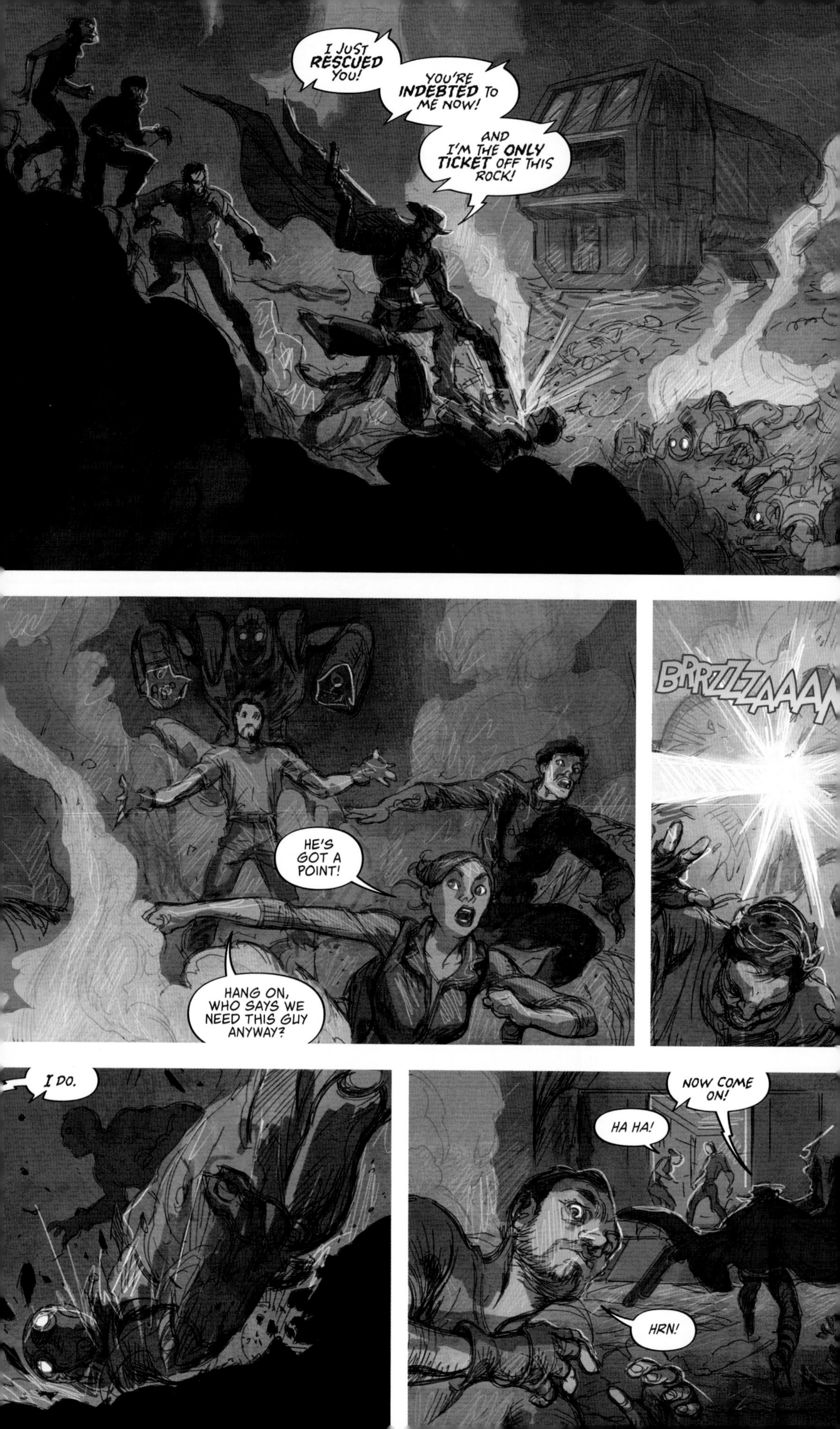
I JUST RESCUED YOU!
YOU'RE INDEBTED TO ME NOW!
AND I'M THE ONLY TICKET OFF THIS ROCK!
HE'S GOT A POINT!
HANG ON, WHO SAYS WE NEED THIS GUY ANYWAY?
BRRZZZAAAA
I DO.
NOW COME ON!
HA HA!
HRN!

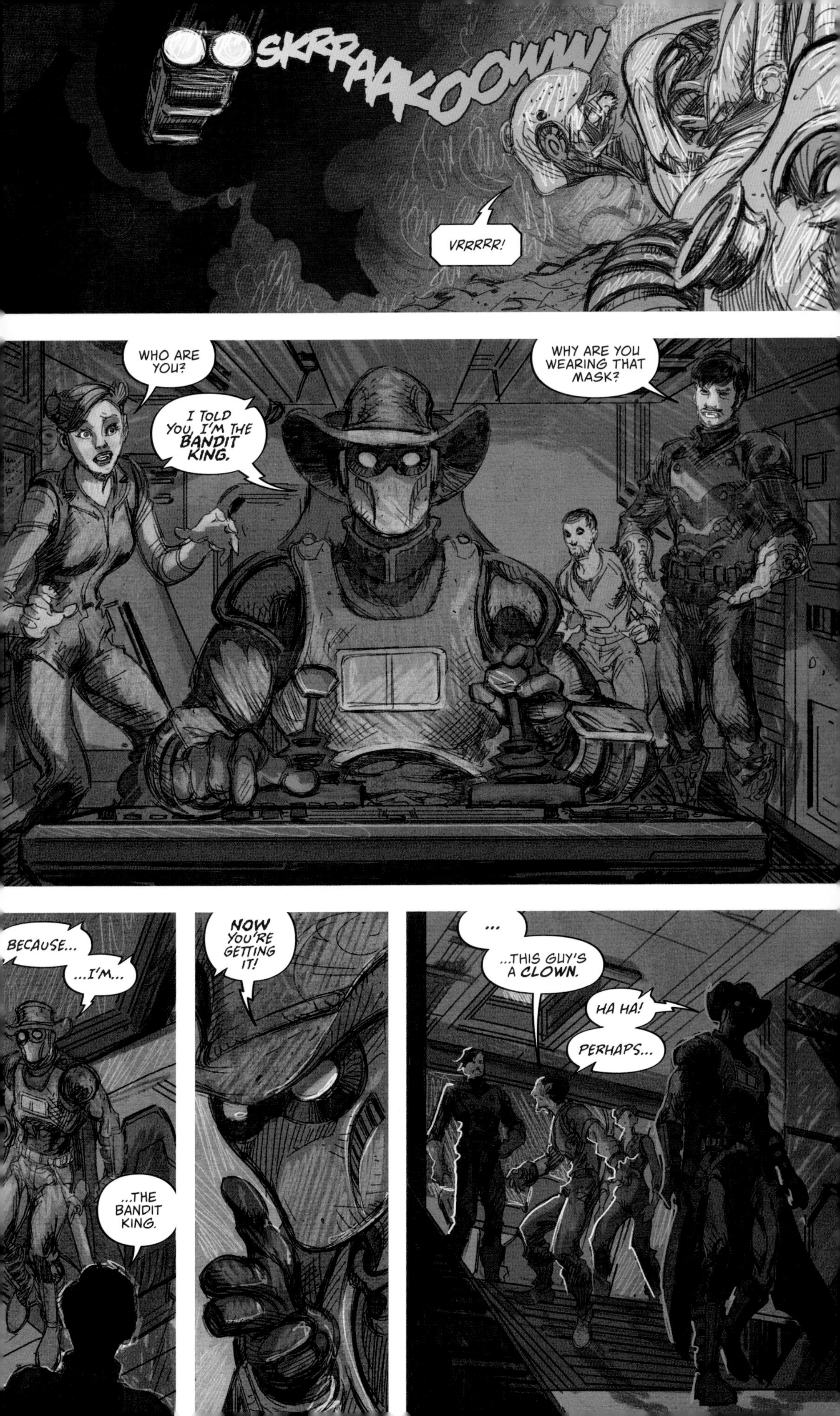
SKRRAAKOOWW
VRRRRR!
WHO ARE YOU?
I TOLD YOU, I'M THE BANDIT KING.
WHY ARE YOU WEARING THAT MASK?
BECAUSE...
...I'M...
...THE BANDIT KING.
NOW YOU'RE GETTING IT!
...
...THIS GUY'S A CLOWN.
HA HA!
PERHAPS...

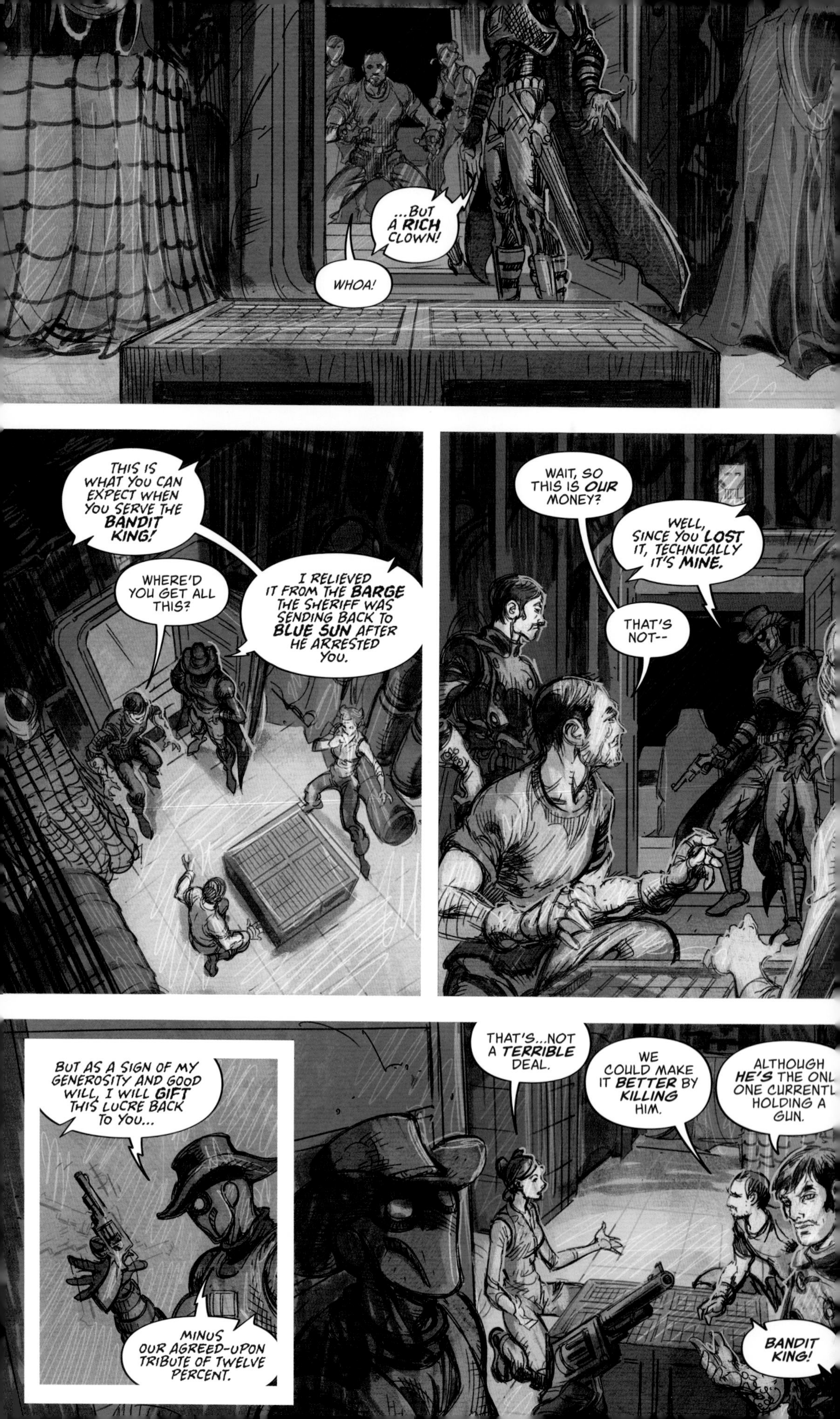
...BUT A RICH CLOWN!
WHOA!
THIS IS WHAT YOU CAN EXPECT WHEN YOU SERVE THE BANDIT KING!
WHERE'D YOU GET ALL THIS?
I RELIEVED IT FROM THE BARGE THE SHERIFF WAS SENDING BACK TO BLUE SUN AFTER HE ARRESTED YOU.
WAIT, SO THIS IS OUR MONEY?
WELL, SINCE YOU LOST IT, TECHNICALLY IT'S MINE.
THAT'S NOT--
BUT AS A SIGN OF MY GENEROSITY AND GOOD WILL, I WILL GIFT THIS LUCRE BACK TO YOU...
MINUS OUR AGREED-UPON TRIBUTE OF TWELVE PERCENT.
THAT'S...NOT A TERRIBLE DEAL.
WE COULD MAKE IT BETTER BY KILLING HIM.
ALTHOUGH HE'S THE ONL ONE CURRENTL HOLDING A GUN.
BANDIT KING!

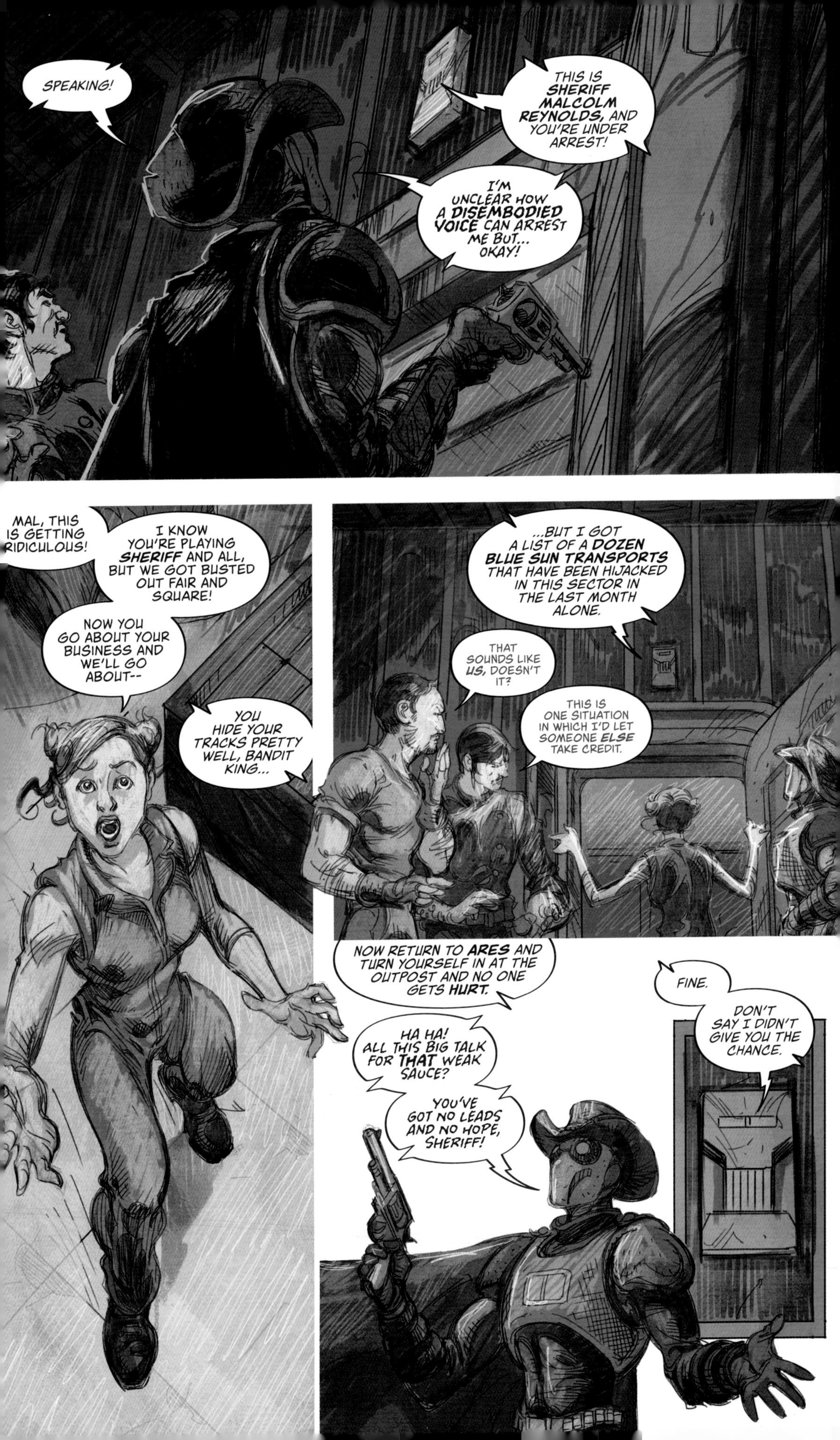
SPEAKING!
THIS IS SHERIFF MALCOLM REYNOLDS, AND YOU'RE UNDER ARREST!
I'M UNCLEAR HOW A DISEMBODIED VOICE CAN ARREST ME BUT... OKAY!
MAL, THIS IS GETTING RIDICULOUS!
I KNOW YOU'RE PLAYING SHERIFF AND ALL, BUT WE GOT BUSTED OUT FAIR AND SQUARE!
NOW YOU GO ABOUT YOUR BUSINESS AND WE'LL GO ABOUT--
YOU HIDE YOUR TRACKS PRETTY WELL, BANDIT KING...
...BUT I GOT A LIST OF A DOZEN BLUE SUN TRANSPORTS THAT HAVE BEEN HIJACKED IN THIS SECTOR IN THE LAST MONTH ALONE.
THAT SOUNDS LIKE US, DOESN'T IT?
THIS IS ONE SITUATION IN WHICH I'D LET SOMEONE ELSE TAKE CREDIT.
NOW RETURN TO ARES AND TURN YOURSELF IN AT THE OUTPOST AND NO ONE GETS HURT.
HA HA! ALL THIS BIG TALK FOR THAT WEAK SAUCE?
YOU'VE GOT NO LEADS AND NO HOPE, SHERIFF!
FINE.
DON'T SAY I DIDN'T GIVE YOU THE CHANCE.

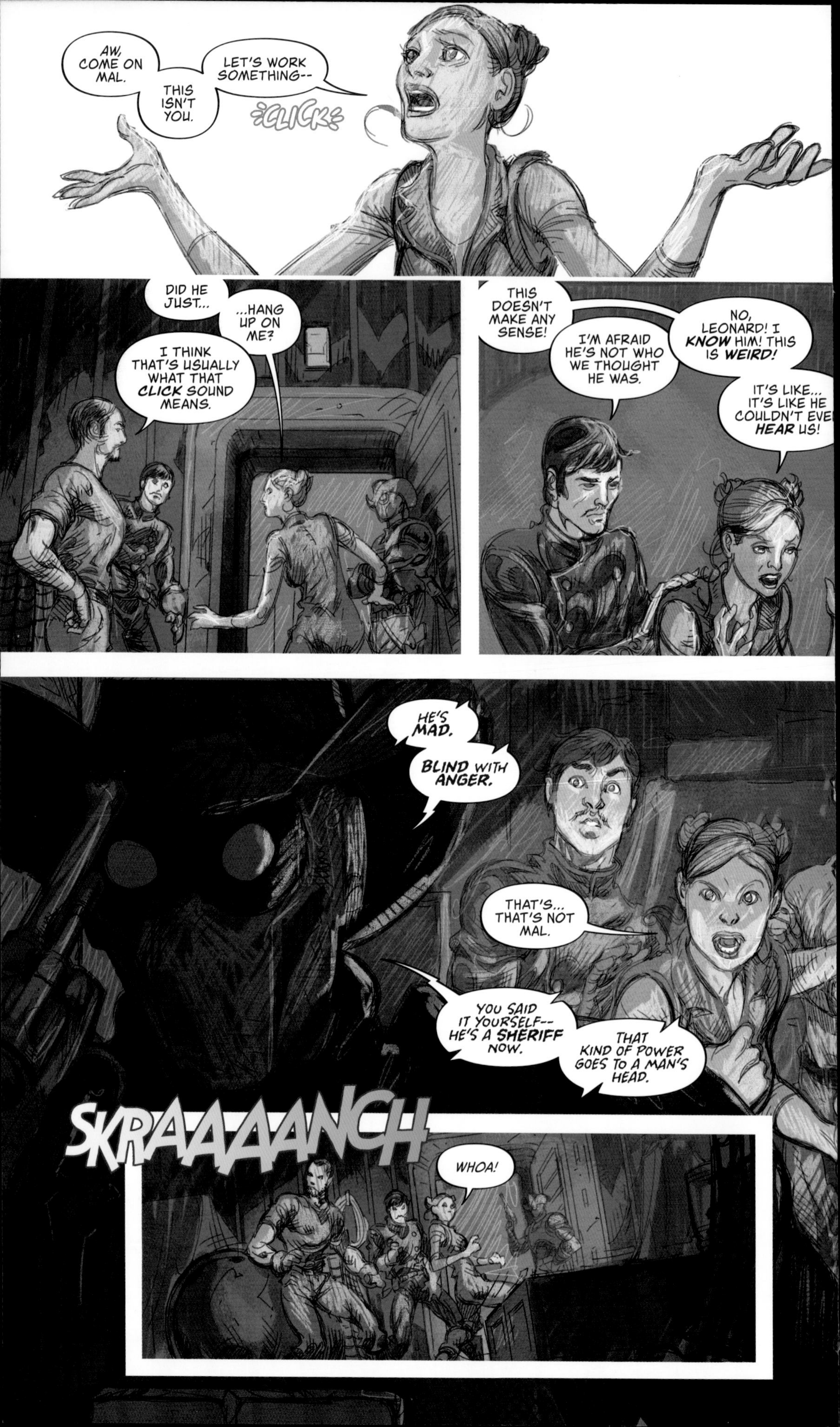
AW, COME ON MAL.
THIS ISN'T YOU.
LET'S WORK SOMETHING--
CLICK
DID HE JUST...
...HANG UP ON ME?
I THINK THAT'S USUALLY WHAT THAT CLICK SOUND MEANS.
THIS DOESN'T MAKE ANY SENSE!
I'M AFRAID HE'S NOT WHO WE THOUGHT HE WAS.
NO, LEONARD! I KNOW HIM! THIS IS WEIRD!
IT'S LIKE... IT'S LIKE HE COULDN'T EVE HEAR US!
HE'S MAD.
BLIND WITH ANGER.
THAT'S... THAT'S NOT MAL.
YOU SAID IT YOURSELF-- HE'S A SHERIFF NOW.
THAT KIND OF POWER GOES TO A MAN'S HEAD.
SKRAAAANCH
WHOA!

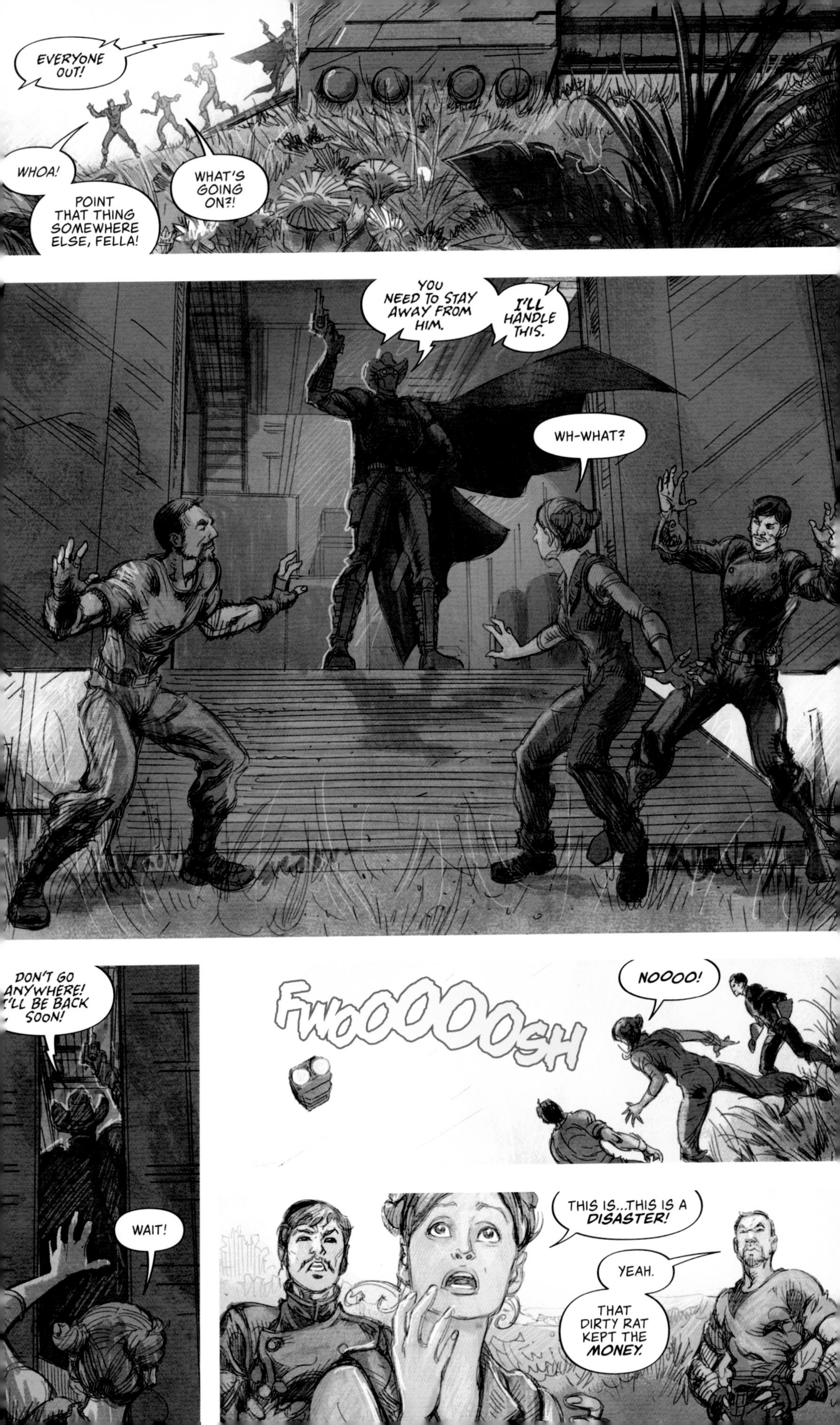
EVERYONE OUT!
WHOA!
POINT THAT THING SOMEWHERE ELSE, FELLA!
WHAT'S GOING ON?!
YOU NEED TO STAY AWAY FROM HIM.
I'LL HANDLE THIS.
WH-WHAT?
DON'T GO ANYWHERE! I'LL BE BACK SOON!
WAIT!
FWOOOOOOSH
NOOOO!
THIS IS...THIS IS A DISASTER!
YEAH.
THAT DIRTY RAT KEPT THE MONEY.

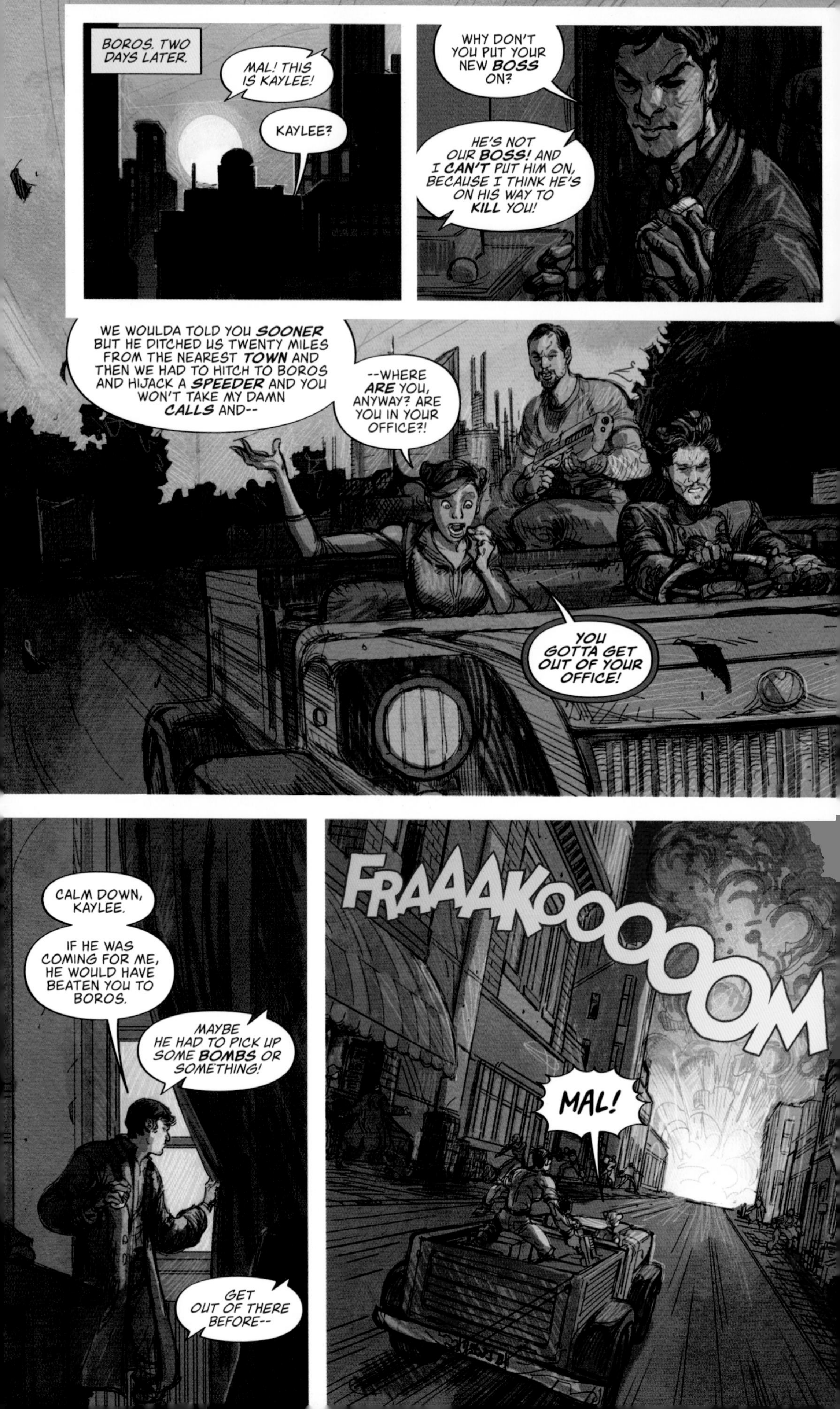
BOROS. TWO DAYS LATER.
MAL! THIS IS KAYLEE!
KAYLEE?
WHY DON'T YOU PUT YOUR NEW BOSS ON?
HE'S NOT OUR BOSS! AND I CAN'T PUT HIM ON, BECAUSE I THINK HE'S ON HIS WAY TO KILL YOU!
WE WOULDA TOLD YOU SOONER BUT HE DITCHED US TWENTY MILES FROM THE NEAREST TOWN AND THEN WE HAD TO HITCH TO BOROS AND HIJACK A SPEEDER AND YOU WON'T TAKE MY DAMN CALLS AND--
--WHERE ARE YOU, ANYWAY? ARE YOU IN YOUR OFFICE?!
YOU GOTTA GET OUT OF YOUR OFFICE!
CALM DOWN, KAYLEE.
IF HE WAS COMING FOR ME, HE WOULD HAVE BEATEN YOU TO BOROS.
MAYBE HE HAD TO PICK UP SOME BOMBS OR SOMETHING!
GET OUT OF THERE BEFORE--
FRAAAKOOOOOOM
MAL!

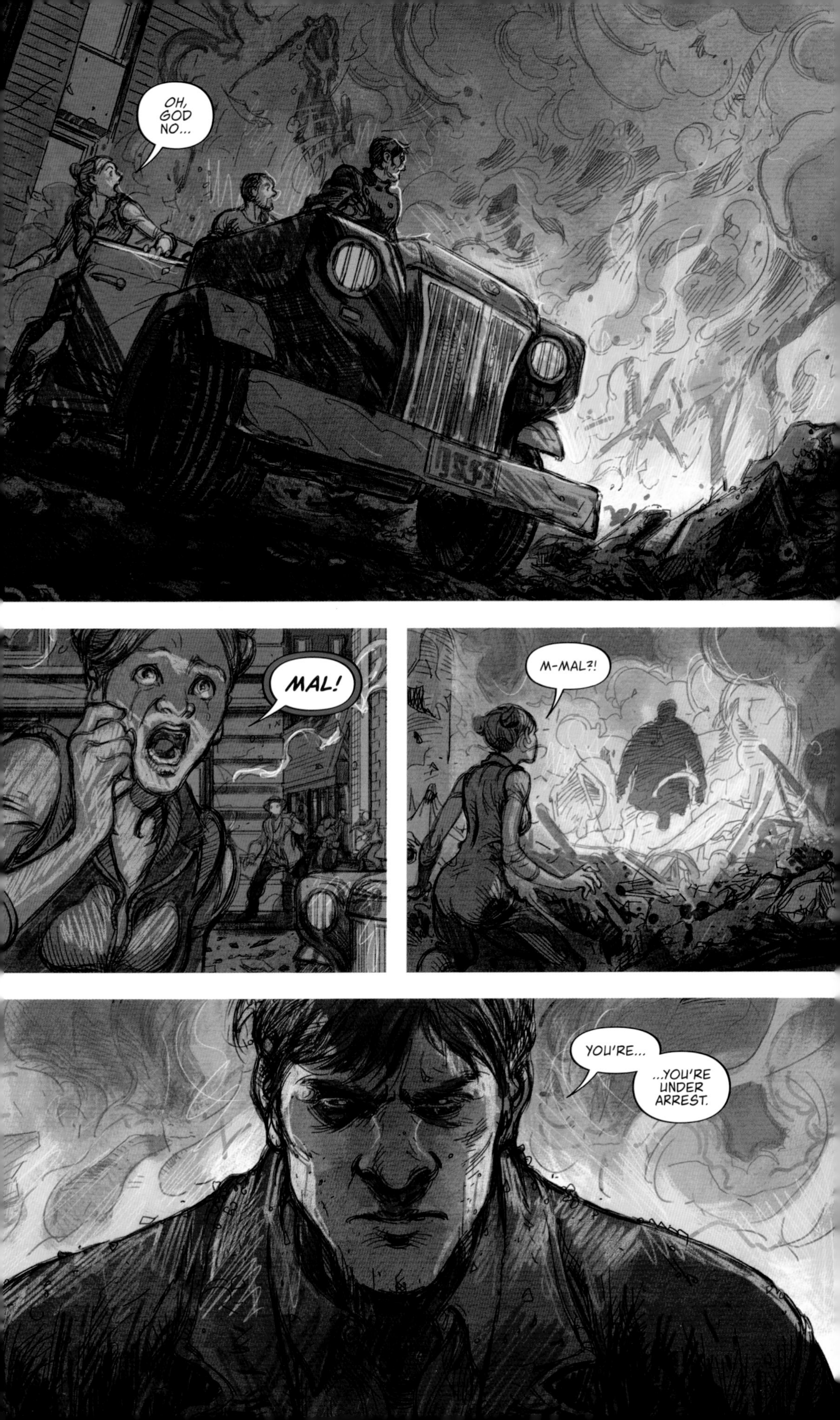
OH, GOD NO...
MAL!
M-MAL?!
YOU'RE...
...YOU'RE UNDER ARREST.

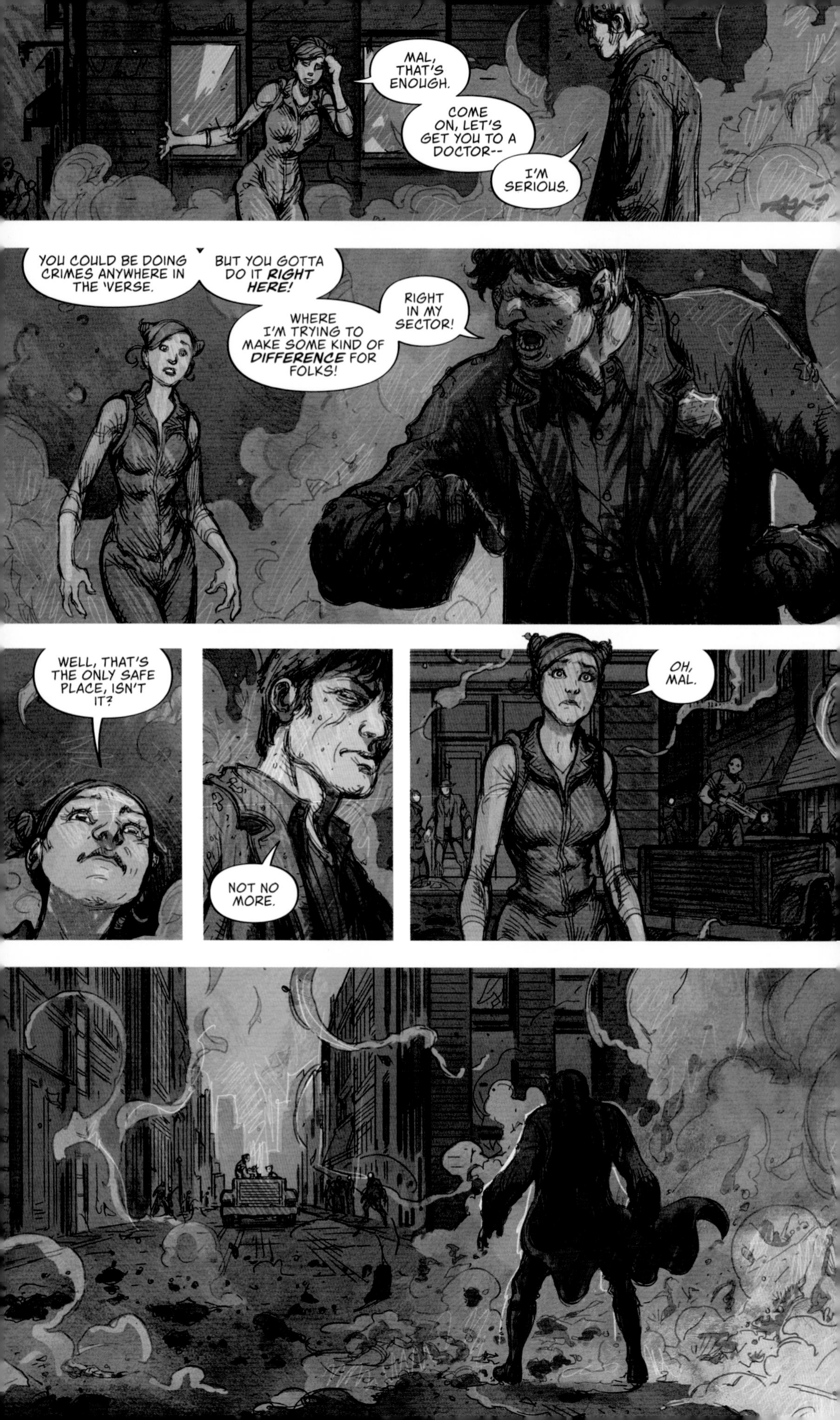
MAL, THAT'S ENOUGH.
COME ON, LET'S GET YOU TO A DOCTOR--
I'M SERIOUS.
YOU COULD BE DOING CRIMES ANYWHERE IN THE 'VERSE.
BUT YOU GOTTA DO IT **RIGHT HERE!**
RIGHT IN MY SECTOR!
WHERE I'M TRYING TO MAKE SOME KIND OF **DIFFERENCE** FOR FOLKS!
WELL, THAT'S THE ONLY SAFE PLACE, ISN'T IT?
NOT NO MORE.
OH, MAL.

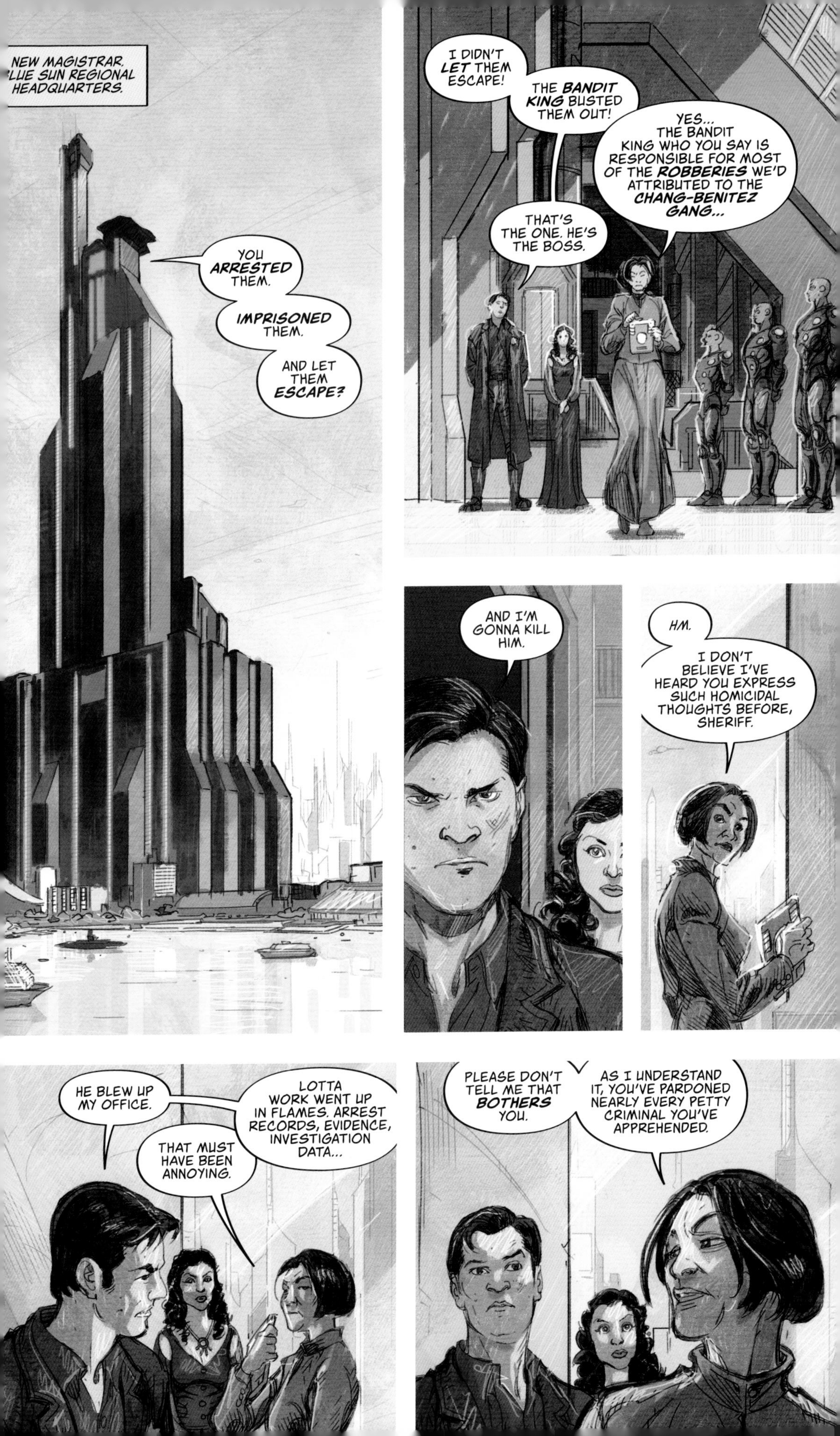

NEW MAGISTRAR. 'LUE SUN REGIONAL HEADQUARTERS.
YOU ARRESTED THEM.
IMPRISONED THEM.
AND LET THEM ESCAPE?
I DIDN'T LET THEM ESCAPE!
THE BANDIT KING BUSTED THEM OUT!
YES... THE BANDIT KING WHO YOU SAY IS RESPONSIBLE FOR MOST OF THE ROBBERIES WE'D ATTRIBUTED TO THE CHANG-BENITEZ GANG...
THAT'S THE ONE. HE'S THE BOSS.
AND I'M GONNA KILL HIM.
HM.
I DON'T BELIEVE I'VE HEARD YOU EXPRESS SUCH HOMICIDAL THOUGHTS BEFORE, SHERIFF.
HE BLEW UP MY OFFICE.
THAT MUST HAVE BEEN ANNOYING.
LOTTA WORK WENT UP IN FLAMES. ARREST RECORDS, EVIDENCE, INVESTIGATION DATA...
PLEASE DON'T TELL ME THAT BOTHERS YOU.
AS I UNDERSTAND IT, YOU'VE PARDONED NEARLY EVERY PETTY CRIMINAL YOU'VE APPREHENDED.

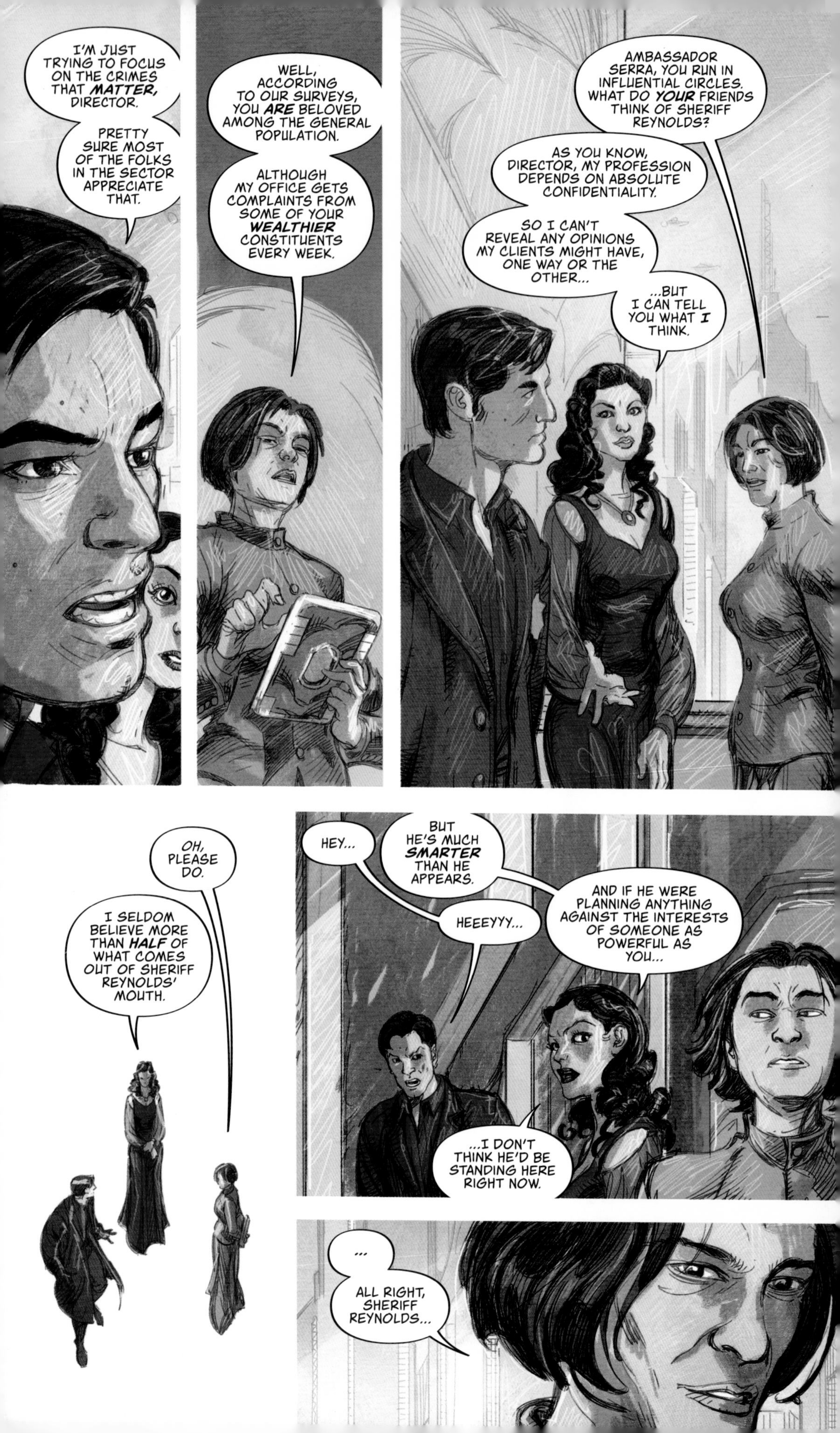

I'M JUST TRYING TO FOCUS ON THE CRIMES THAT *MATTER,* DIRECTOR.
PRETTY SURE MOST OF THE FOLKS IN THE SECTOR APPRECIATE THAT.
WELL, ACCORDING TO OUR SURVEYS, YOU *ARE* BELOVED AMONG THE GENERAL POPULATION.
ALTHOUGH MY OFFICE GETS COMPLAINTS FROM SOME OF YOUR *WEALTHIER* CONSTITUENTS EVERY WEEK.
AMBASSADOR SERRA, YOU RUN IN INFLUENTIAL CIRCLES. WHAT DO *YOUR* FRIENDS THINK OF SHERIFF REYNOLDS?
AS YOU KNOW, DIRECTOR, MY PROFESSION DEPENDS ON ABSOLUTE CONFIDENTIALITY.
SO I CAN'T REVEAL ANY OPINIONS MY CLIENTS MIGHT HAVE, ONE WAY OR THE OTHER...
...BUT I CAN TELL YOU WHAT *I* THINK.
OH, PLEASE DO.
I SELDOM BELIEVE MORE THAN *HALF* OF WHAT COMES OUT OF SHERIFF REYNOLDS' MOUTH.
HEY...
BUT HE'S MUCH *SMARTER* THAN HE APPEARS.
HEEEYYY...
AND IF HE WERE PLANNING ANYTHING AGAINST THE INTERESTS OF SOMEONE AS POWERFUL AS YOU...
...I DON'T THINK HE'D BE STANDING HERE RIGHT NOW.
...
ALL RIGHT, SHERIFF REYNOLDS...

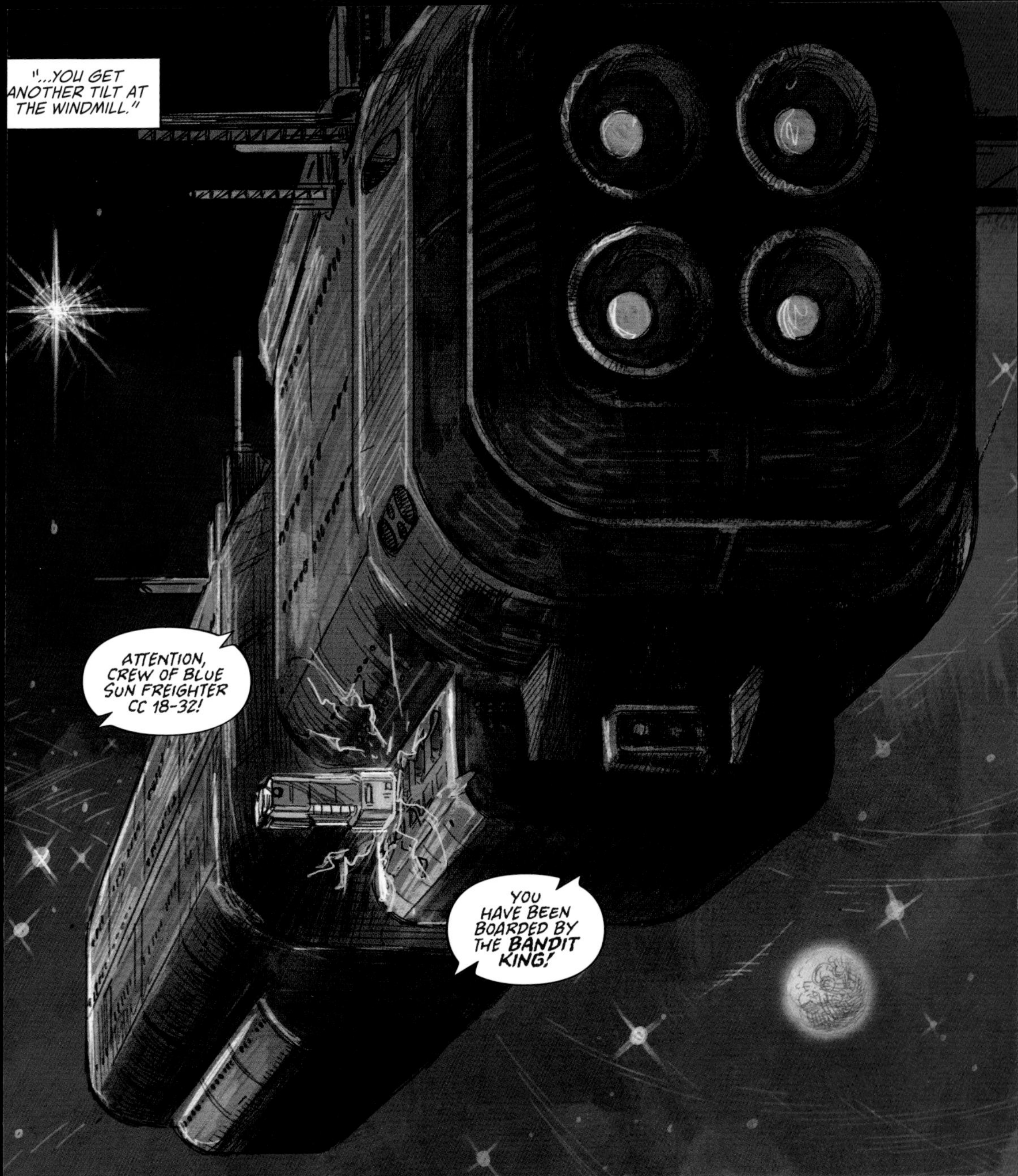
"...YOU GET ANOTHER TILT AT THE WINDMILL."
ATTENTION, CREW OF BLUE SUN FREIGHTER CC 18-32!
YOU HAVE BEEN BOARDED BY THE BANDIT KING!
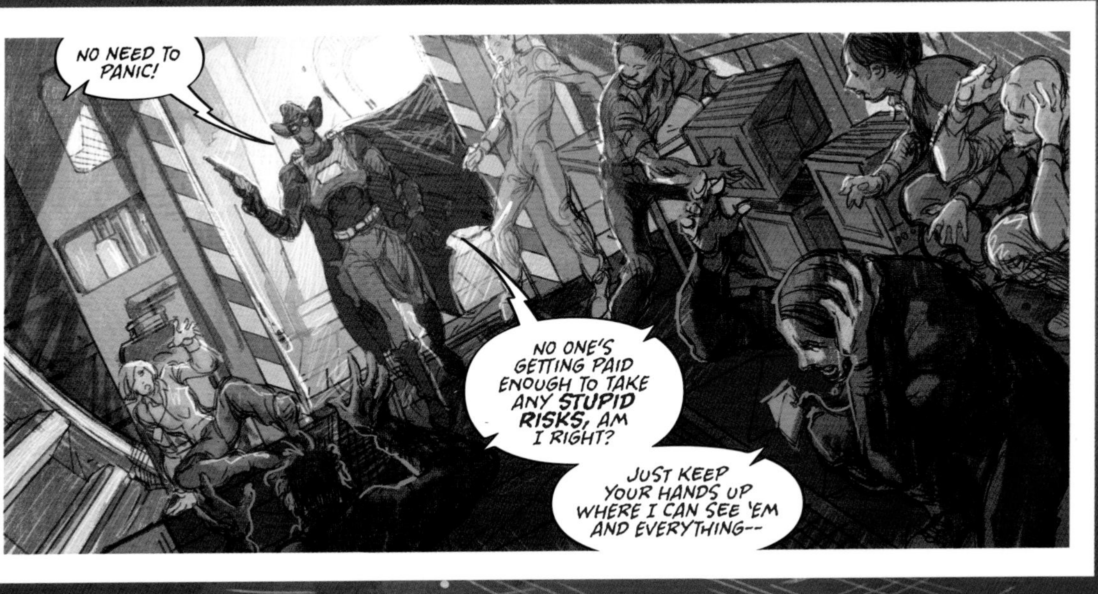
NO NEED TO PANIC!
NO ONE'S GETTING PAID ENOUGH TO TAKE ANY STUPID RISKS, AM I RIGHT?
JUST KEEP YOUR HANDS UP WHERE I CAN SEE 'EM AND EVERYTHING--

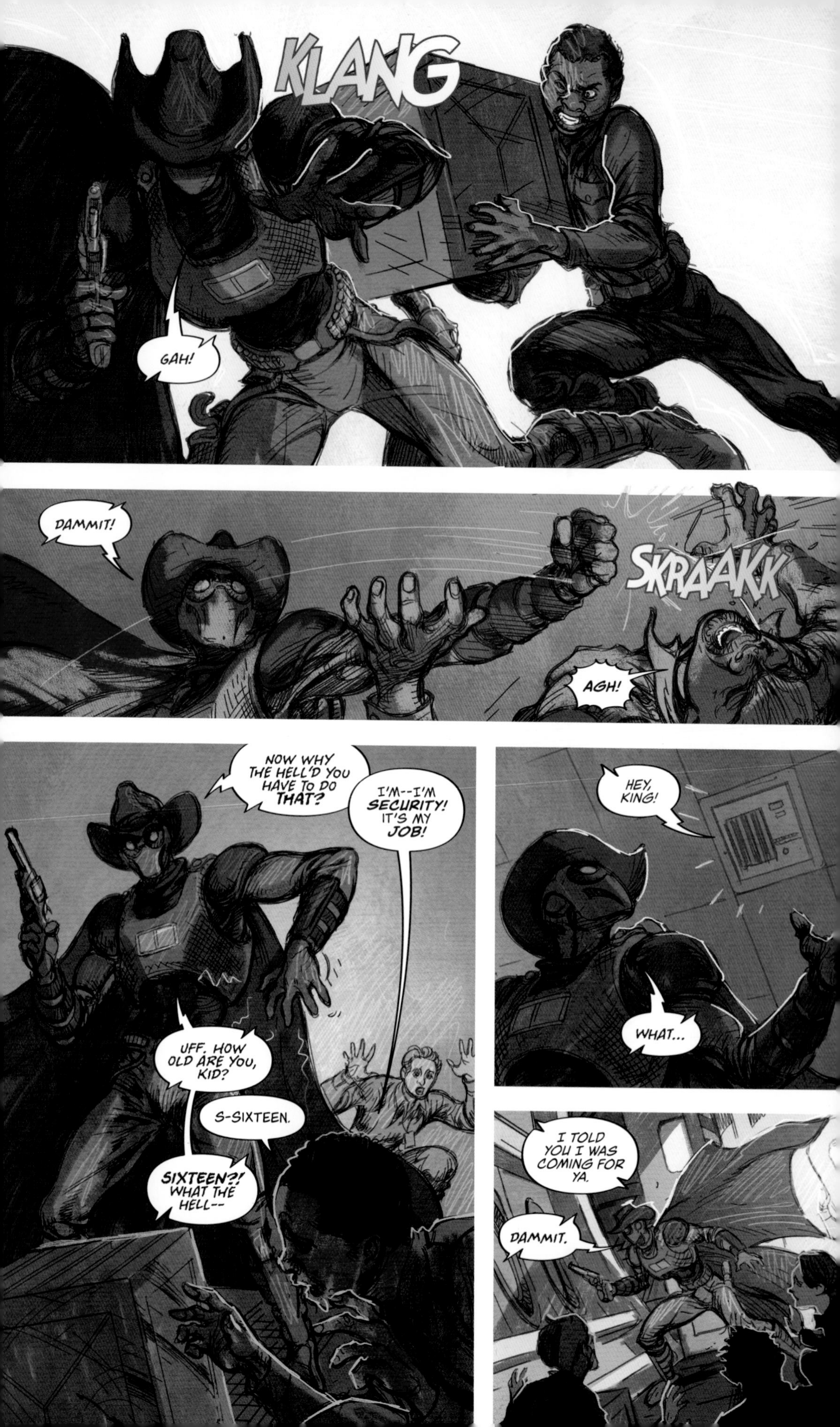
KLANG
GAH!
DAMMIT!
SKRAAKK
AGH!
NOW WHY THE HELL'D YOU HAVE TO DO THAT?
I'M--I'M SECURITY! IT'S MY JOB!
UFF. HOW OLD ARE YOU, KID?
S-SIXTEEN.
SIXTEEN?! WHAT THE HELL--
HEY, KING!
WHAT...
I TOLD YOU I WAS COMING FOR YA.
DAMMIT.

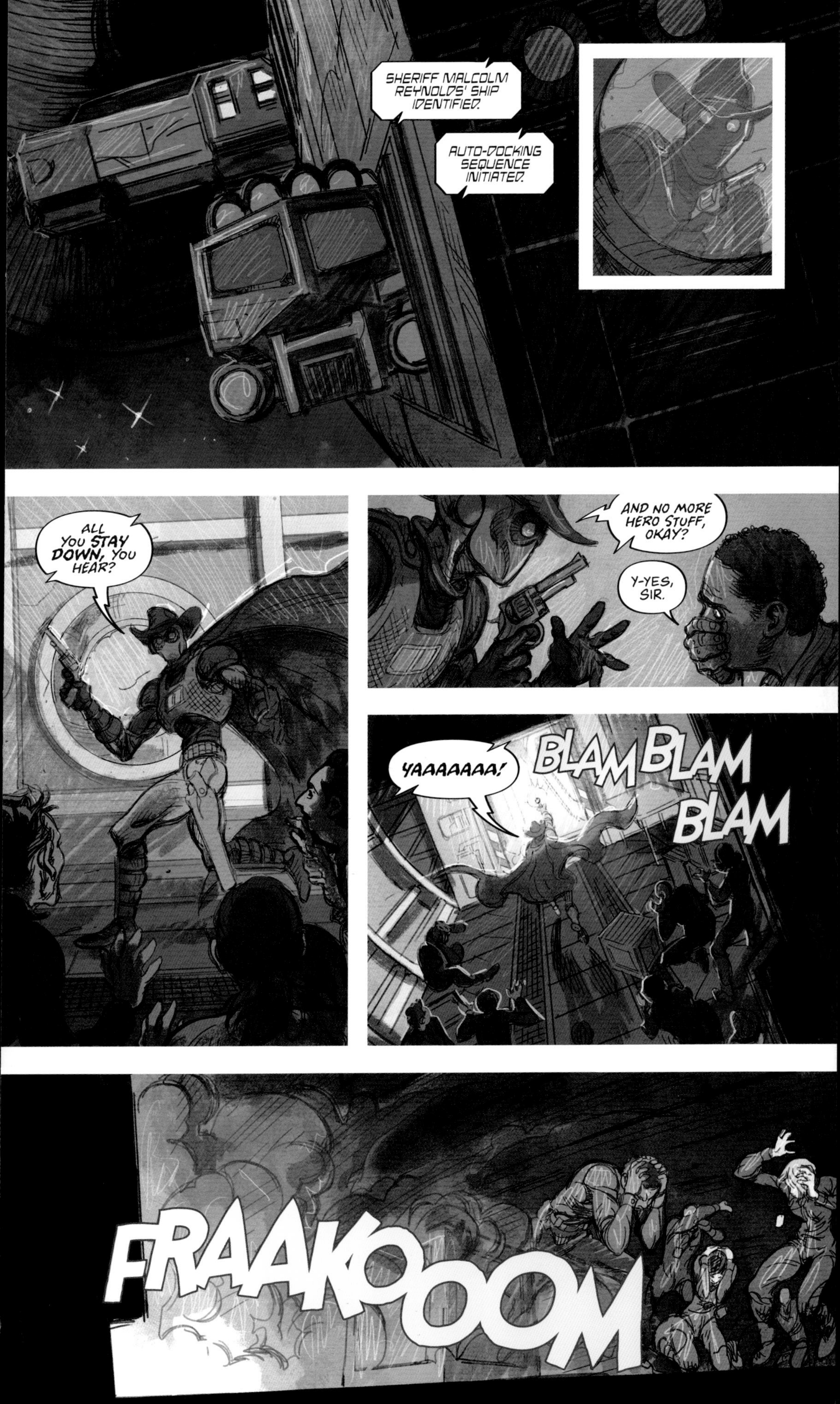

SHERIFF MALCOLM REYNOLDS' SHIP IDENTIFIED.
AUTO-DOCKING SEQUENCE INITIATED.
ALL YOU STAY DOWN, YOU HEAR?
AND NO MORE HERO STUFF, OKAY?
Y-YES, SIR.
YAAAAAAA!
BLAM BLAM BLAM BLAM
FRAAKOOOM

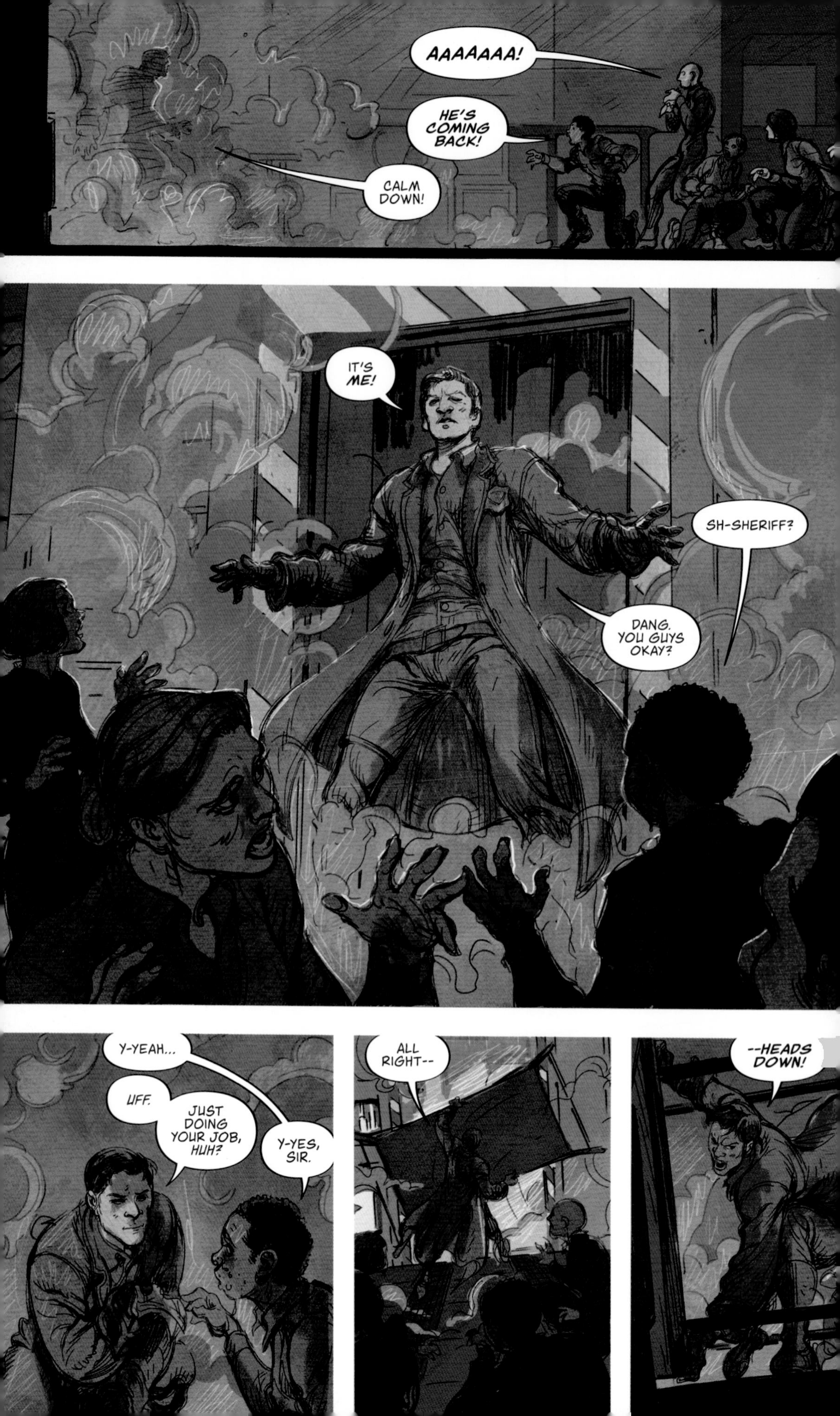
AAAAAAA!
HE'S COMING BACK!
CALM DOWN!
IT'S ME!
SH-SHERIFF?
DANG. YOU GUYS OKAY?
Y-YEAH...
UFF.
JUST DOING YOUR JOB, HUH?
Y-YES, SIR.
ALL RIGHT--
--HEADS DOWN!

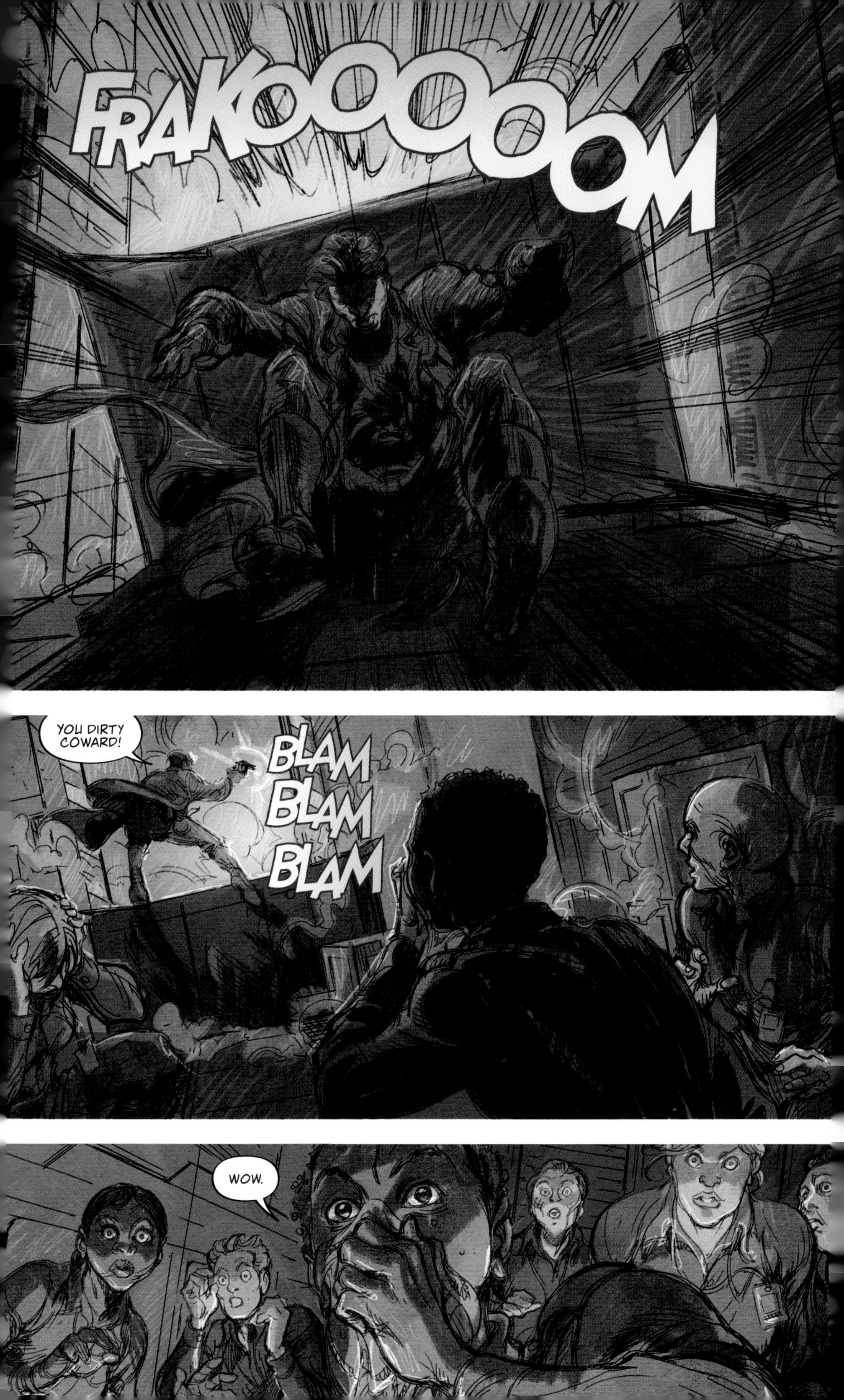
FRAKOOOOOOOM
YOU DIRTY COWARD!
BLAM
BLAM
BLAM
WOW.

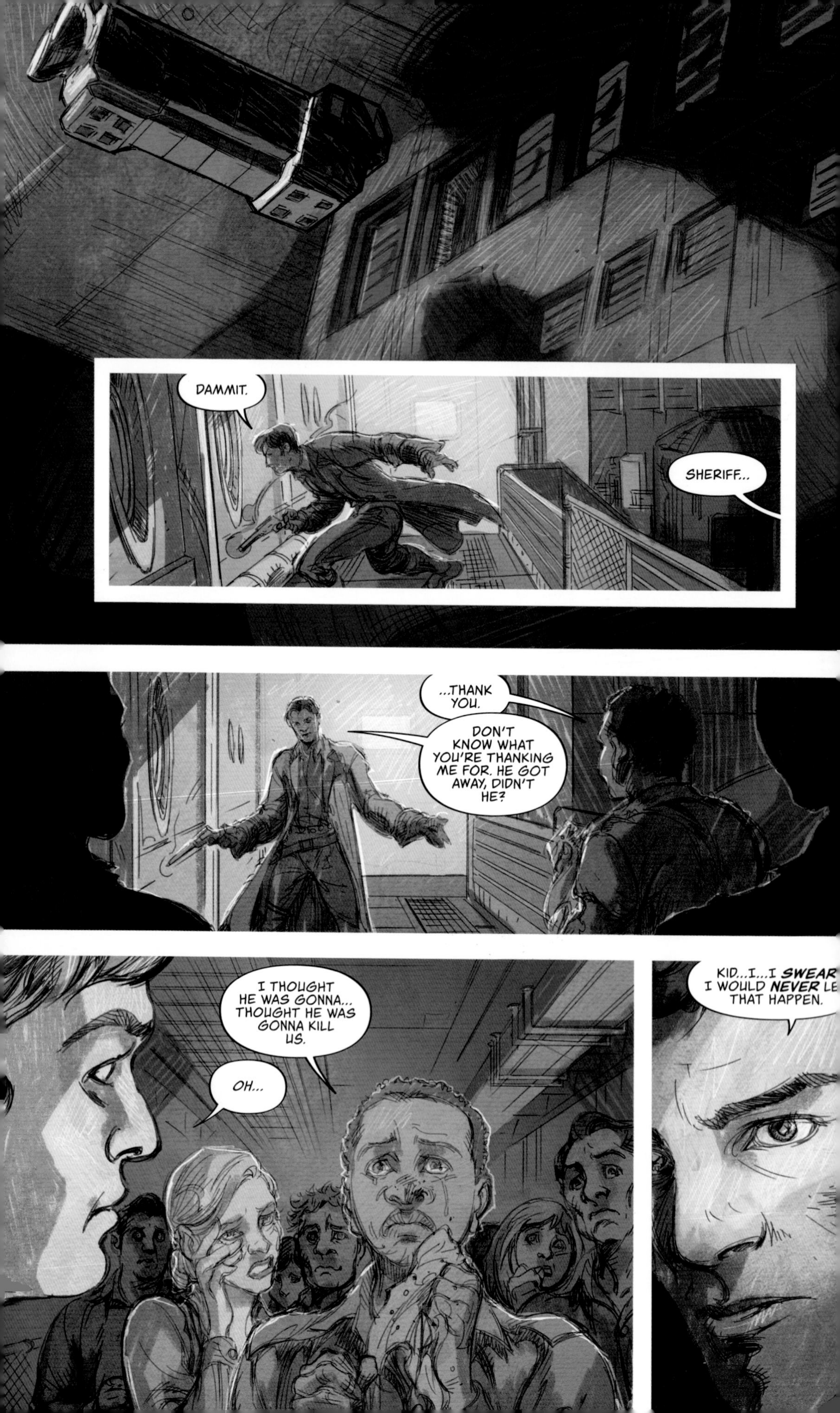
DAMMIT.
SHERIFF...
...THANK YOU.
DON'T KNOW WHAT YOU'RE THANKING ME FOR. HE GOT AWAY, DIDN'T HE?
I THOUGHT HE WAS GONNA... THOUGHT HE WAS GONNA KILL US.
OH...
KID...I...I *SWEAR* I WOULD *NEVER* LE THAT HAPPEN.

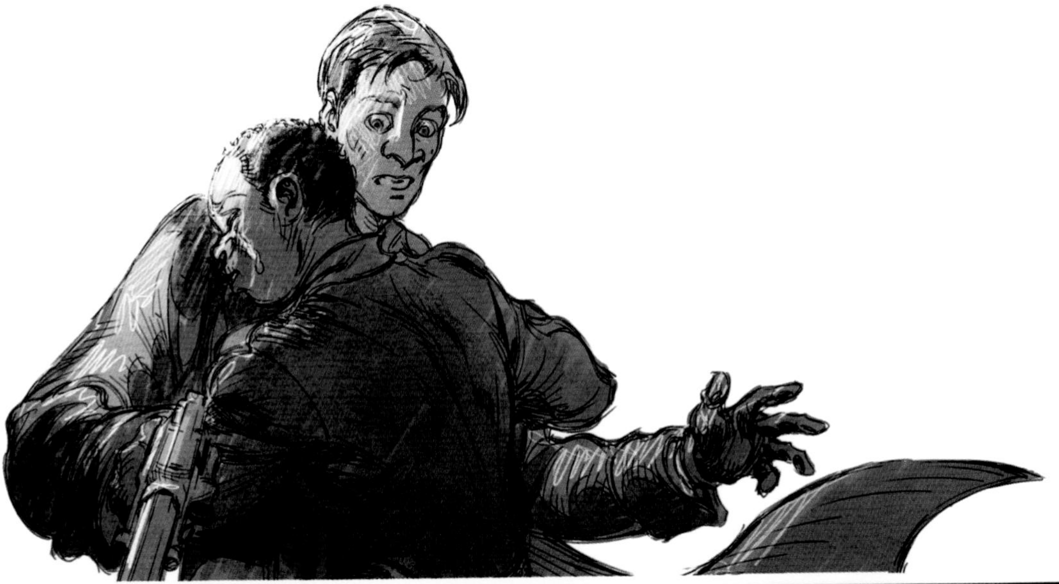

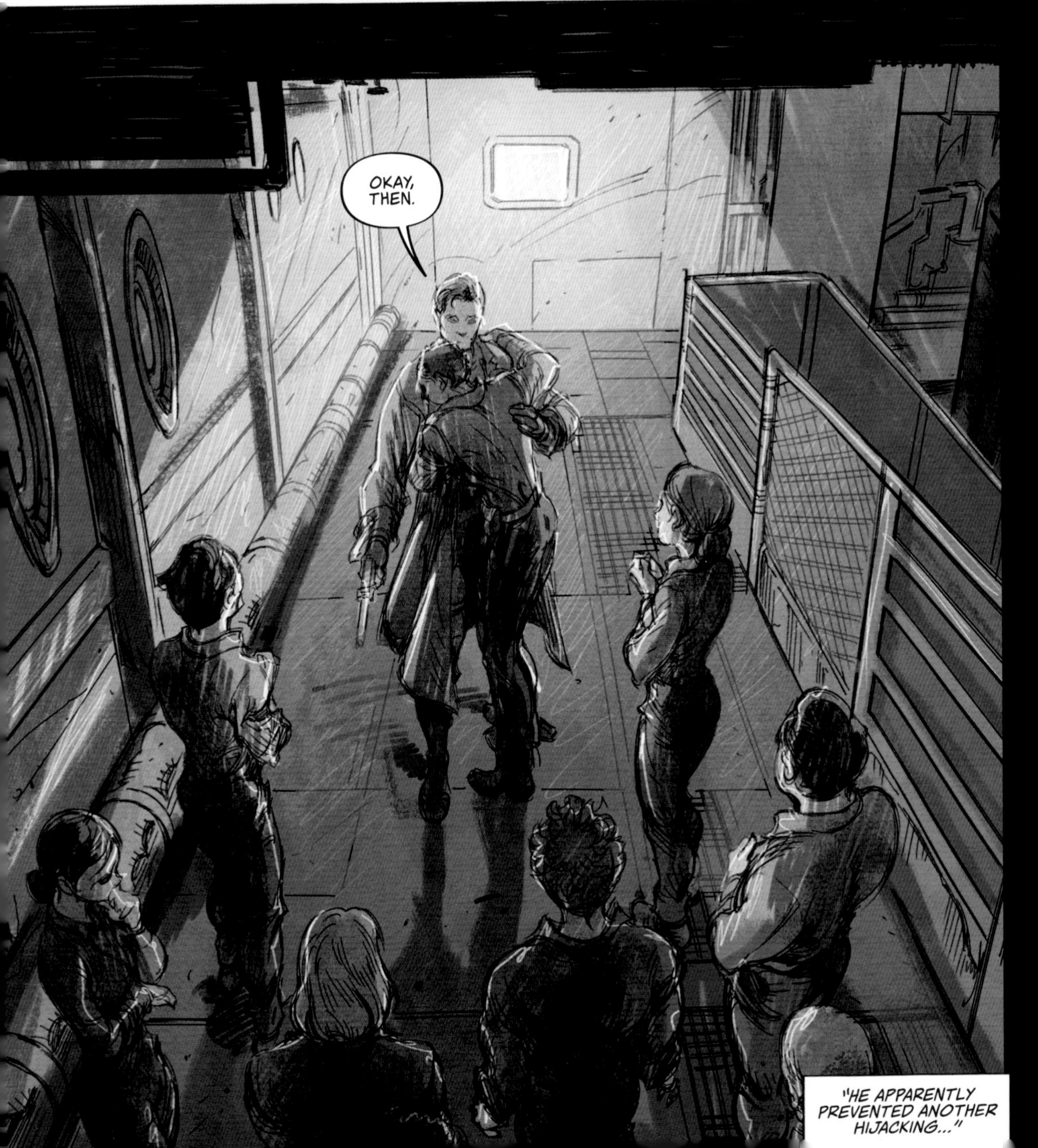
OKAY, THEN.
"HE APPARENTLY PREVENTED ANOTHER HIJACKING..."

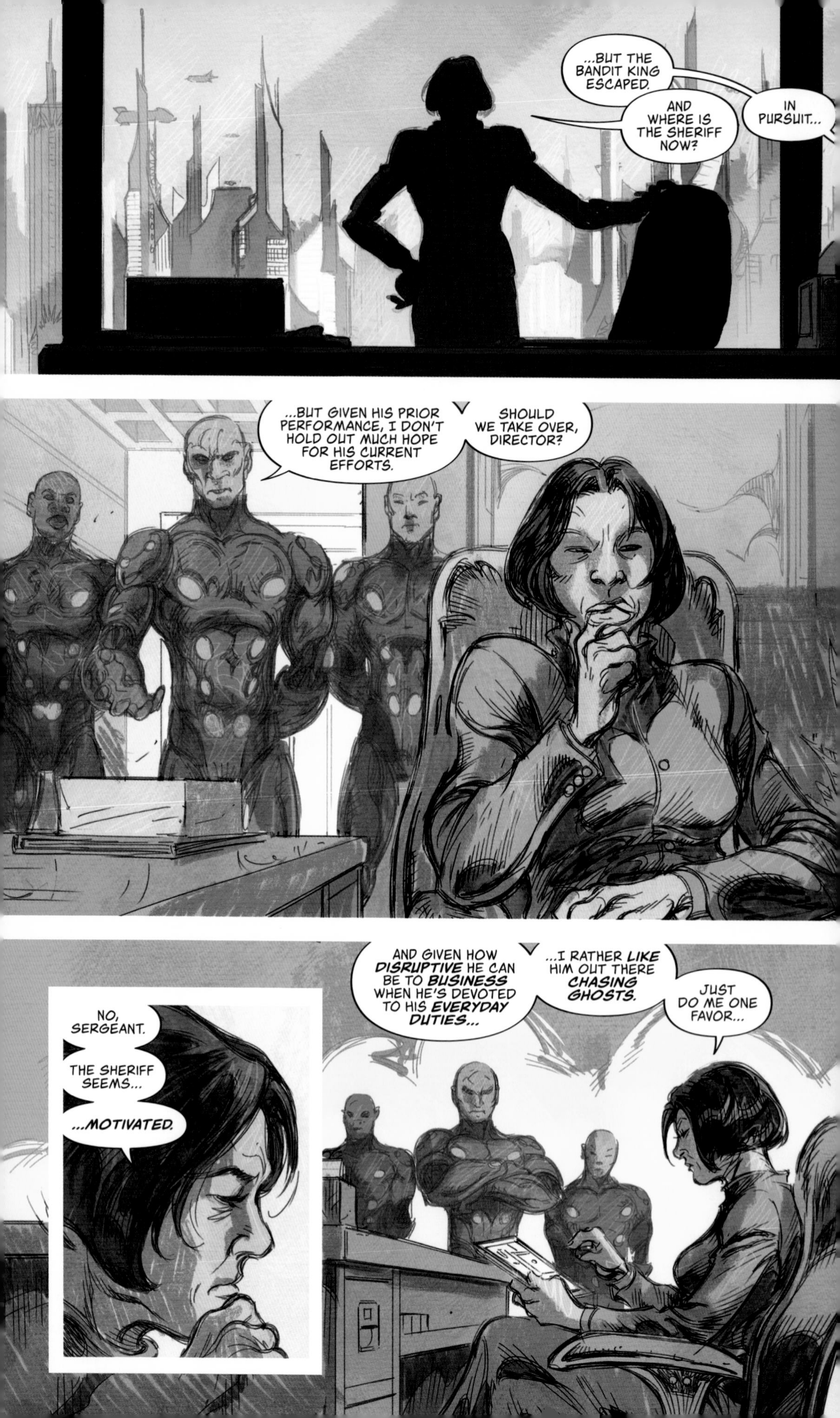
...BUT THE BANDIT KING ESCAPED.
AND WHERE IS THE SHERIFF NOW?
IN PURSUIT...
...BUT GIVEN HIS PRIOR PERFORMANCE, I DON'T HOLD OUT MUCH HOPE FOR HIS CURRENT EFFORTS.
SHOULD WE TAKE OVER, DIRECTOR?
NO, SERGEANT.
THE SHERIFF SEEMS...
...MOTIVATED.
AND GIVEN HOW DISRUPTIVE HE CAN BE TO BUSINESS WHEN HE'S DEVOTED TO HIS EVERYDAY DUTIES...
...I RATHER LIKE HIM OUT THERE CHASING GHOSTS.
JUST DO ME ONE FAVOR...

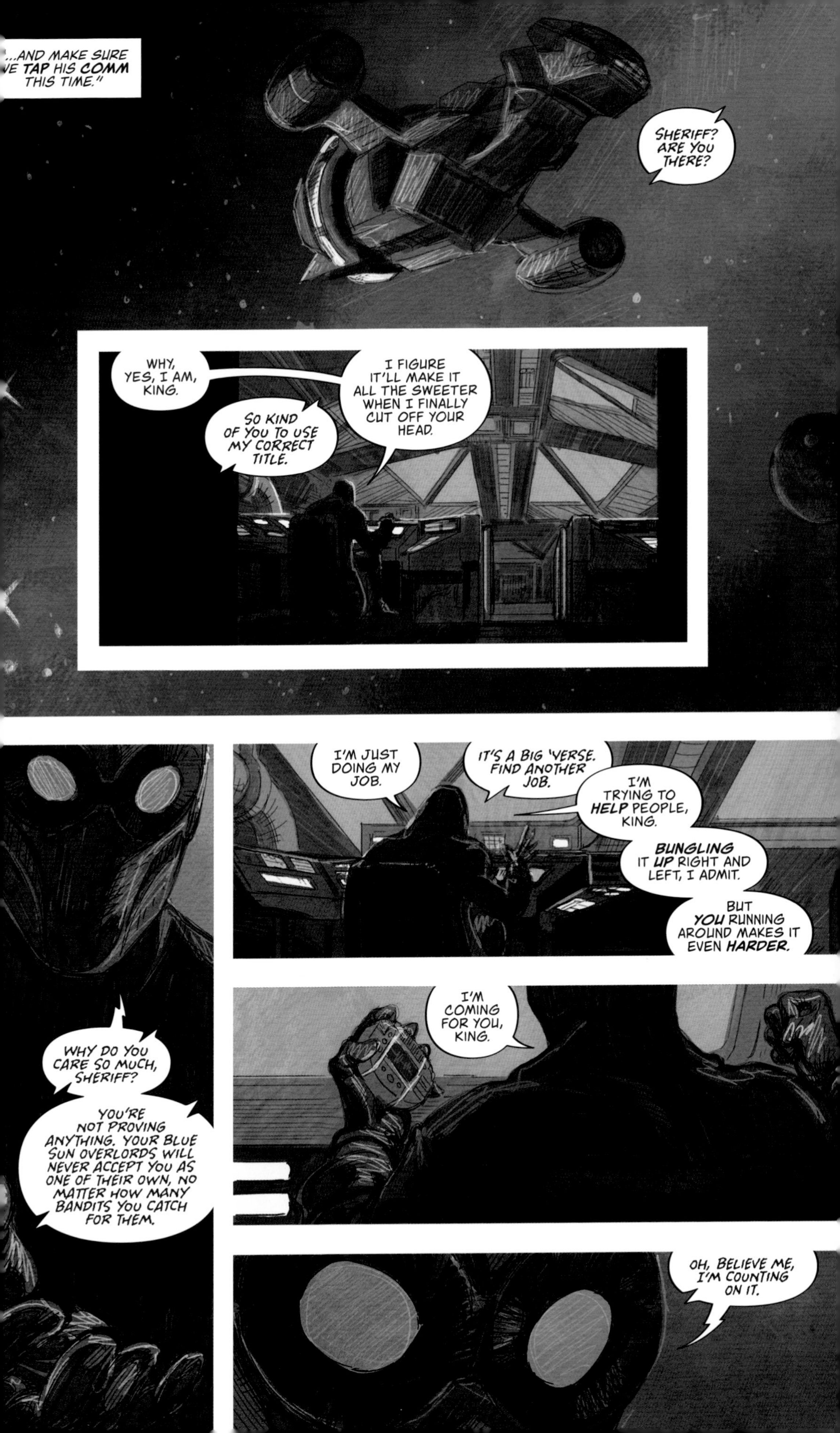
...AND MAKE SURE WE TAP HIS COMM THIS TIME."
SHERIFF? ARE YOU THERE?
WHY, YES, I AM, KING.
SO KIND OF YOU TO USE MY CORRECT TITLE.
I FIGURE IT'LL MAKE IT ALL THE SWEETER WHEN I FINALLY CUT OFF YOUR HEAD.
I'M JUST DOING MY JOB.
IT'S A BIG 'VERSE. FIND ANOTHER JOB.
I'M TRYING TO HELP PEOPLE, KING.
BUNGLING IT UP RIGHT AND LEFT, I ADMIT.
BUT YOU RUNNING AROUND MAKES IT EVEN HARDER.
WHY DO YOU CARE SO MUCH, SHERIFF?
YOU'RE NOT PROVING ANYTHING. YOUR BLUE SUN OVERLORDS WILL NEVER ACCEPT YOU AS ONE OF THEIR OWN, NO MATTER HOW MANY BANDITS YOU CATCH FOR THEM.
I'M COMING FOR YOU, KING.
OH, BELIEVE ME, I'M COUNTING ON IT.

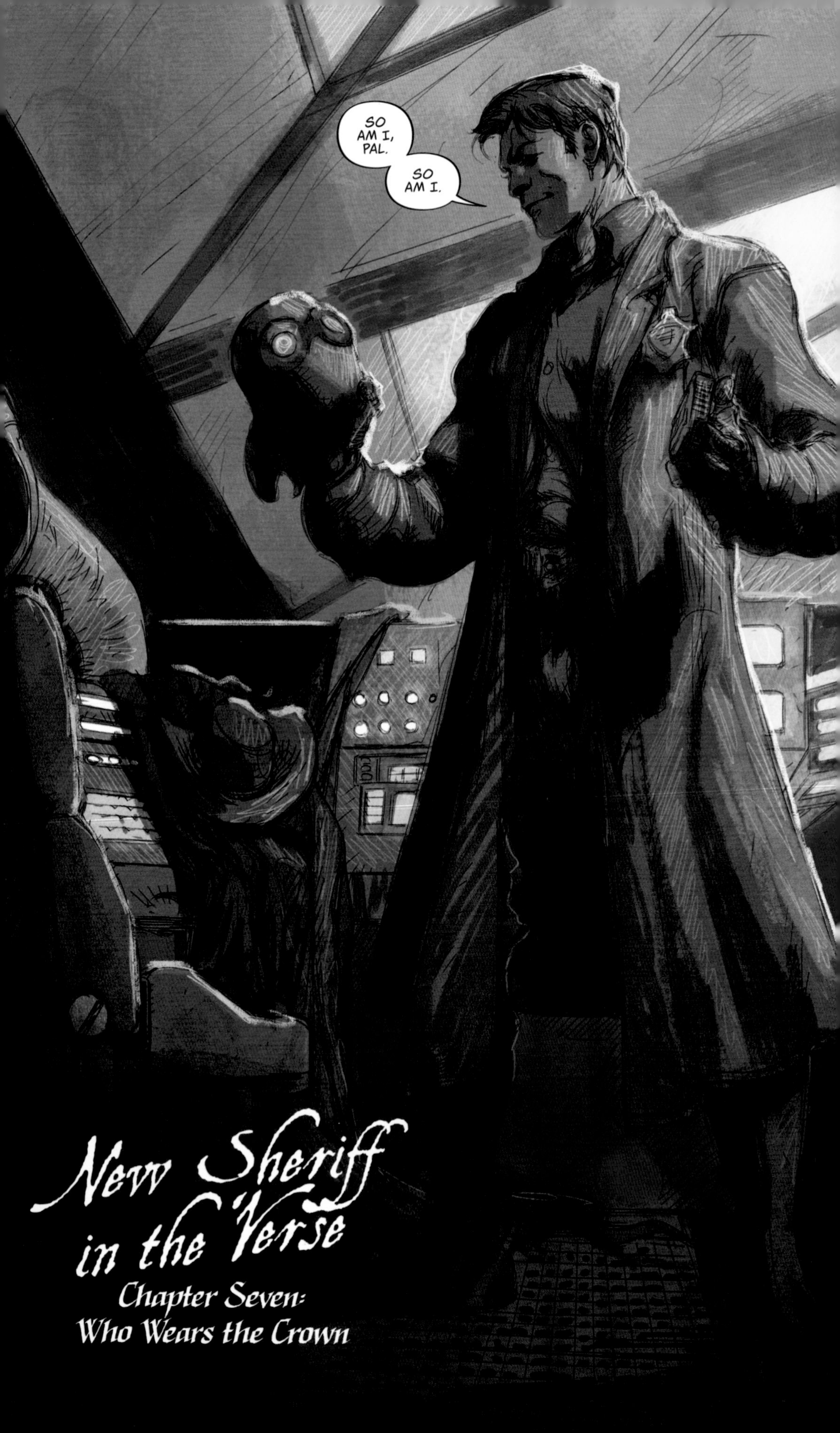
SO AM I, PAL.
SO AM I.
New Sheriff in the 'Verse
Chapter Seven: Who Wears the Crown

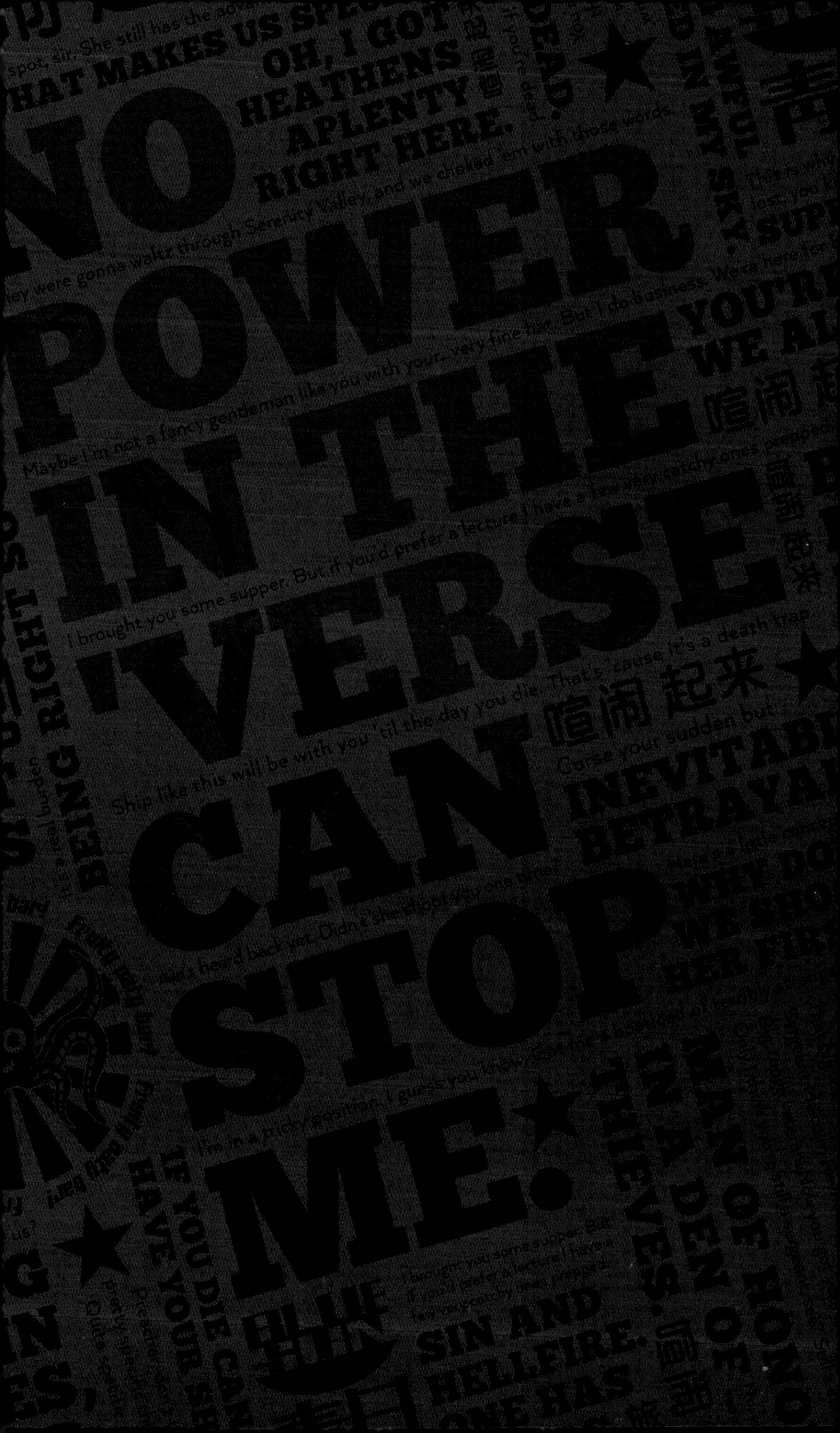
NO POWER IN THE 'VERSE CAN STOP ME.
OH, I GOT HEATHENS APLENTY RIGHT HERE.
They were gonna waltz through Serenity Valley, and we choked 'em with those words.
Maybe I'm not a fancy gentleman like you with your very fine hat. But I do business.
I brought you some supper. But if you'd prefer a lecture, I have a few very catchy ones prepped.
Ship like this will be with you 'til the day you die. That's 'cause it's a death trap.
Curse your sudden but inevitable betrayal!
SIN AND HELLFIRE.

CHAPTER EIGHT

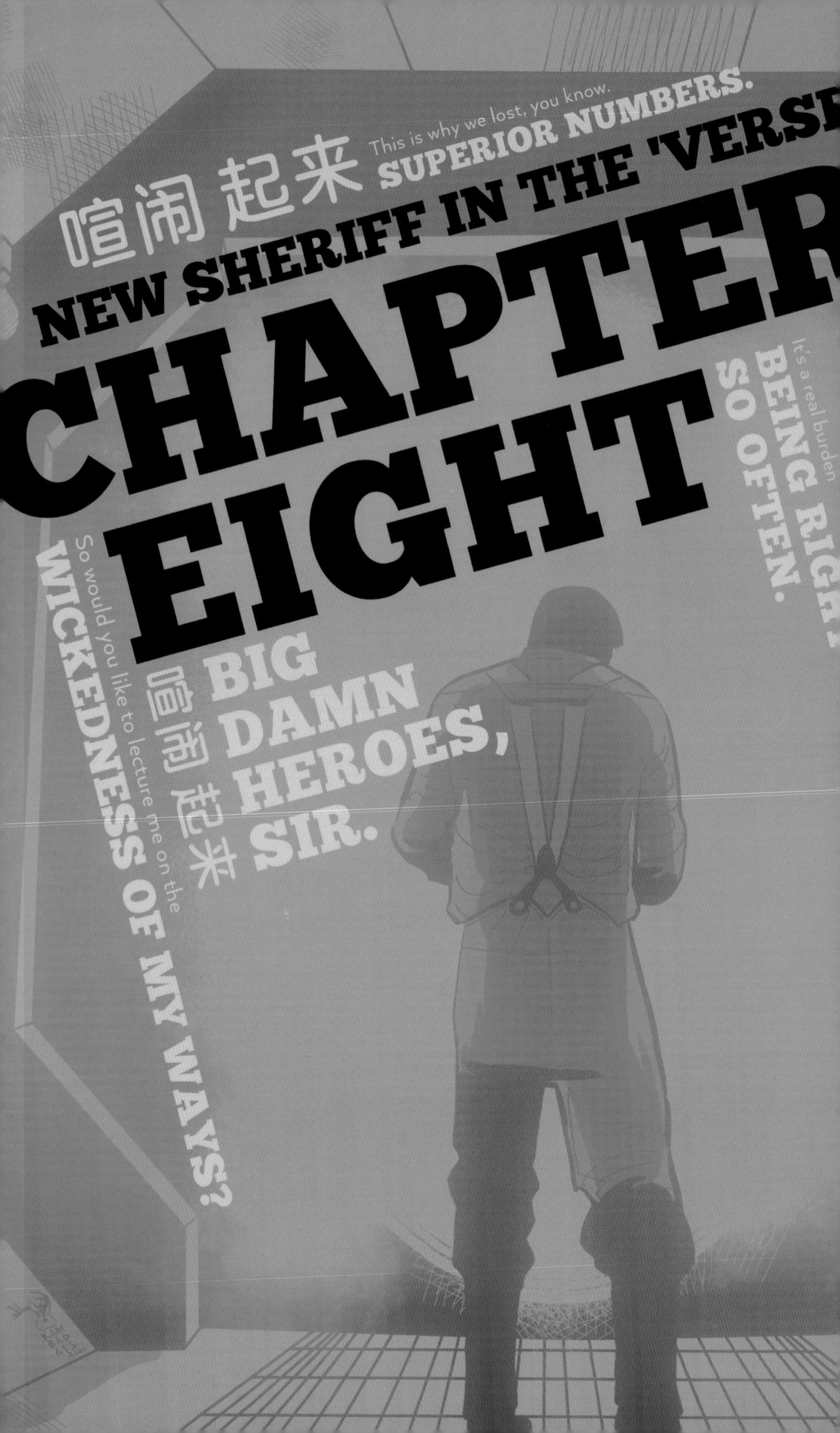

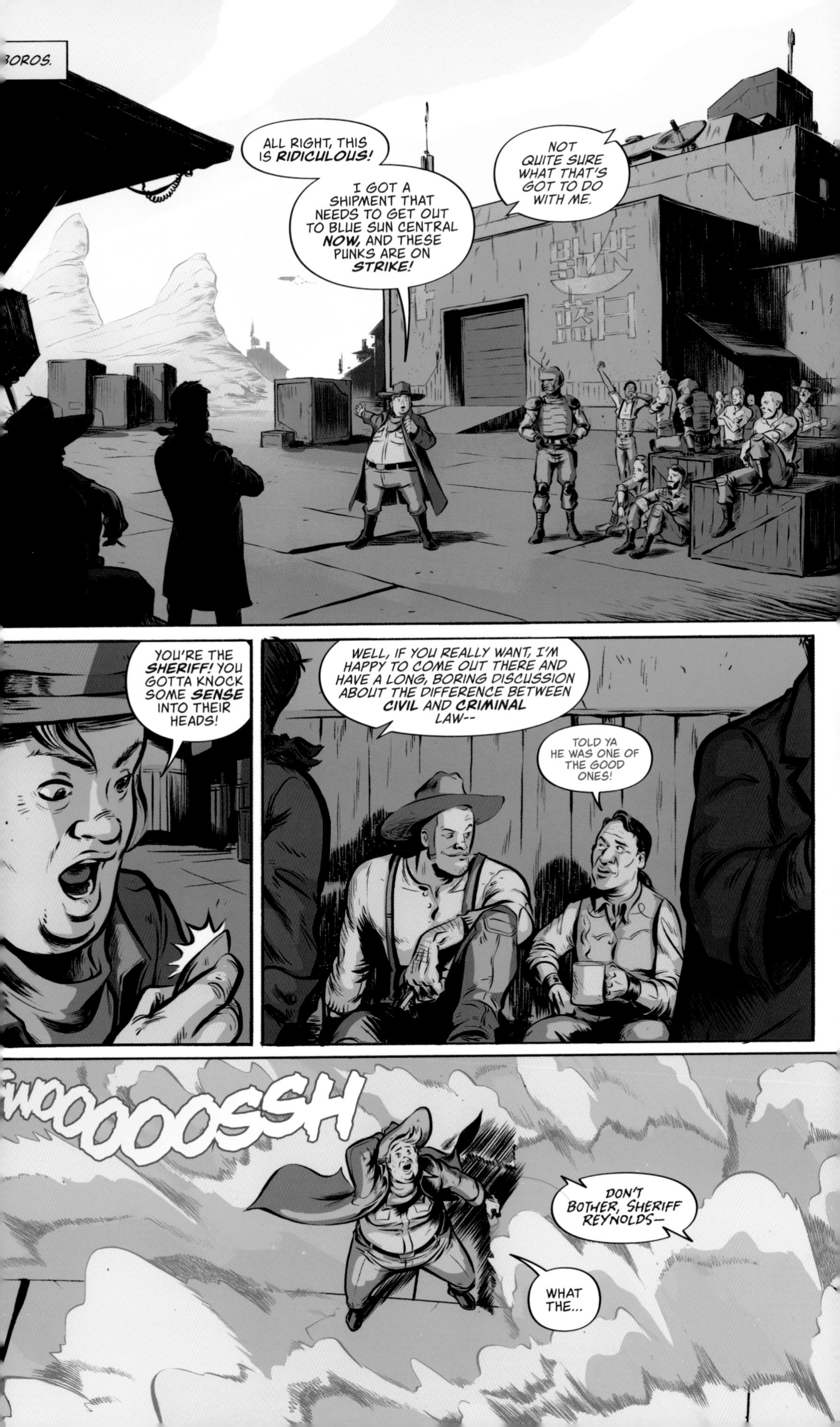

BOROS.
ALL RIGHT, THIS IS RIDICULOUS!
I GOT A SHIPMENT THAT NEEDS TO GET OUT TO BLUE SUN CENTRAL NOW, AND THESE PUNKS ARE ON STRIKE!
NOT QUITE SURE WHAT THAT'S GOT TO DO WITH ME.
YOU'RE THE SHERIFF! YOU GOTTA KNOCK SOME SENSE INTO THEIR HEADS!
WELL, IF YOU REALLY WANT, I'M HAPPY TO COME OUT THERE AND HAVE A LONG, BORING DISCUSSION ABOUT THE DIFFERENCE BETWEEN CIVIL AND CRIMINAL LAW--
TOLD YA HE WAS ONE OF THE GOOD ONES!
WOOOOOOSSH
DON'T BOTHER, SHERIFF REYNOLDS—
WHAT THE...

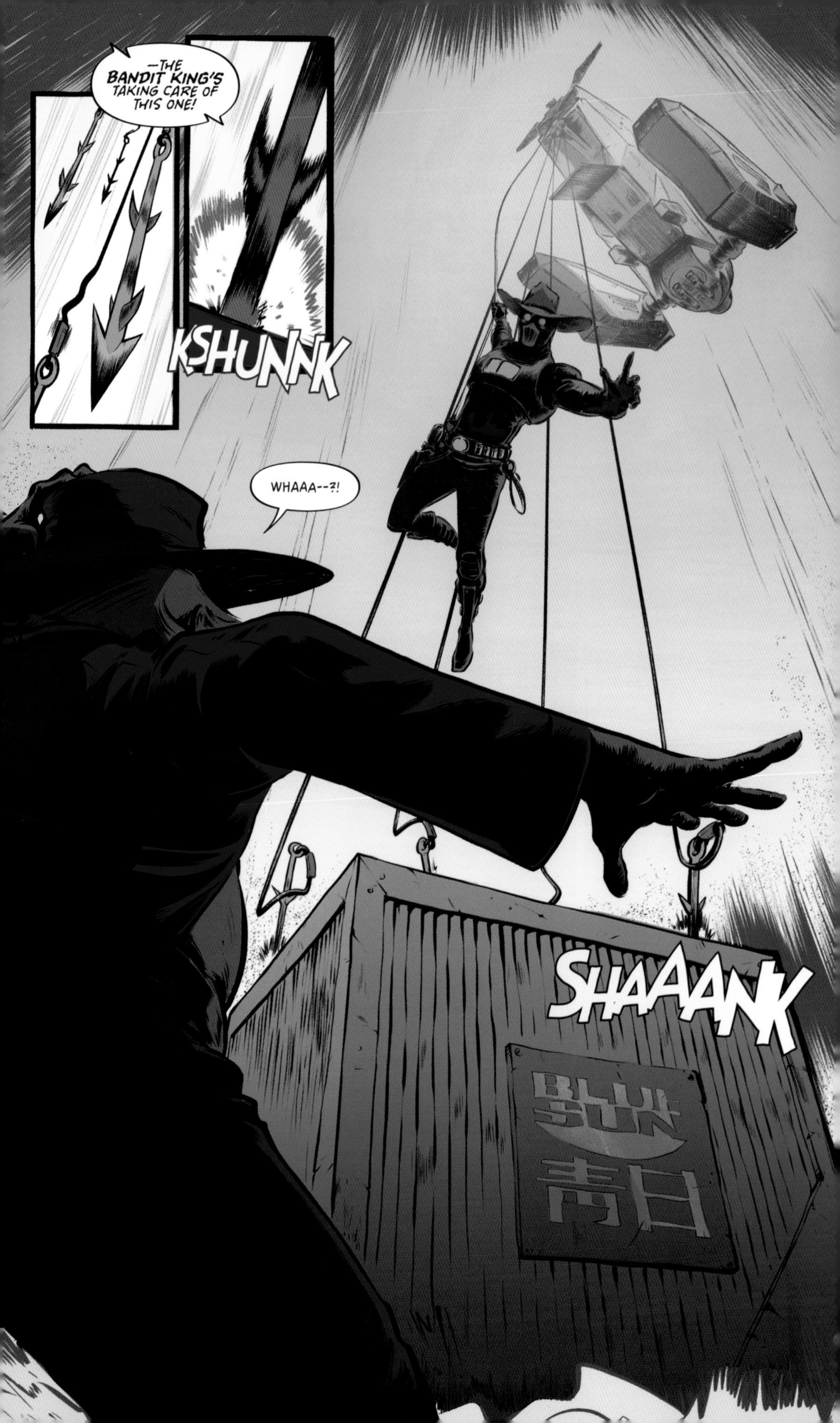
—THE BANDIT KING'S TAKING CARE OF THIS ONE!
KSHUNNK
WHAAA--?!
SHAAANK

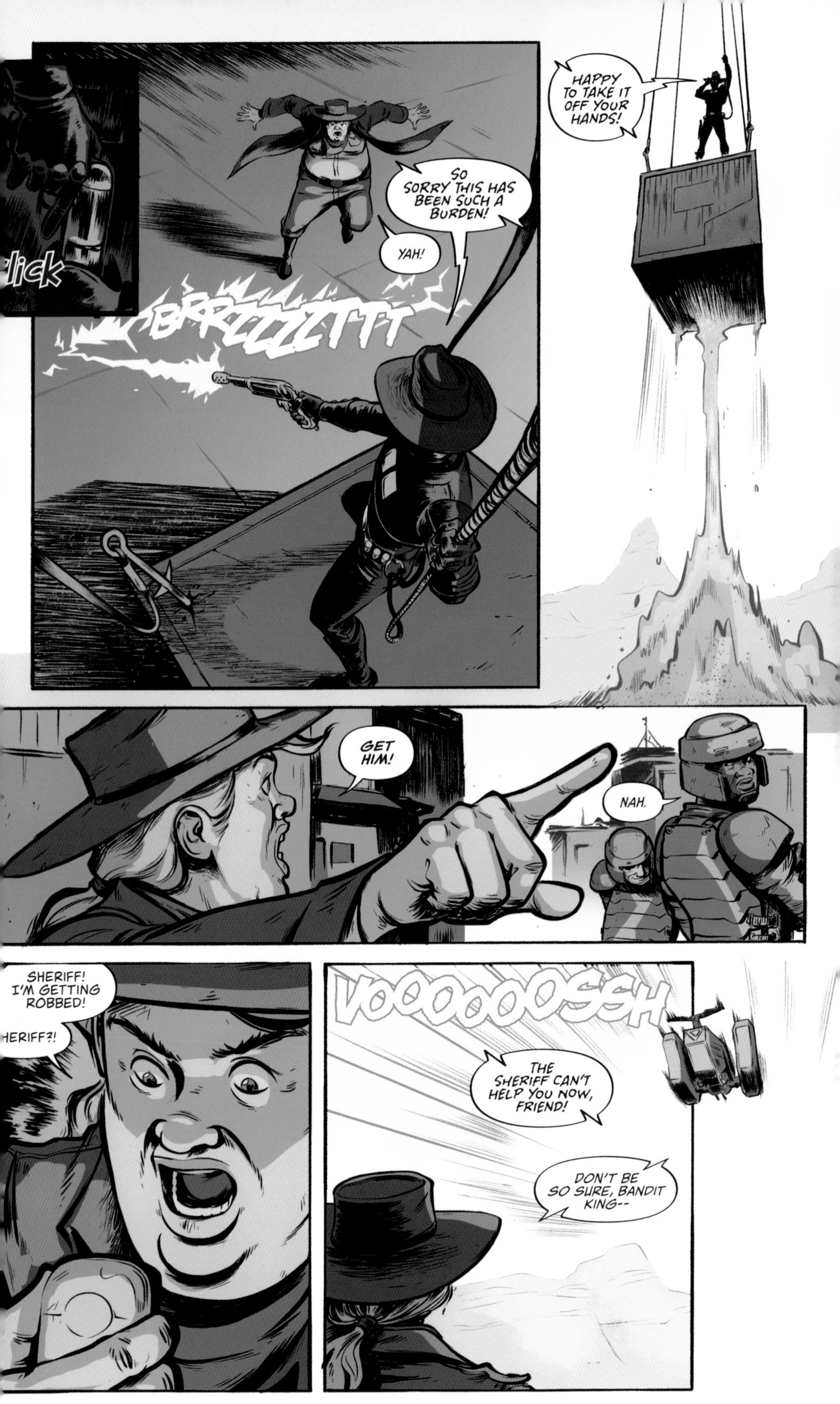

lick
SO SORRY THIS HAS BEEN SUCH A BURDEN!
YAH!
BRRZZZZTTTT
HAPPY TO TAKE IT OFF YOUR HANDS!
GET HIM!
NAH.
SHERIFF! I'M GETTING ROBBED!
HERIFF?!
VOOOOOOOSSH
THE SHERIFF CAN'T HELP YOU NOW, FRIEND!
DON'T BE SO SURE, BANDIT KING--

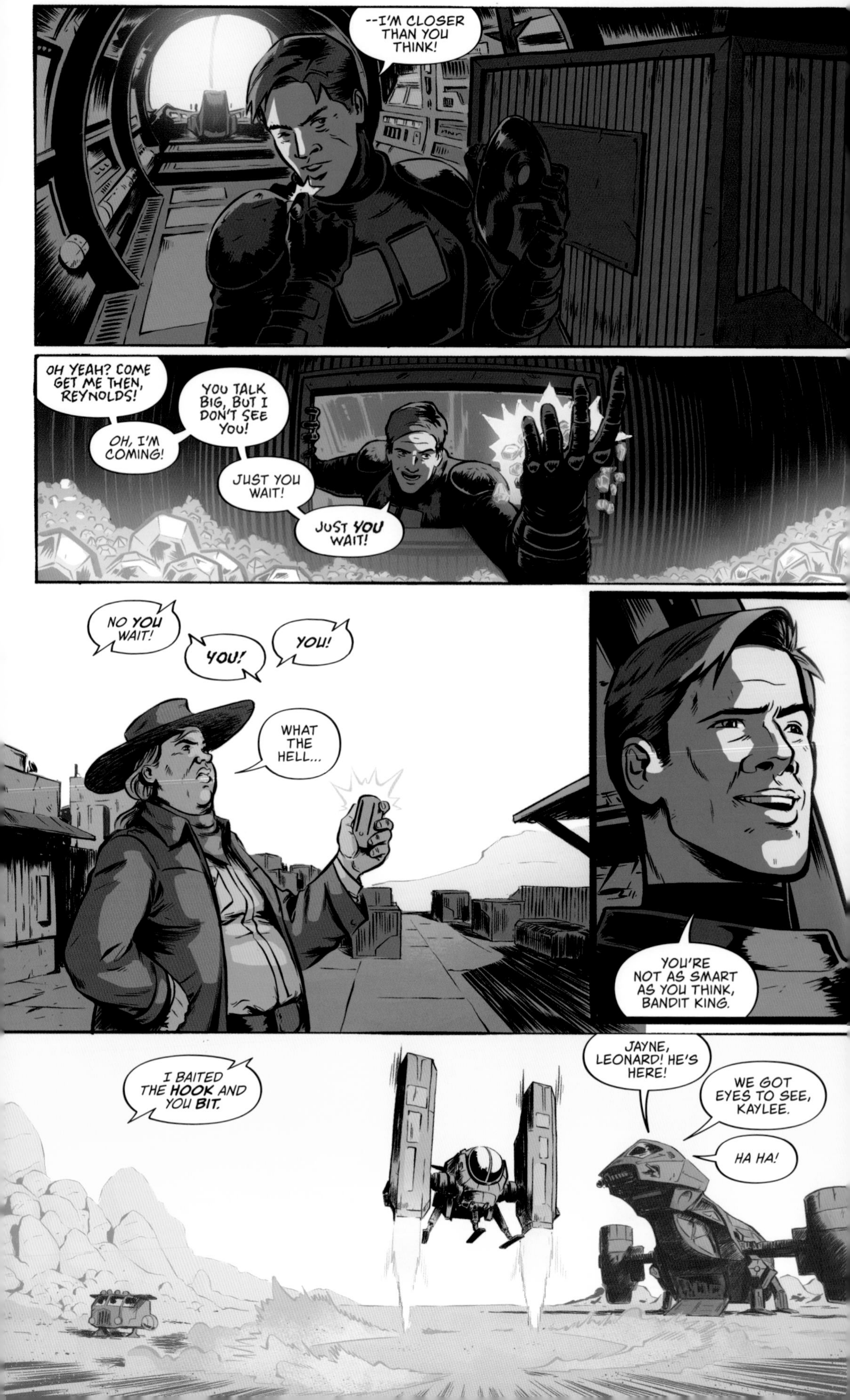
--I'M CLOSER THAN YOU THINK!
OH YEAH? COME GET ME THEN, REYNOLDS!
OH, I'M COMING!
YOU TALK BIG, BUT I DON'T SEE YOU!
JUST YOU WAIT!
JUST YOU WAIT!
NO YOU WAIT!
YOU!
YOU!
WHAT THE HELL...
YOU'RE NOT AS SMART AS YOU THINK, BANDIT KING.
I BAITED THE HOOK AND YOU BIT.
JAYNE, LEONARD! HE'S HERE!
WE GOT EYES TO SEE, KAYLEE.
HA HA!

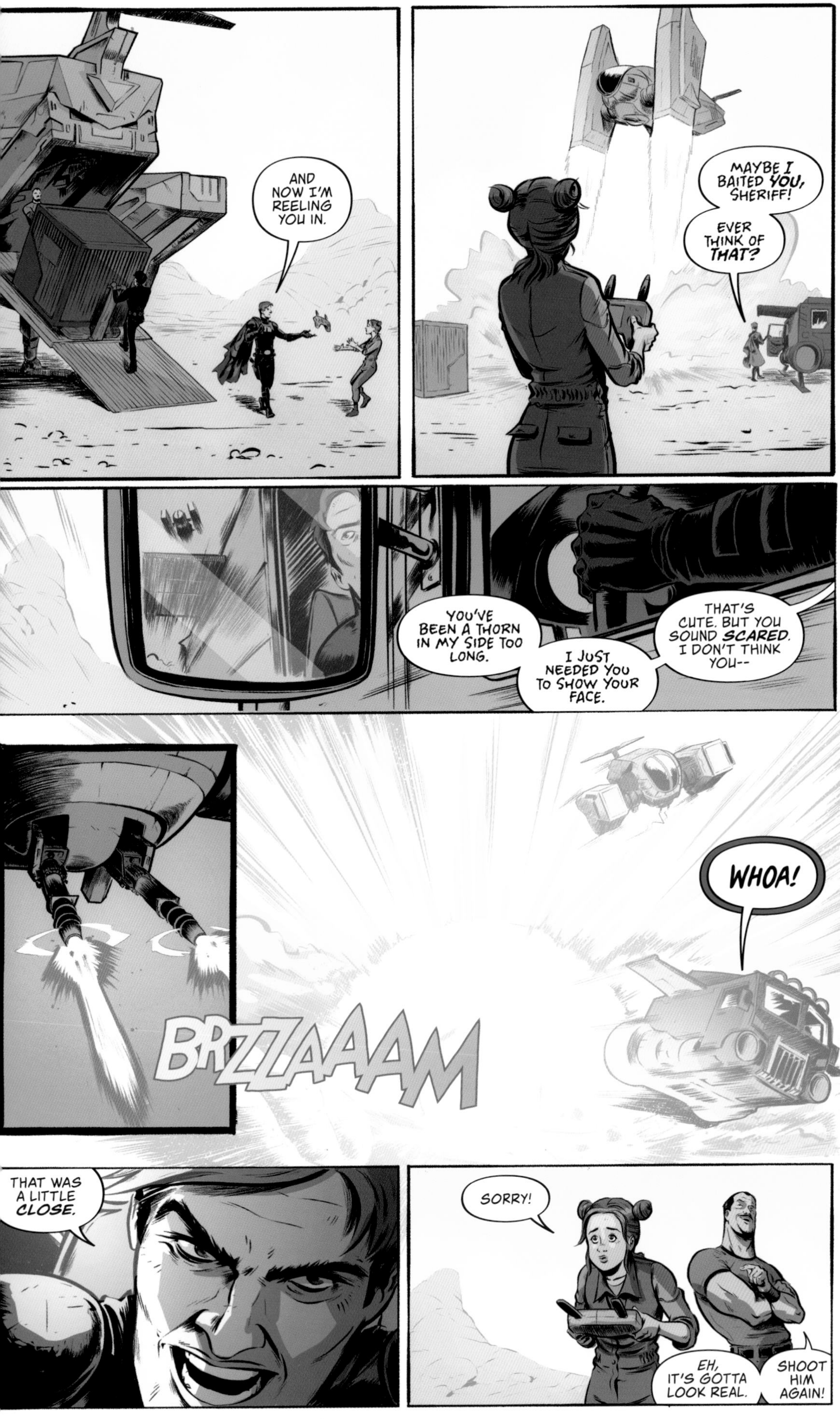
AND NOW I'M REELING YOU IN.
MAYBE I BAITED YOU, SHERIFF!
EVER THINK OF THAT?
YOU'VE BEEN A THORN IN MY SIDE TOO LONG.
I JUST NEEDED YOU TO SHOW YOUR FACE.
THAT'S CUTE. BUT YOU SOUND SCARED. I DON'T THINK YOU--
BRZZAAAAM
WHOA!
THAT WAS A LITTLE CLOSE.
SORRY!
EH, IT'S GOTTA LOOK REAL.
SHOOT HIM AGAIN!

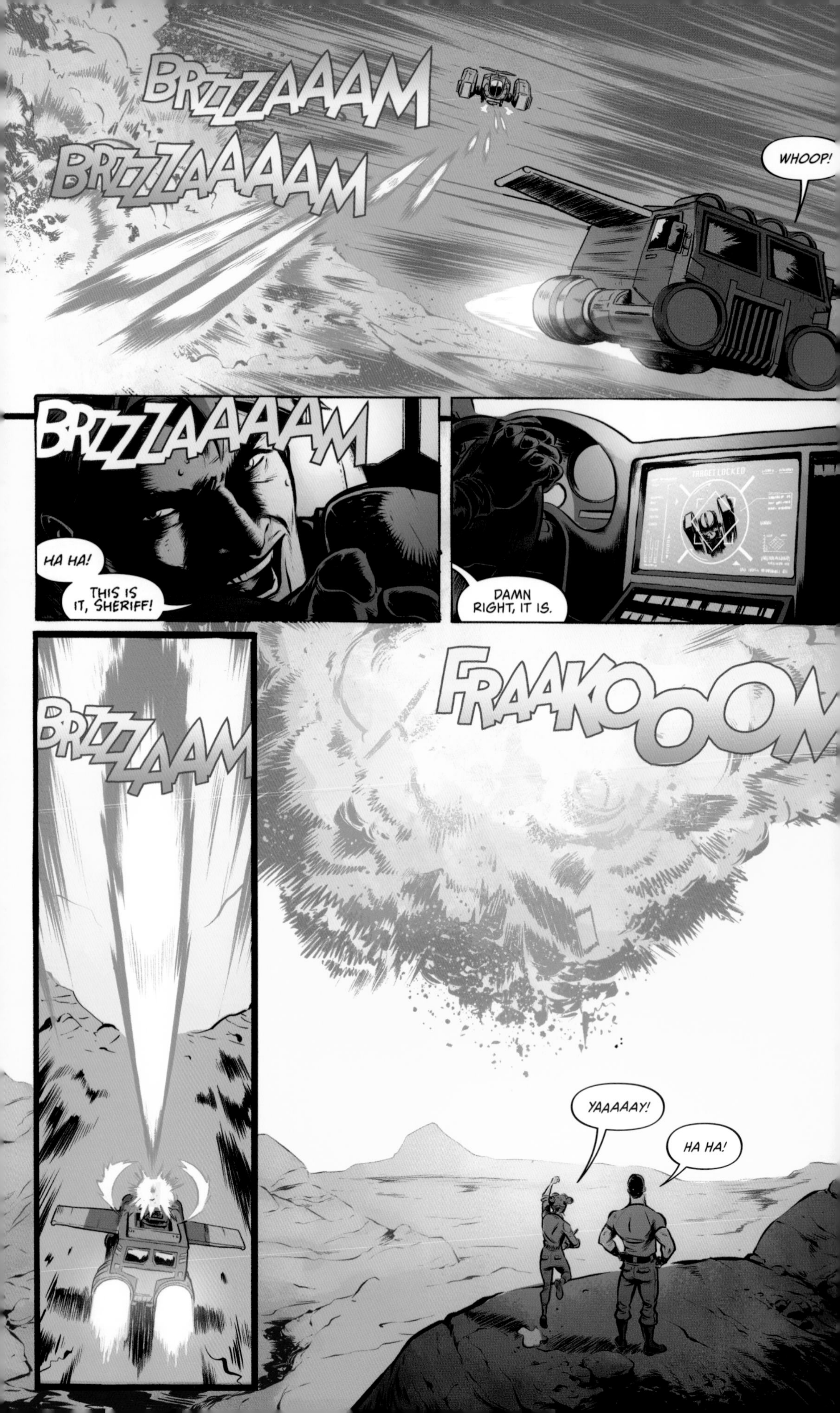
BRZZAAAM
BRZZZAAAAAM
WHOOP!
BRZZZAAAAAM
HA HA!
THIS IS IT, SHERIFF!
DAMN RIGHT, IT IS.
BRZZZAAM
FRAAKOOOOM
YAAAAAY!
HA HA!

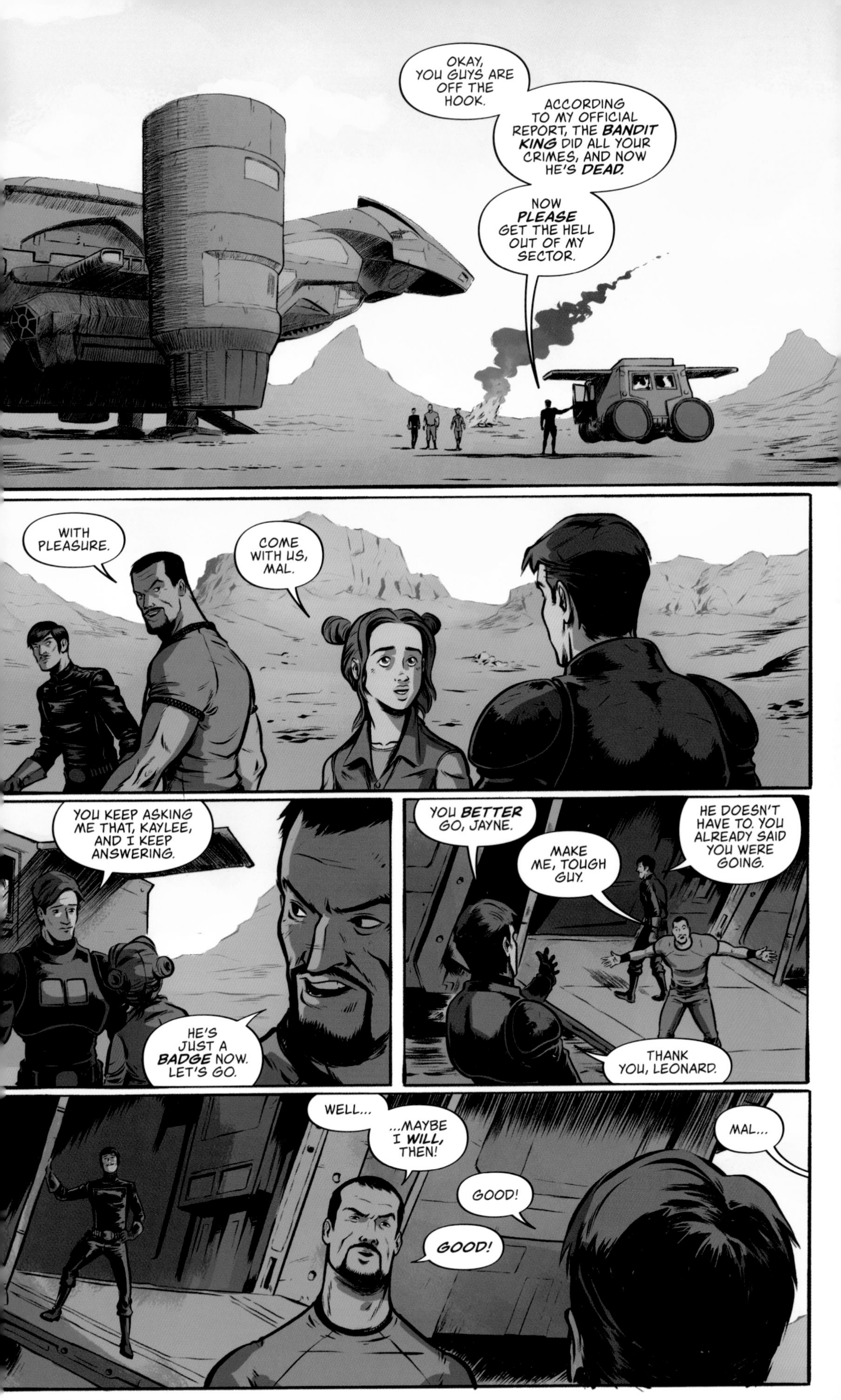
OKAY, YOU GUYS ARE OFF THE HOOK.
ACCORDING TO MY OFFICIAL REPORT, THE **BANDIT KING** DID ALL YOUR CRIMES, AND NOW HE'S **DEAD.**
NOW **PLEASE** GET THE HELL OUT OF MY SECTOR.
WITH PLEASURE.
COME WITH US, MAL.
YOU KEEP ASKING ME THAT, KAYLEE, AND I KEEP ANSWERING.
HE'S JUST A **BADGE** NOW. LET'S GO.
YOU **BETTER** GO, JAYNE.
MAKE ME, TOUGH GUY.
HE DOESN'T HAVE TO. YOU ALREADY SAID YOU WERE GOING.
THANK YOU, LEONARD.
WELL...
...MAYBE I **WILL,** THEN!
MAL...
GOOD!
GOOD!

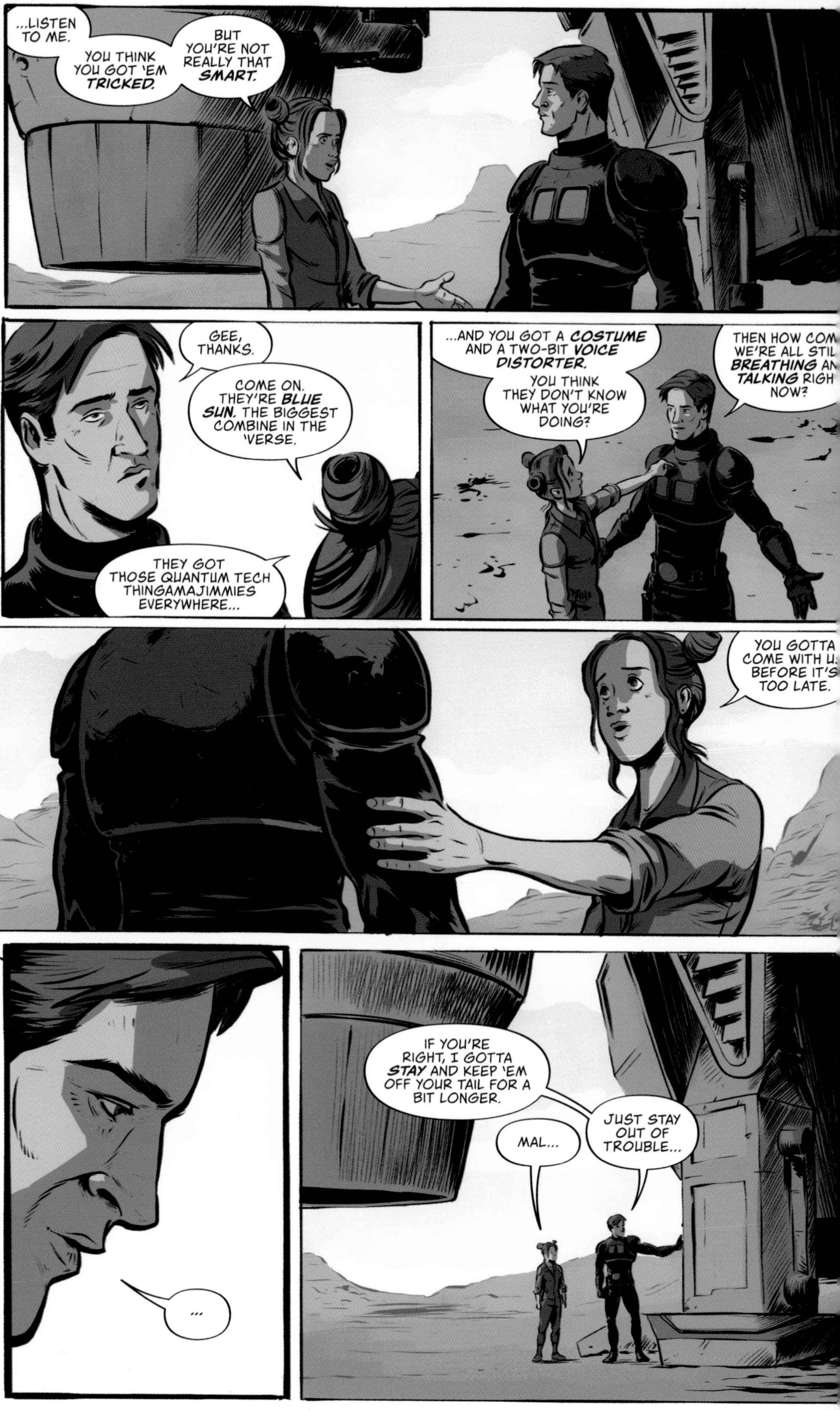
...LISTEN TO ME.
YOU THINK YOU GOT 'EM TRICKED.
BUT YOU'RE NOT REALLY THAT SMART.
GEE, THANKS.
COME ON. THEY'RE BLUE SUN. THE BIGGEST COMBINE IN THE 'VERSE.
THEY GOT THOSE QUANTUM TECH THINGAMAJIMMIES EVERYWHERE...
...AND YOU GOT A COSTUME AND A TWO-BIT VOICE DISTORTER.
YOU THINK THEY DON'T KNOW WHAT YOU'RE DOING?
THEN HOW COM WE'RE ALL STIL BREATHING AN TALKING RIGH NOW?
YOU GOTTA COME WITH U BEFORE IT'S TOO LATE.
...
IF YOU'RE RIGHT, I GOTTA STAY AND KEEP 'EM OFF YOUR TAIL FOR A BIT LONGER.
MAL...
JUST STAY OUT OF TROUBLE...

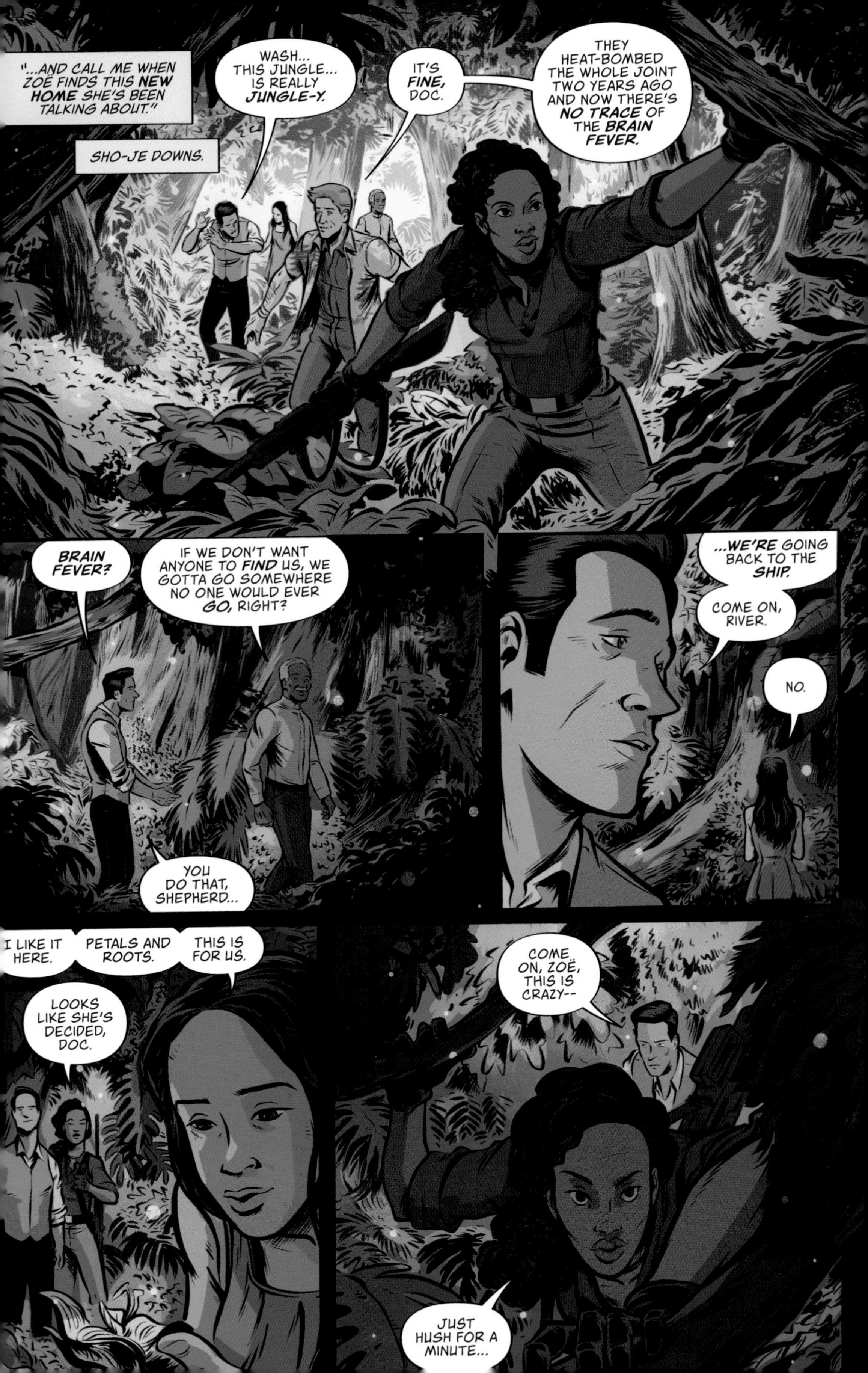
"...AND CALL ME WHEN ZOË FINDS THIS NEW HOME SHE'S BEEN TALKING ABOUT."
SHO-JE DOWNS.
WASH... THIS JUNGLE... IS REALLY JUNGLE-Y.
IT'S FINE, DOC.
THEY HEAT-BOMBED THE WHOLE JOINT TWO YEARS AGO AND NOW THERE'S NO TRACE OF THE BRAIN FEVER.
BRAIN FEVER?
IF WE DON'T WANT ANYONE TO FIND US, WE GOTTA GO SOMEWHERE NO ONE WOULD EVER GO, RIGHT?
YOU DO THAT, SHEPHERD...
...WE'RE GOING BACK TO THE SHIP.
COME ON, RIVER.
NO.
I LIKE IT HERE.
PETALS AND ROOTS.
THIS IS FOR US.
LOOKS LIKE SHE'S DECIDED, DOC.
COME ON, ZOË, THIS IS CRAZY--
JUST HUSH FOR A MINUTE...

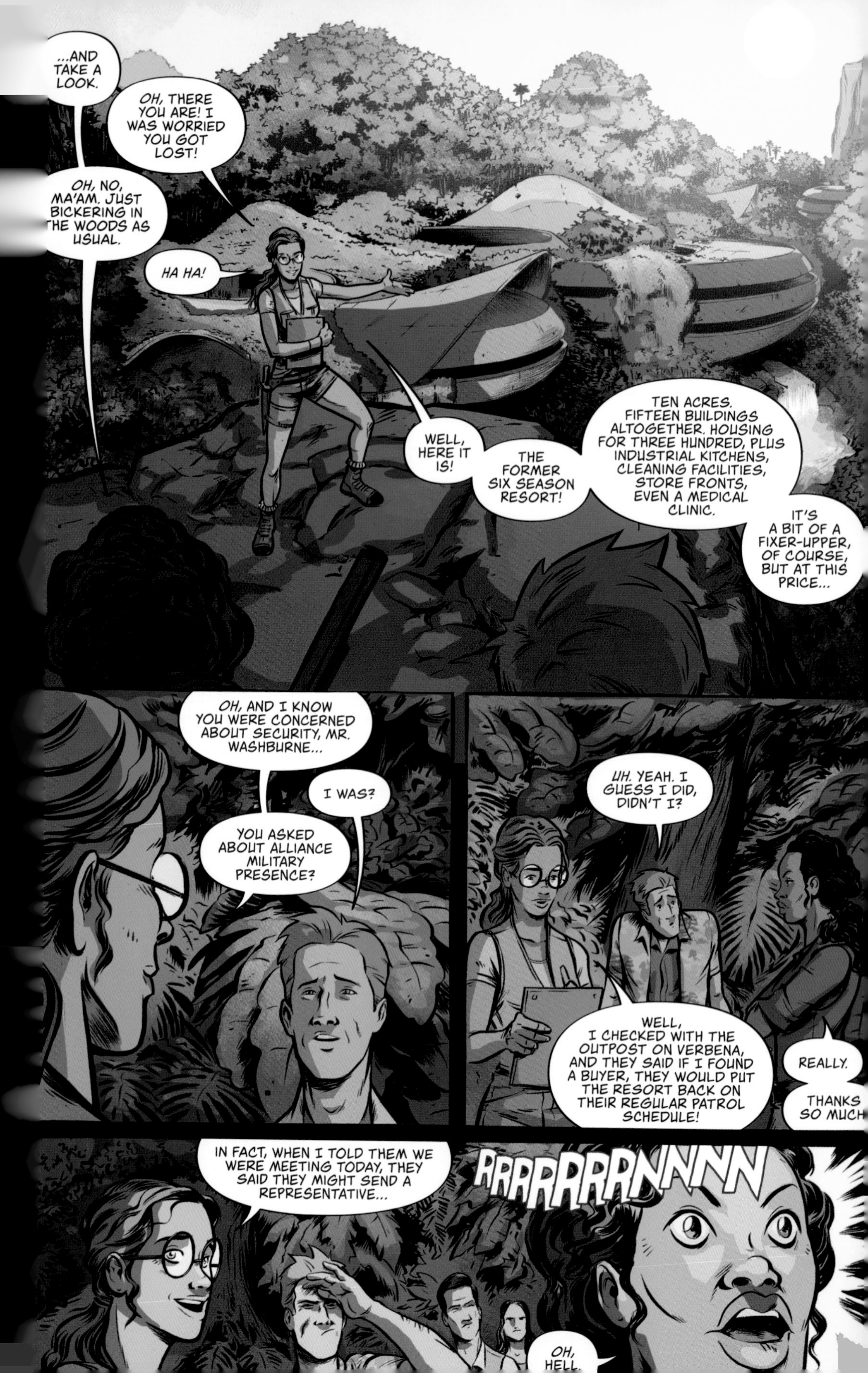
...AND TAKE A LOOK.
OH, THERE YOU ARE! I WAS WORRIED YOU GOT LOST!
OH, NO, MA'AM. JUST BICKERING IN THE WOODS AS USUAL.
HA HA!
WELL, HERE IT IS!
THE FORMER SIX SEASON RESORT!
TEN ACRES. FIFTEEN BUILDINGS ALTOGETHER. HOUSING FOR THREE HUNDRED, PLUS INDUSTRIAL KITCHENS, CLEANING FACILITIES, STORE FRONTS, EVEN A MEDICAL CLINIC.
IT'S A BIT OF A FIXER-UPPER, OF COURSE, BUT AT THIS PRICE...
OH, AND I KNOW YOU WERE CONCERNED ABOUT SECURITY, MR. WASHBURNE...
I WAS?
YOU ASKED ABOUT ALLIANCE MILITARY PRESENCE?
UH. YEAH. I GUESS I DID, DIDN'T I?
WELL, I CHECKED WITH THE OUTPOST ON VERBENA, AND THEY SAID IF I FOUND A BUYER, THEY WOULD PUT THE RESORT BACK ON THEIR REGULAR PATROL SCHEDULE!
REALLY.
THANKS SO MUCH
IN FACT, WHEN I TOLD THEM WE WERE MEETING TODAY, THEY SAID THEY MIGHT SEND A REPRESENTATIVE...
RRRRRRRNNNNN
OH, HELL.

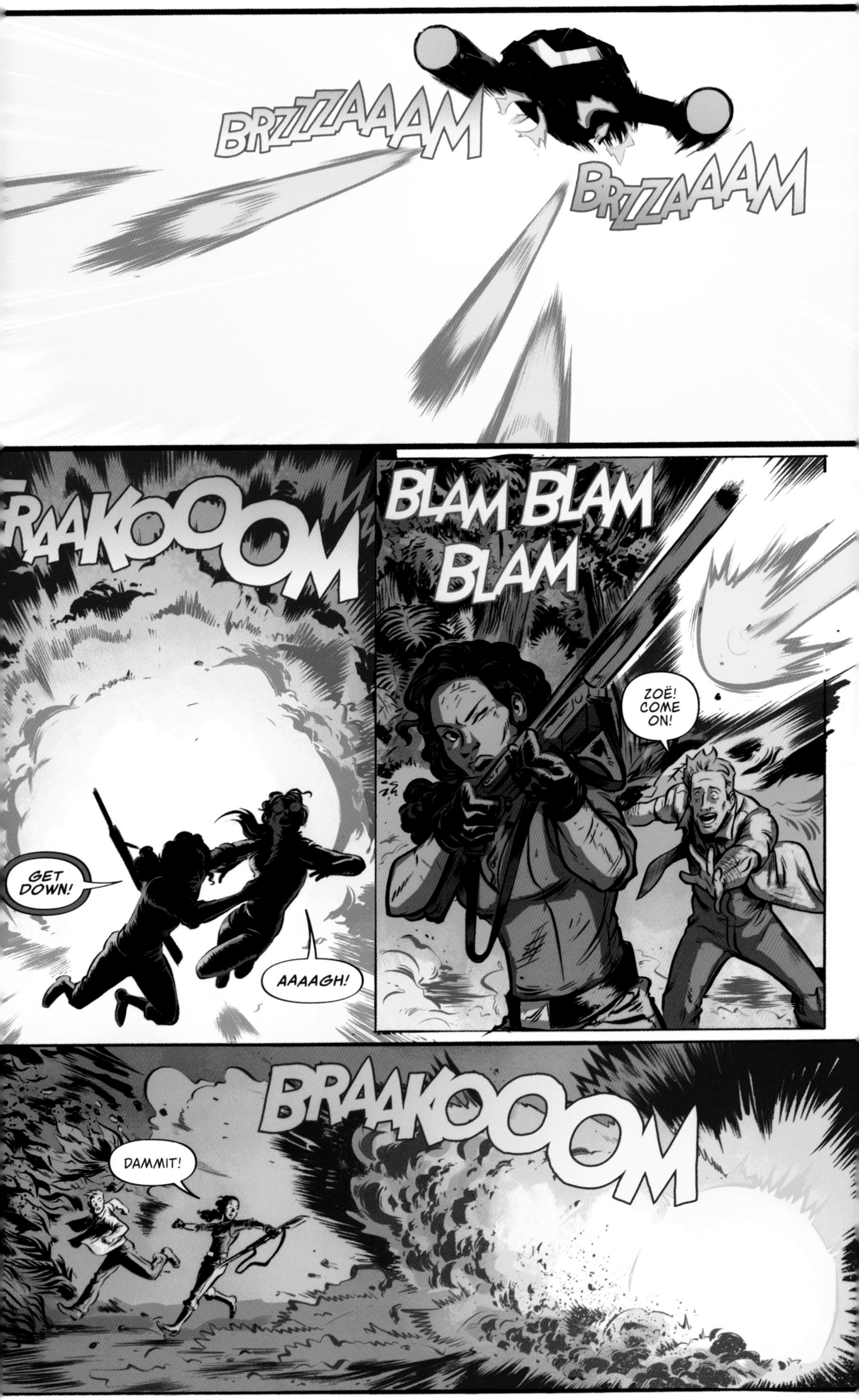
BRZZZAAAM
BRZZAAAM
RAAKOOOOM
GET DOWN!
AAAAGH!
BLAM BLAM BLAM
ZOË! COME ON!
BRAAKOOOOM
DAMMIT!

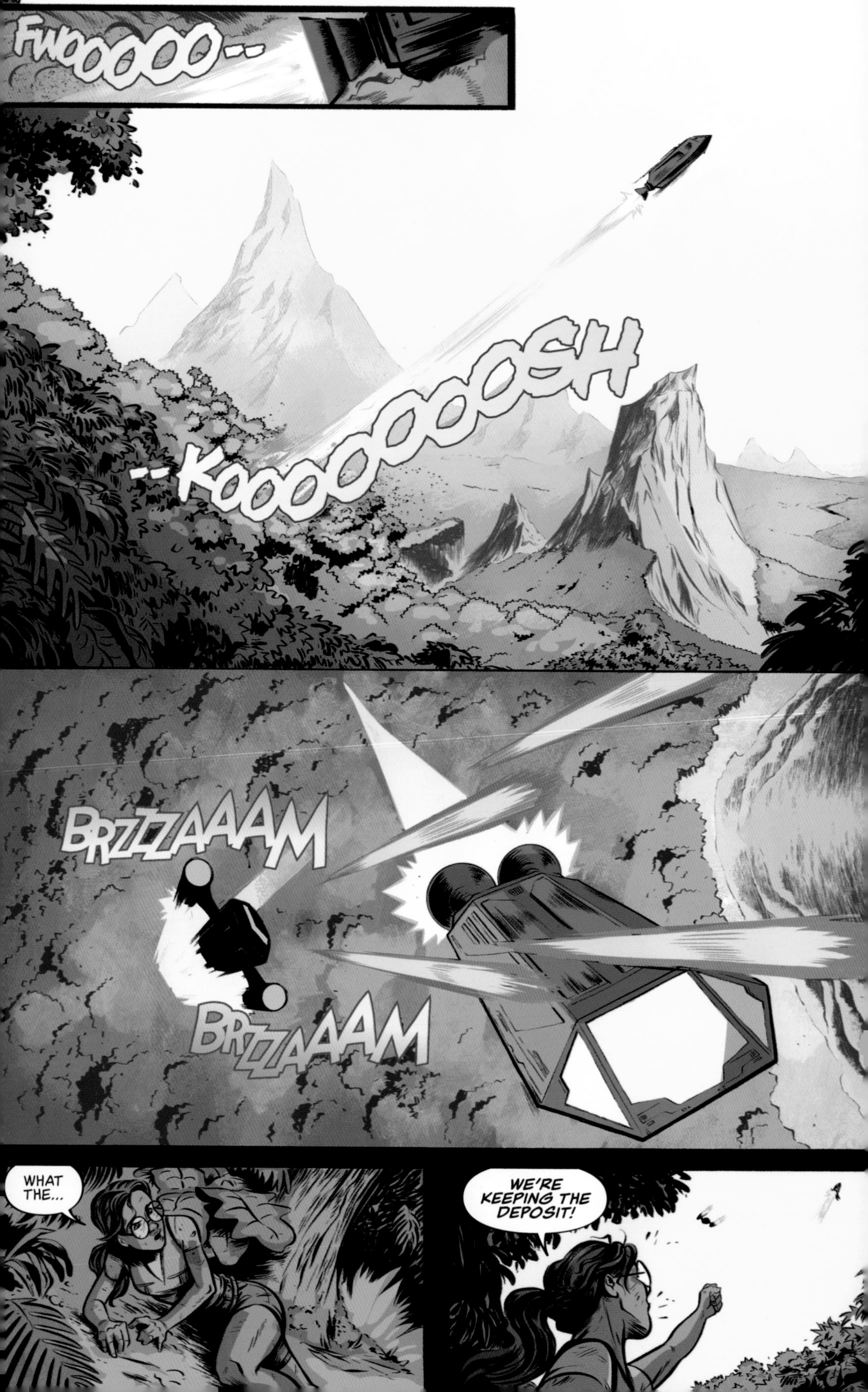
FWOOOOO--
--KOOOOOOOOOSH
BRZZZAAAM
BRZZAAAM
WHAT THE...
WE'RE KEEPING THE DEPOSIT!

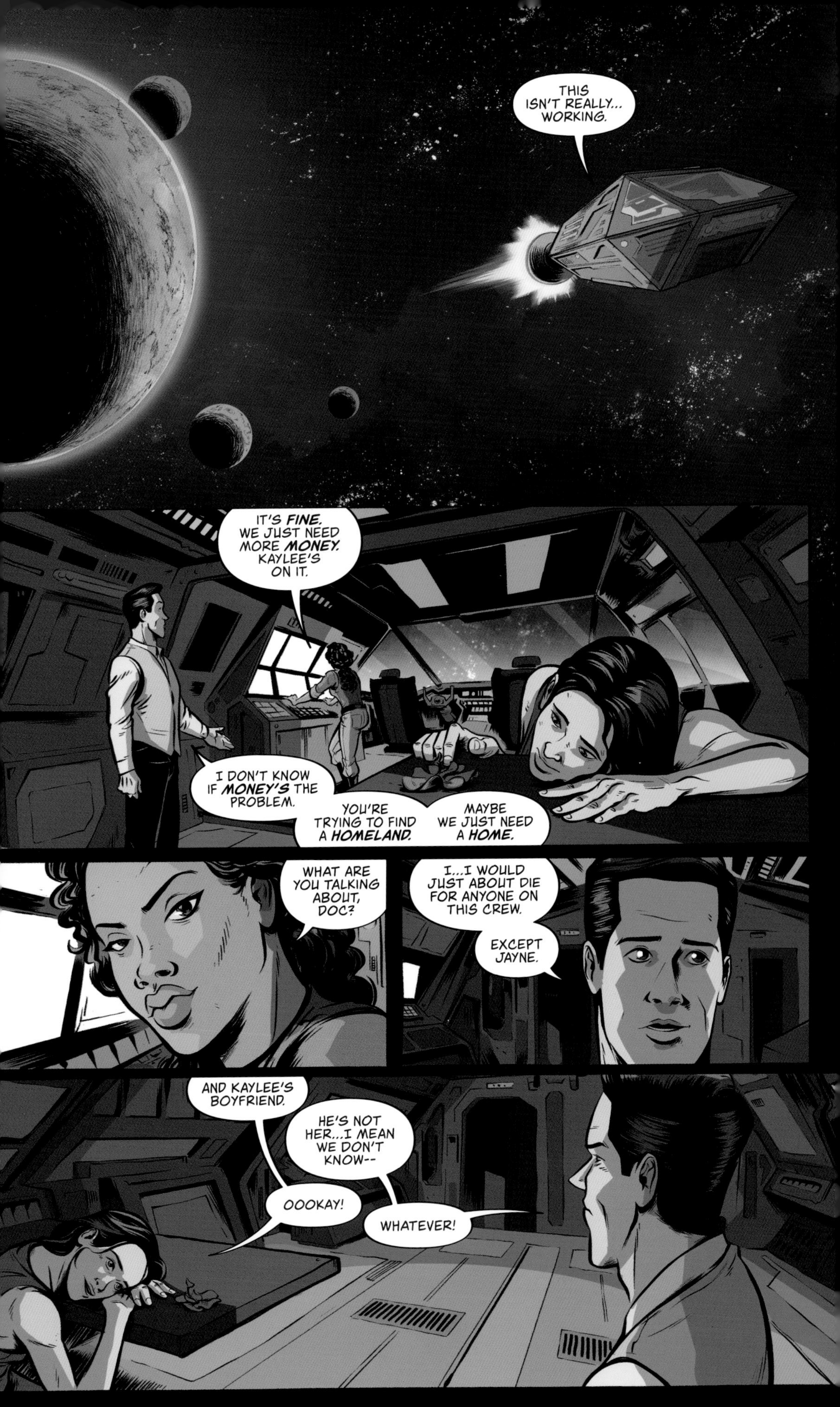
THIS ISN'T REALLY... WORKING.
IT'S FINE. WE JUST NEED MORE MONEY. KAYLEE'S ON IT.
I DON'T KNOW IF MONEY'S THE PROBLEM.
YOU'RE TRYING TO FIND A HOMELAND.
MAYBE WE JUST NEED A HOME.
WHAT ARE YOU TALKING ABOUT, DOC?
I...I WOULD JUST ABOUT DIE FOR ANYONE ON THIS CREW.
EXCEPT JAYNE.
AND KAYLEE'S BOYFRIEND.
HE'S NOT HER...I MEAN WE DON'T KNOW--
OOOKAY!
WHATEVER!

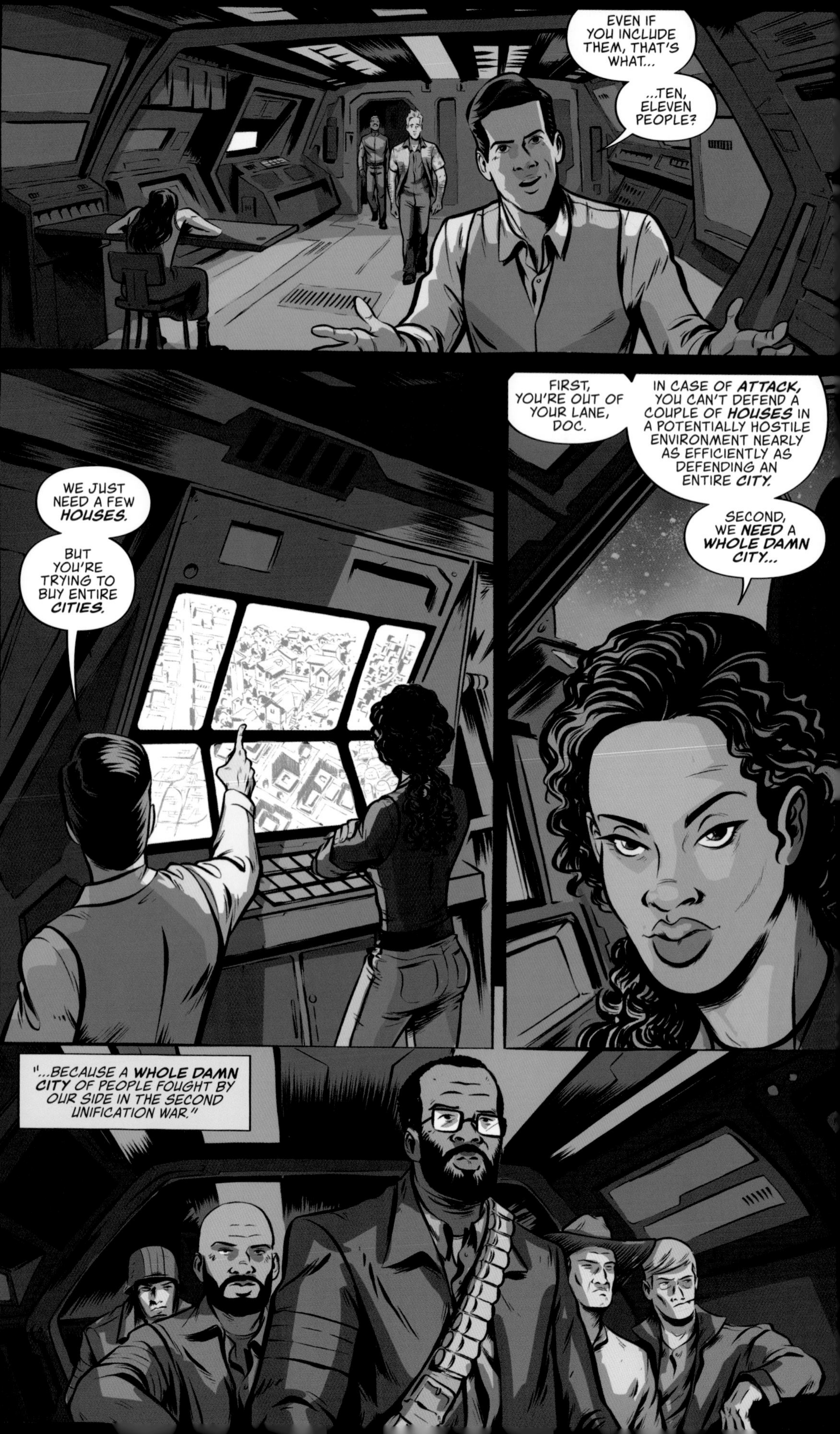
EVEN IF YOU INCLUDE THEM, THAT'S WHAT...
...TEN, ELEVEN PEOPLE?
WE JUST NEED A FEW **HOUSES.**
BUT YOU'RE TRYING TO BUY ENTIRE **CITIES.**
FIRST, YOU'RE OUT OF YOUR LANE, DOC.
IN CASE OF **ATTACK,** YOU CAN'T DEFEND A COUPLE OF **HOUSES** IN A POTENTIALLY HOSTILE ENVIRONMENT NEARLY AS EFFICIENTLY AS DEFENDING AN ENTIRE **CITY.**
SECOND, WE **NEED** A **WHOLE DAMN CITY...**
"...BECAUSE A **WHOLE DAMN CITY** OF PEOPLE FOUGHT BY OUR SIDE IN THE SECOND UNIFICATION WAR."

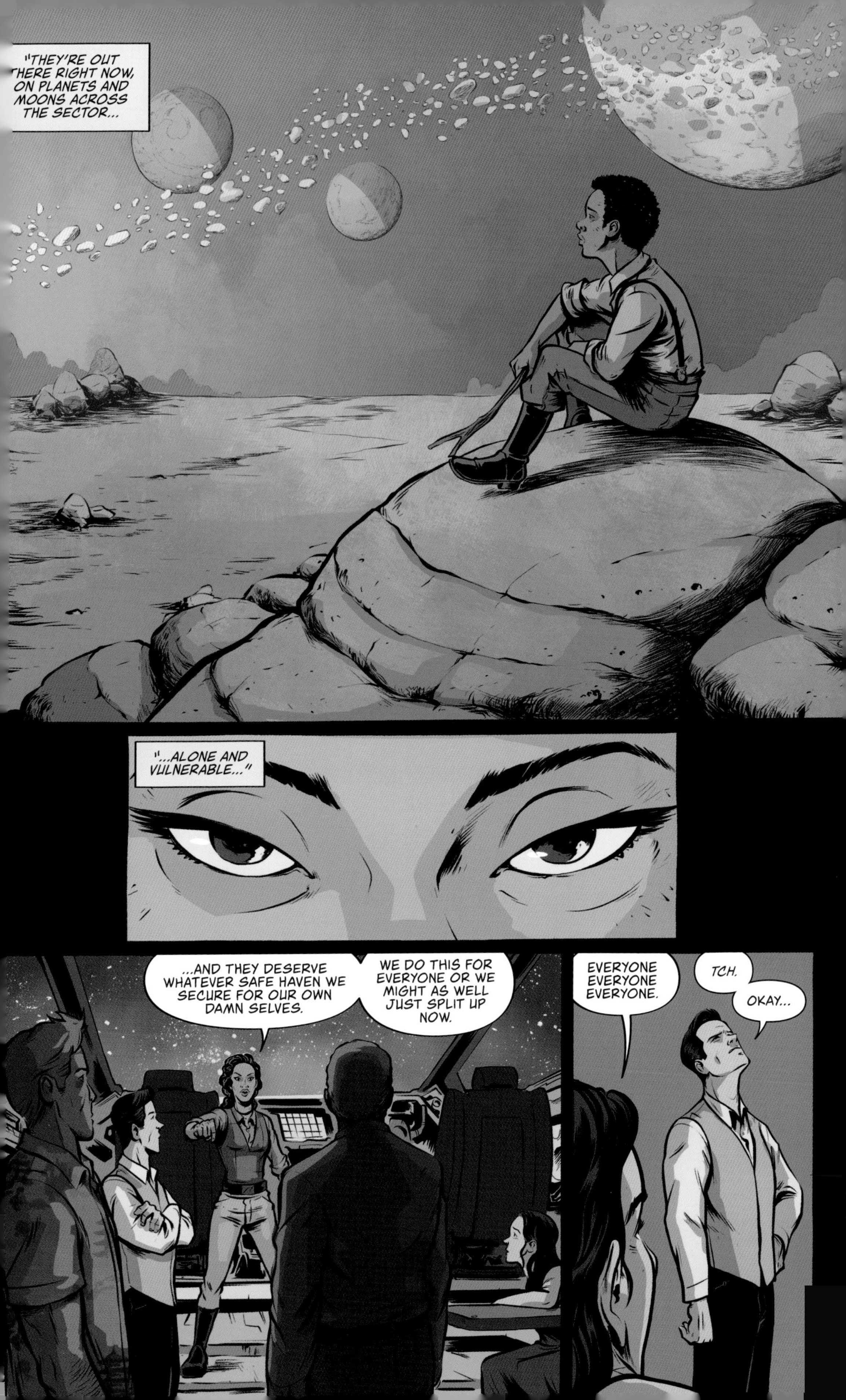
"THEY'RE OUT THERE RIGHT NOW, ON PLANETS AND MOONS ACROSS THE SECTOR...
"...ALONE AND VULNERABLE..."
...AND THEY DESERVE WHATEVER SAFE HAVEN WE SECURE FOR OUR OWN DAMN SELVES.
WE DO THIS FOR EVERYONE OR WE MIGHT AS WELL JUST SPLIT UP NOW.
EVERYONE EVERYONE EVERYONE.
TCH.
OKAY...

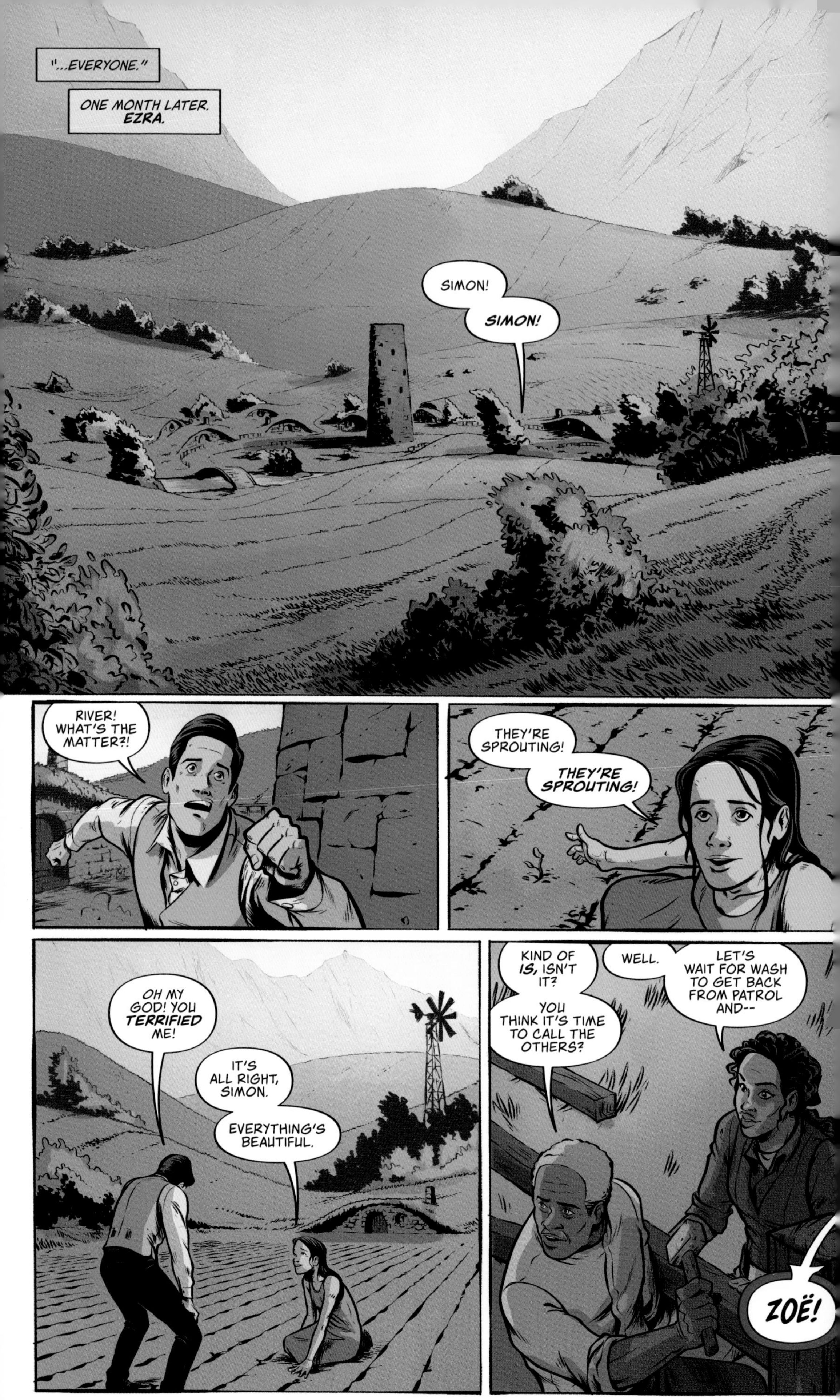
"...EVERYONE."
ONE MONTH LATER. EZRA.
SIMON!
SIMON!
RIVER! WHAT'S THE MATTER?!
THEY'RE SPROUTING!
THEY'RE SPROUTING!
OH MY GOD! YOU TERRIFIED ME!
IT'S ALL RIGHT, SIMON.
EVERYTHING'S BEAUTIFUL.
KIND OF IS, ISN'T IT?
YOU THINK IT'S TIME TO CALL THE OTHERS?
WELL.
LET'S WAIT FOR WASH TO GET BACK FROM PATROL AND--
ZOË!

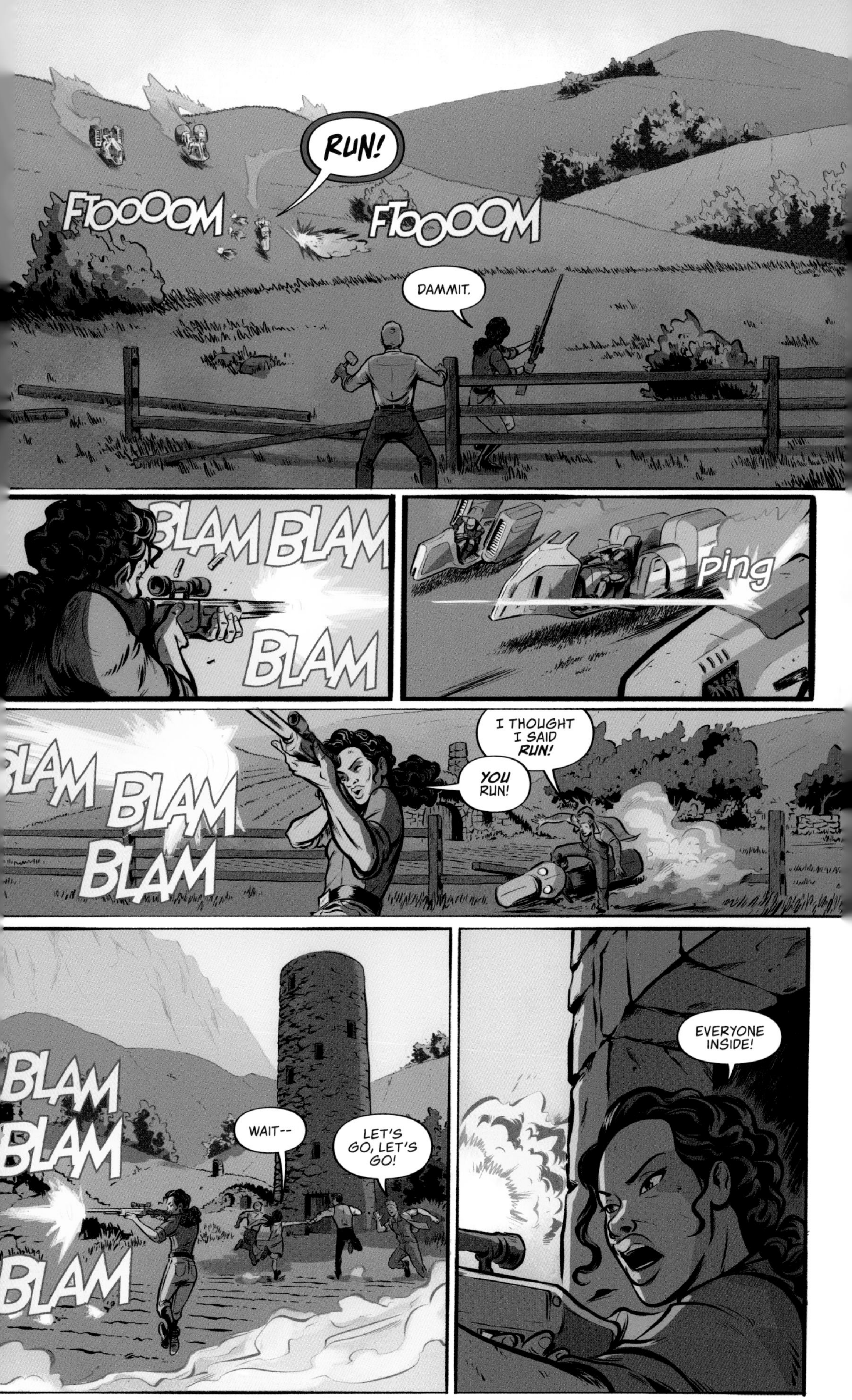
RUN!
FTOOOOM
FTOOOOM
DAMMIT.
BLAM BLAM
BLAM
ping
BLAM
BLAM
BLAM
I THOUGHT I SAID RUN!
YOU RUN!
BLAM
BLAM
BLAM
WAIT--
LET'S GO, LET'S GO!
EVERYONE INSIDE!

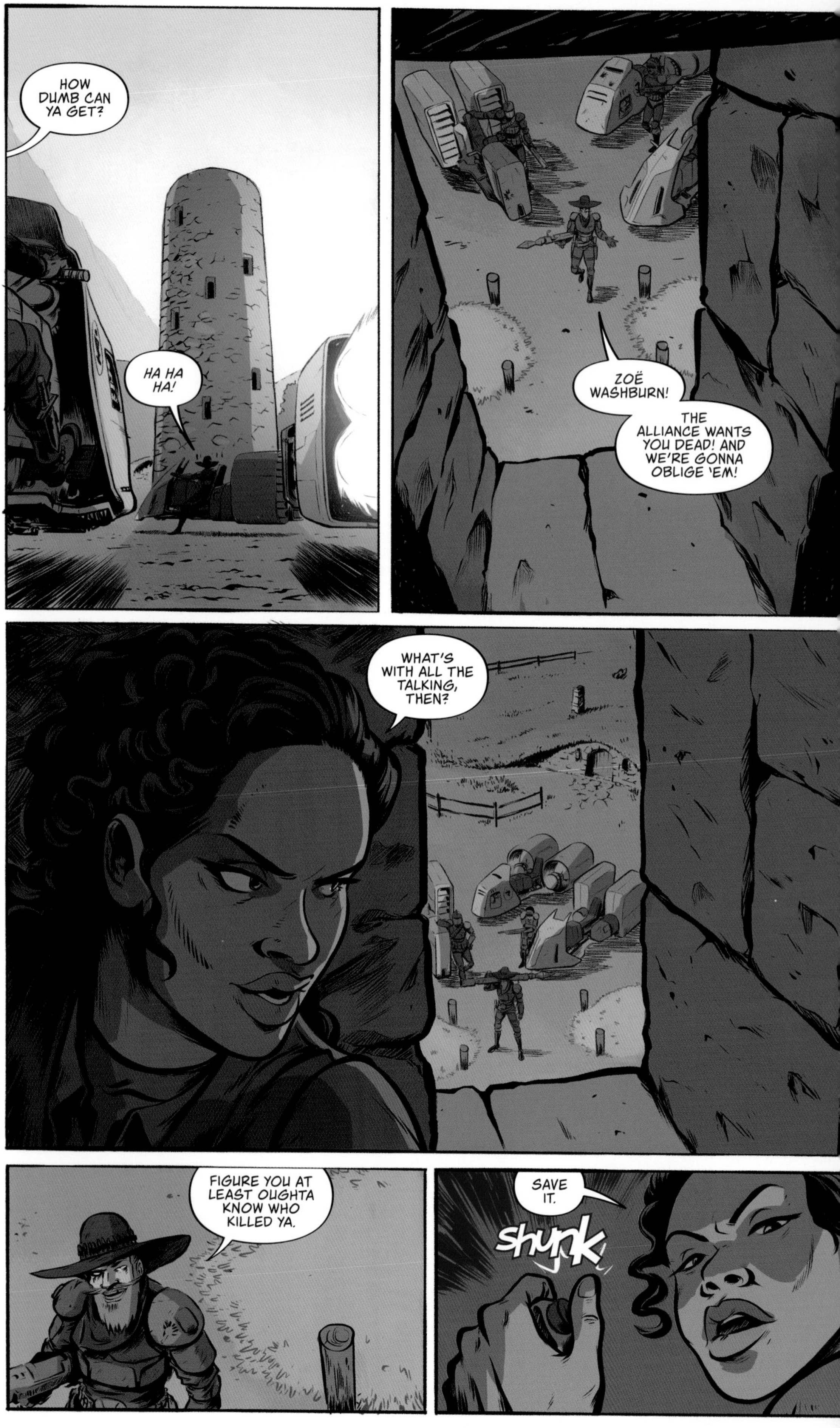
HOW DUMB CAN YA GET?
HA HA HA!
ZOË WASHBURN!
THE ALLIANCE WANTS YOU DEAD! AND WE'RE GONNA OBLIGE 'EM!
WHAT'S WITH ALL THE TALKING, THEN?
FIGURE YOU AT LEAST OUGHTA KNOW WHO KILLED YA.
SAVE IT.
SHUNK

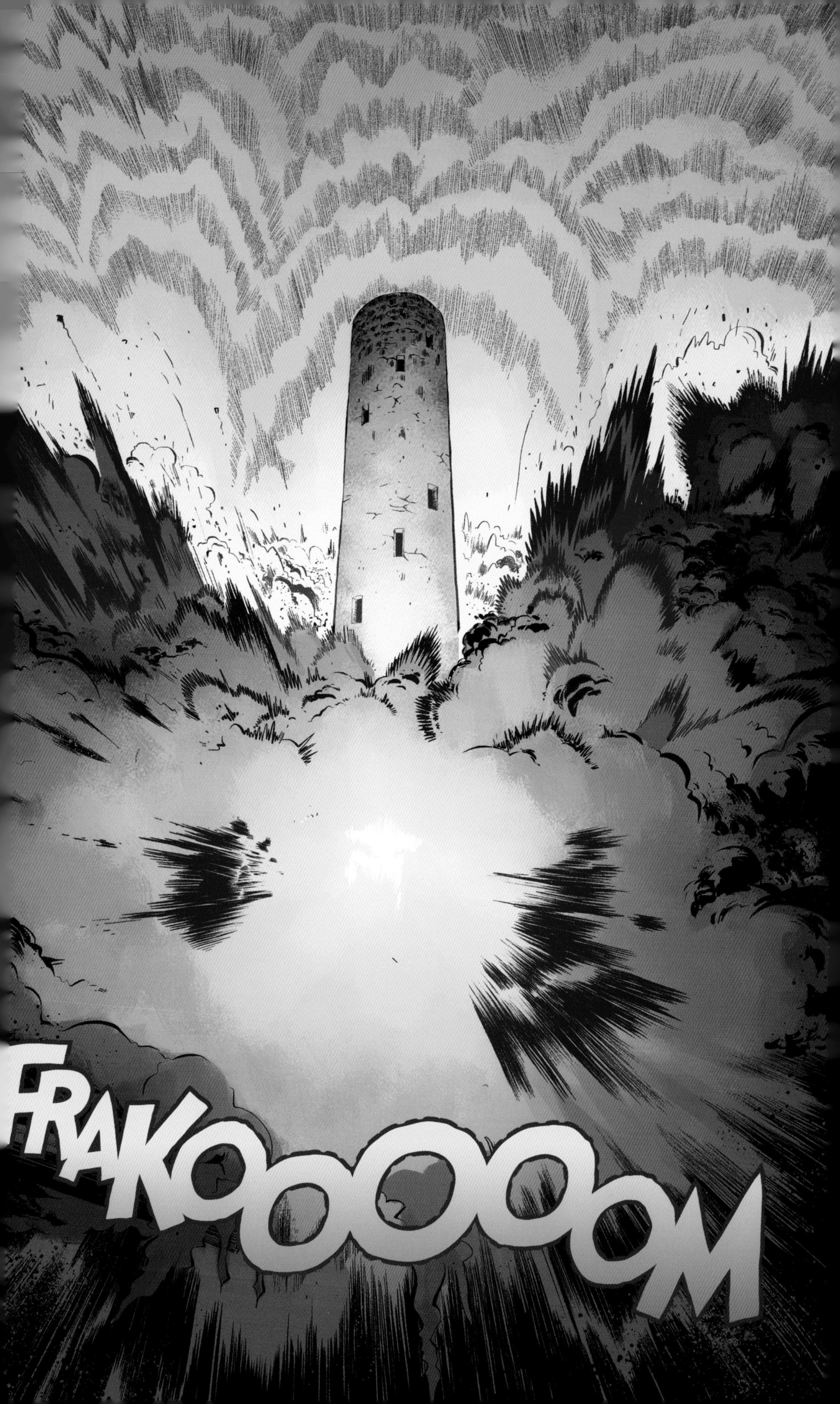
FRAKOOOOOOM

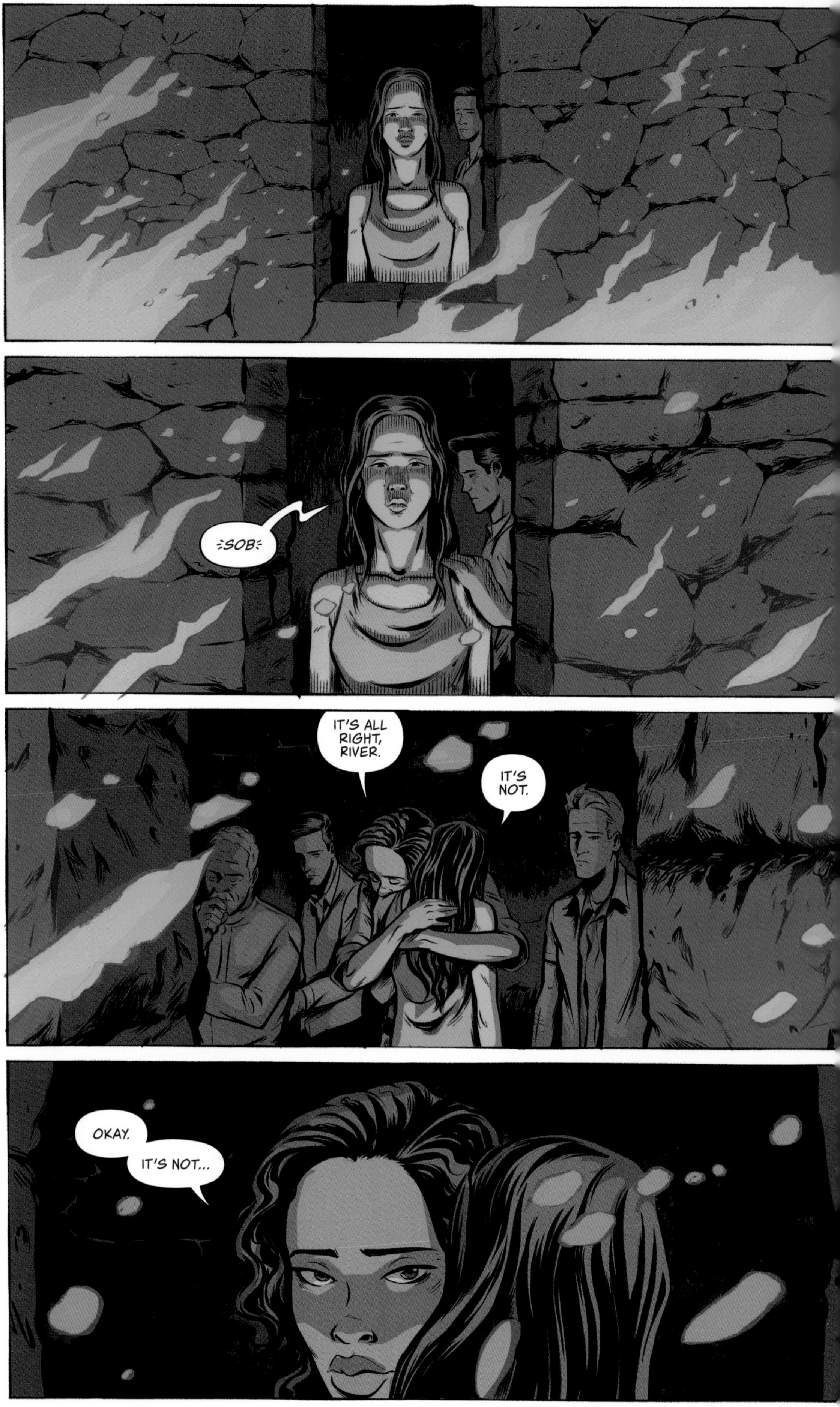
SOB
IT'S ALL RIGHT, RIVER.
IT'S NOT.
OKAY.
IT'S NOT...

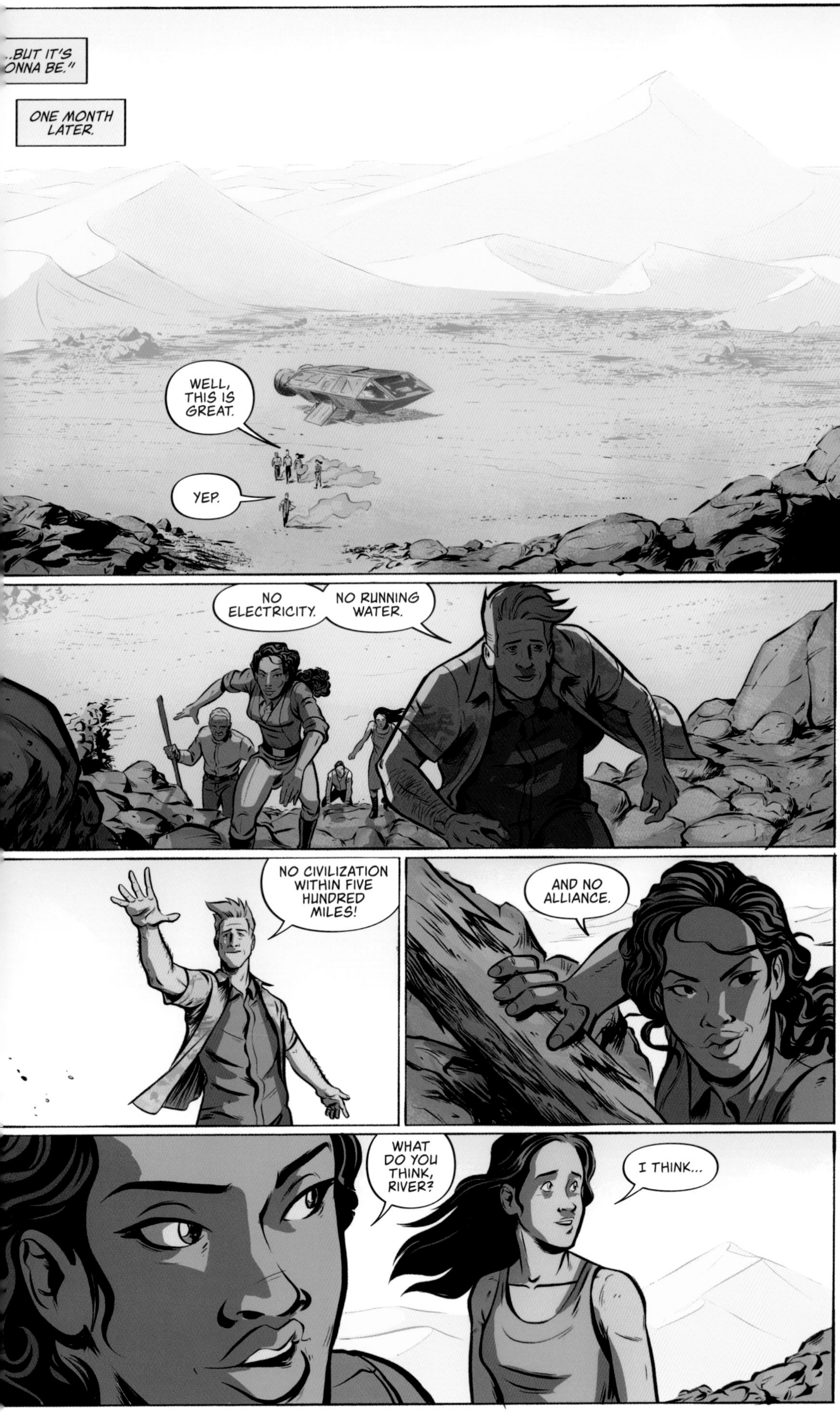
..BUT IT'S
ONNA BE."
ONE MONTH LATER.
WELL, THIS IS GREAT.
YEP.
NO ELECTRICITY.
NO RUNNING WATER.
NO CIVILIZATION WITHIN FIVE HUNDRED MILES!
AND NO ALLIANCE.
WHAT DO YOU THINK, RIVER?
I THINK...

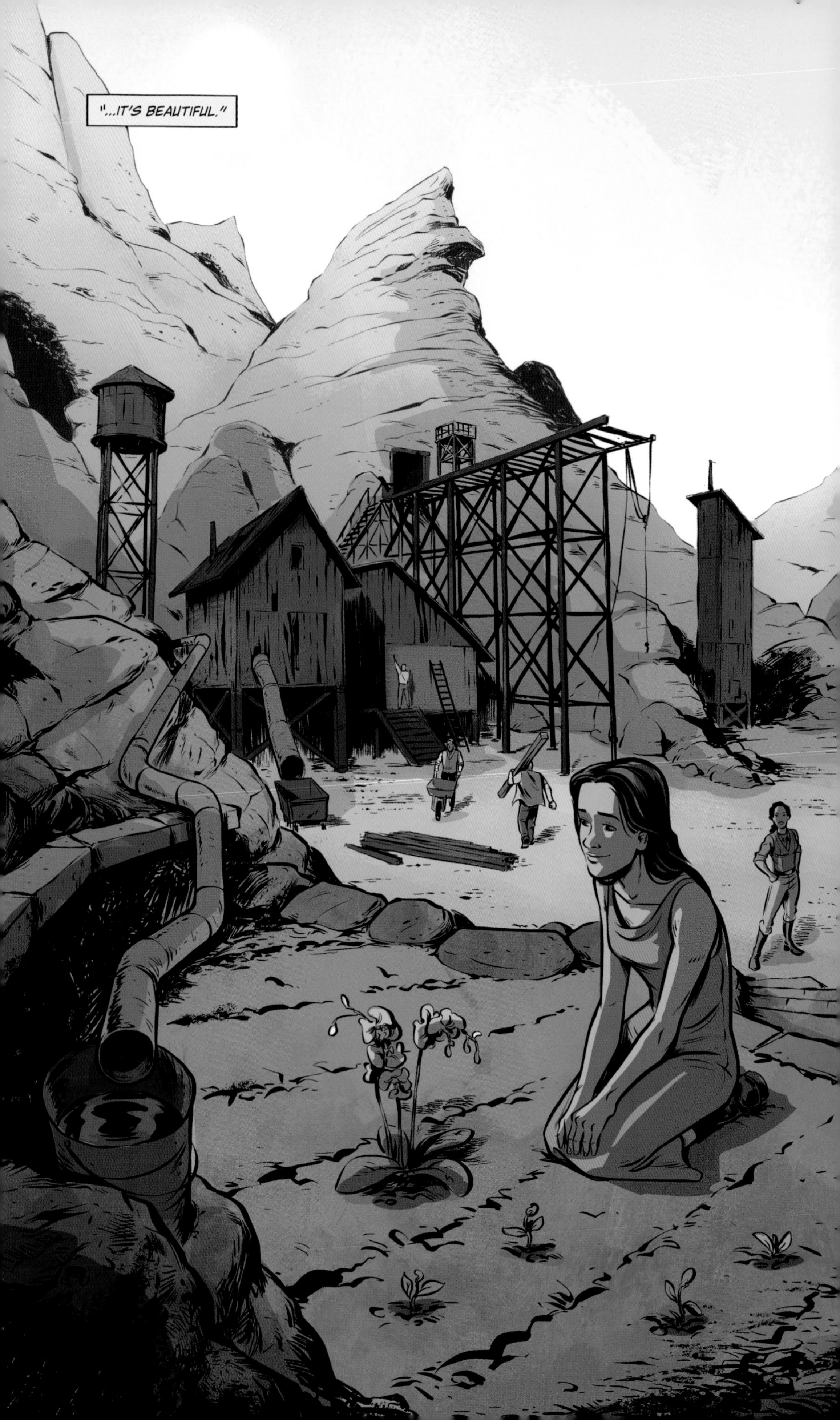
"...IT'S BEAUTIFUL."

COVER GALLERY

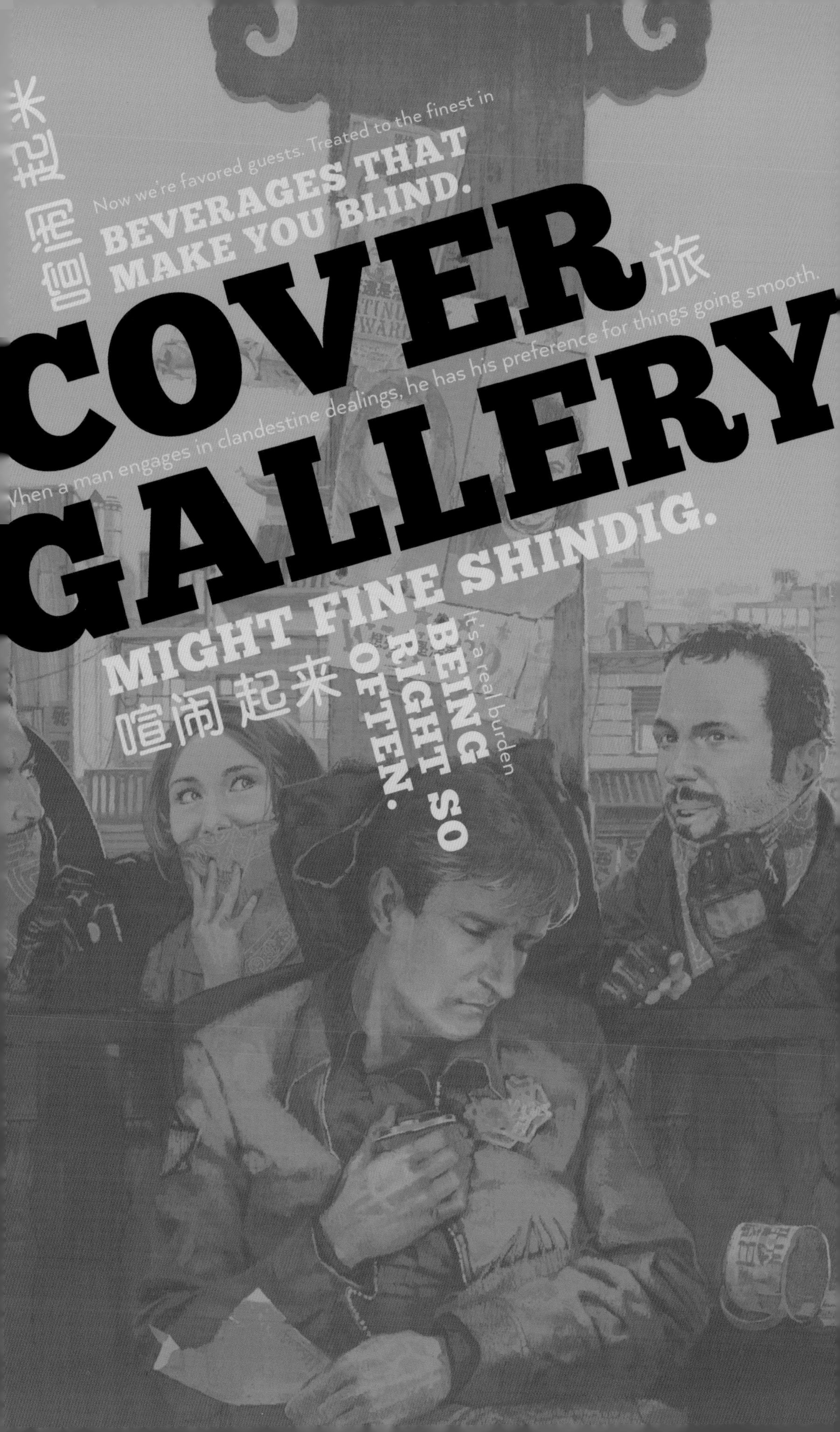

Now we're favored guests. Treated to the finest in
BEVERAGES THAT MAKE YOU BLIND.
When a man engages in clandestine dealings, he has his preference for things going smooth.
MIGHT FINE SHINDIG.
喧闹起来
It's a real burden
BEING RIGHT SO OFTEN.

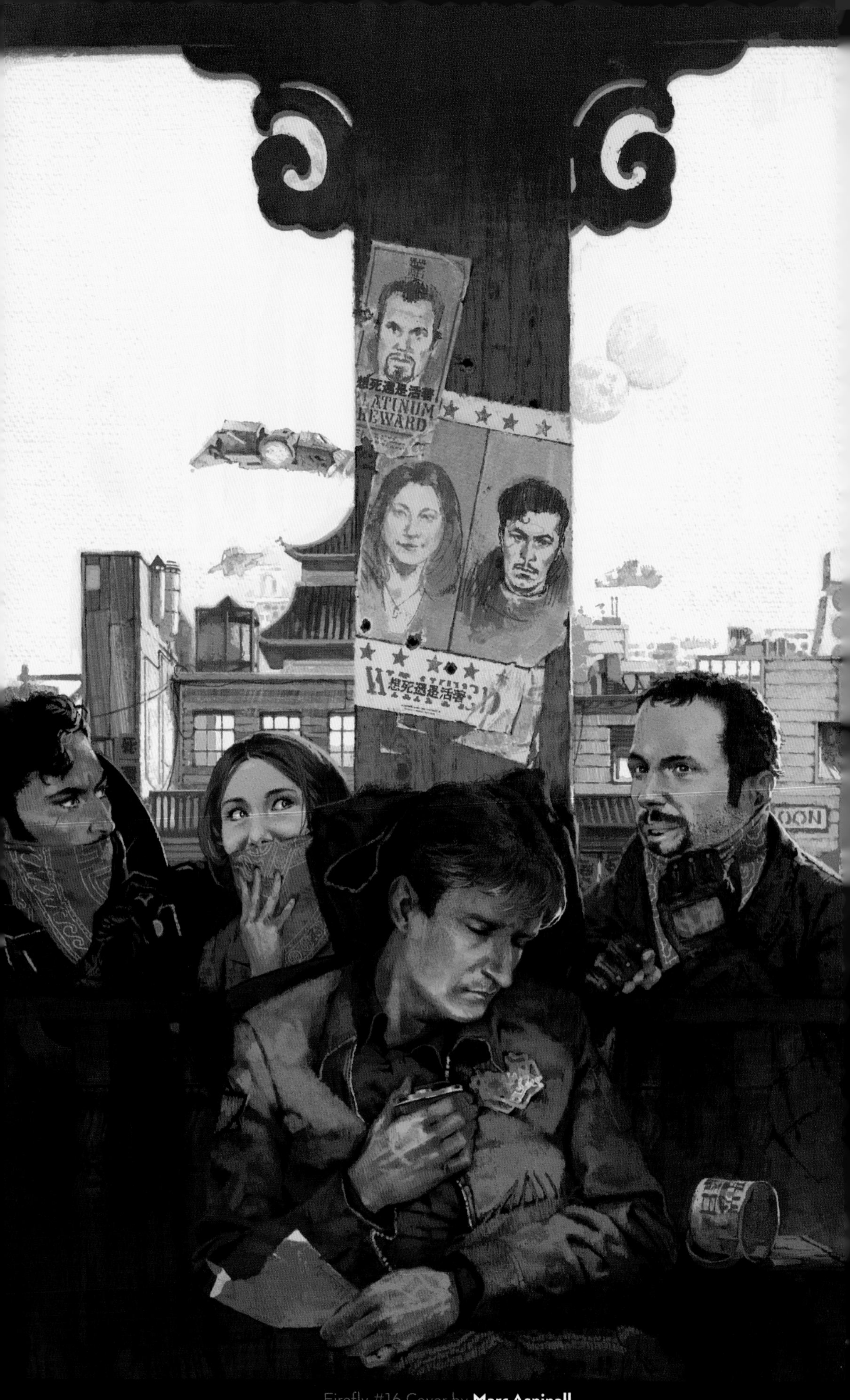

Firefly #16 Cover by **Marc Aspinall**

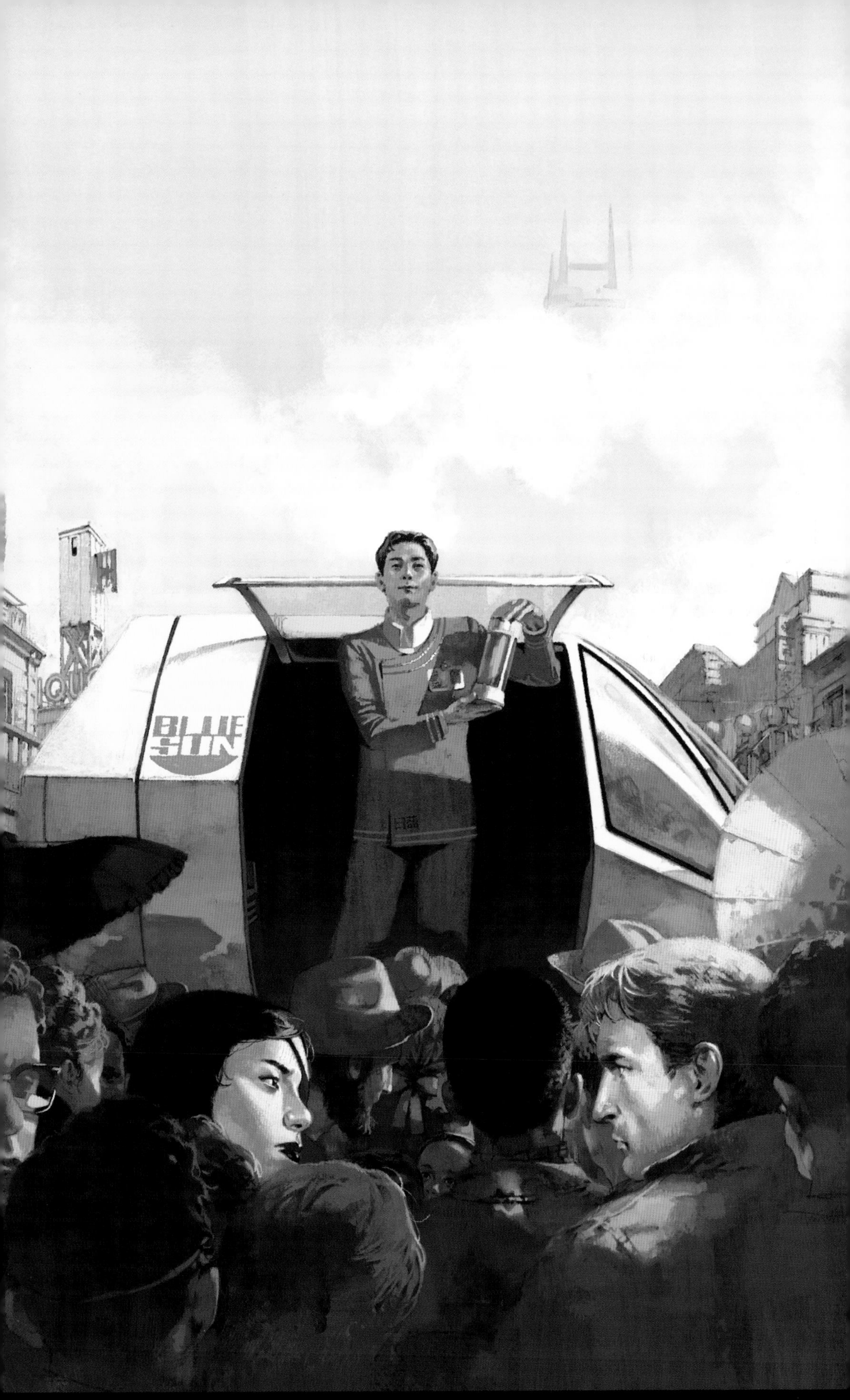
BLUE SUN

Firefly #17 Cover by **Marc Aspinall**

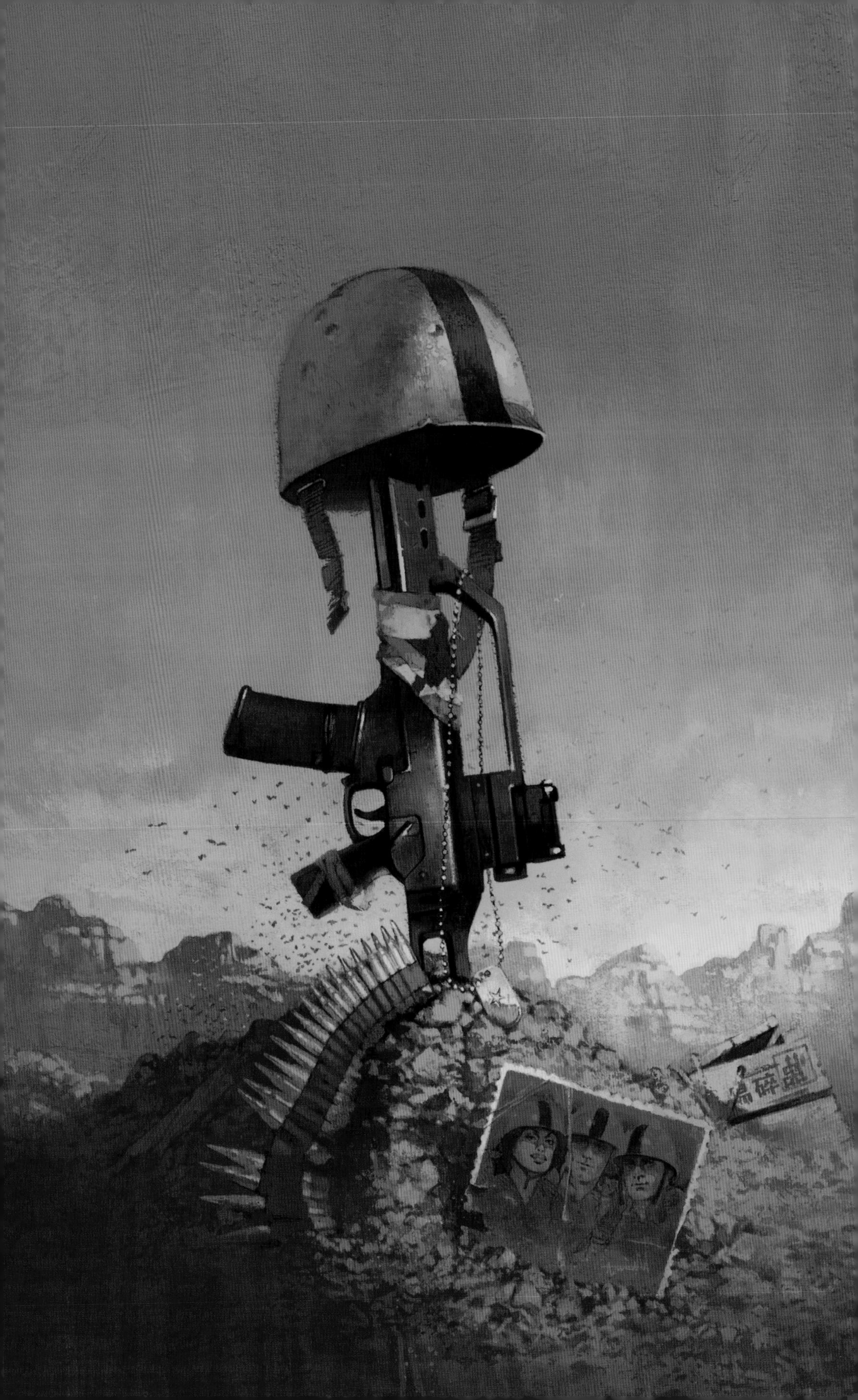

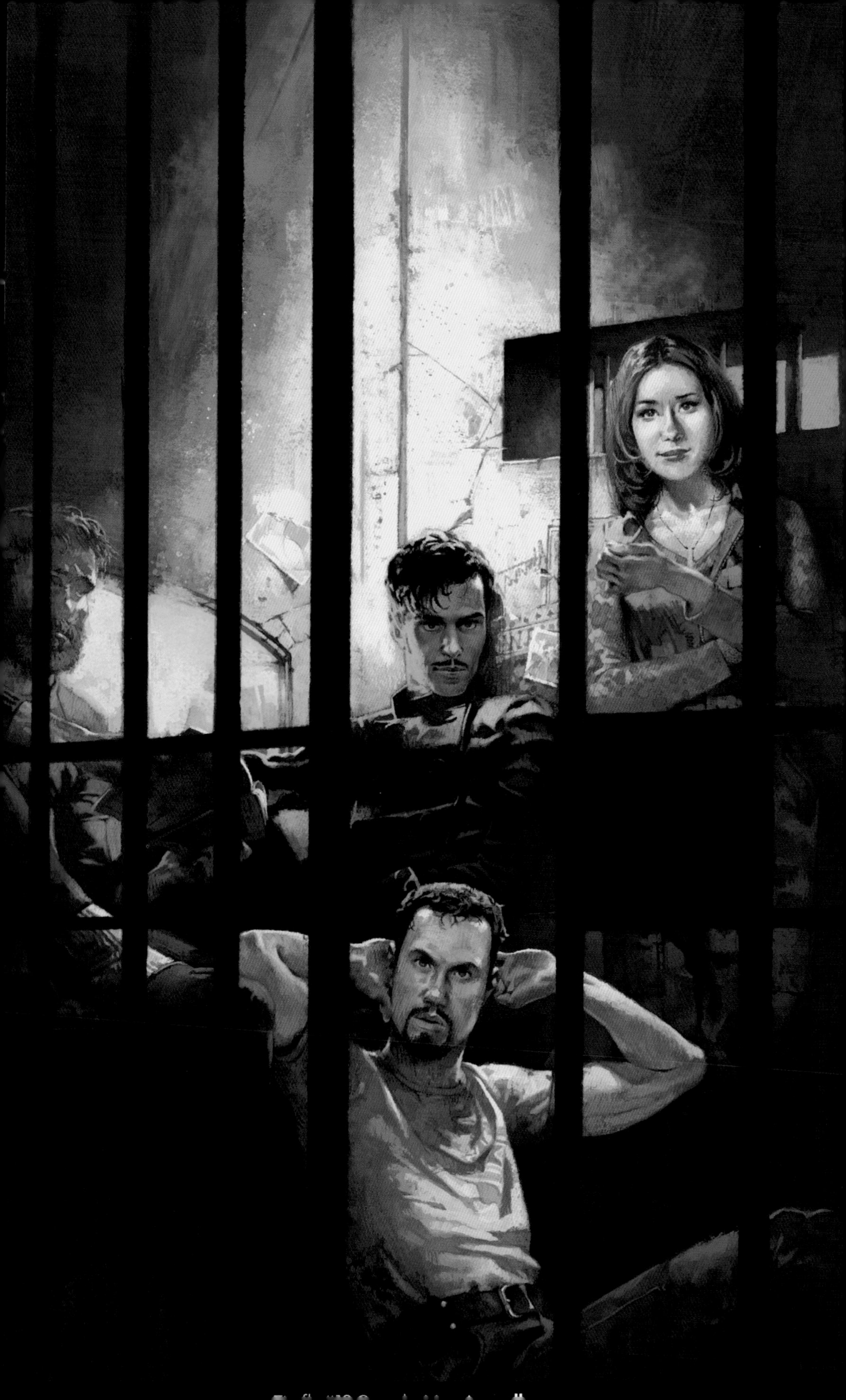

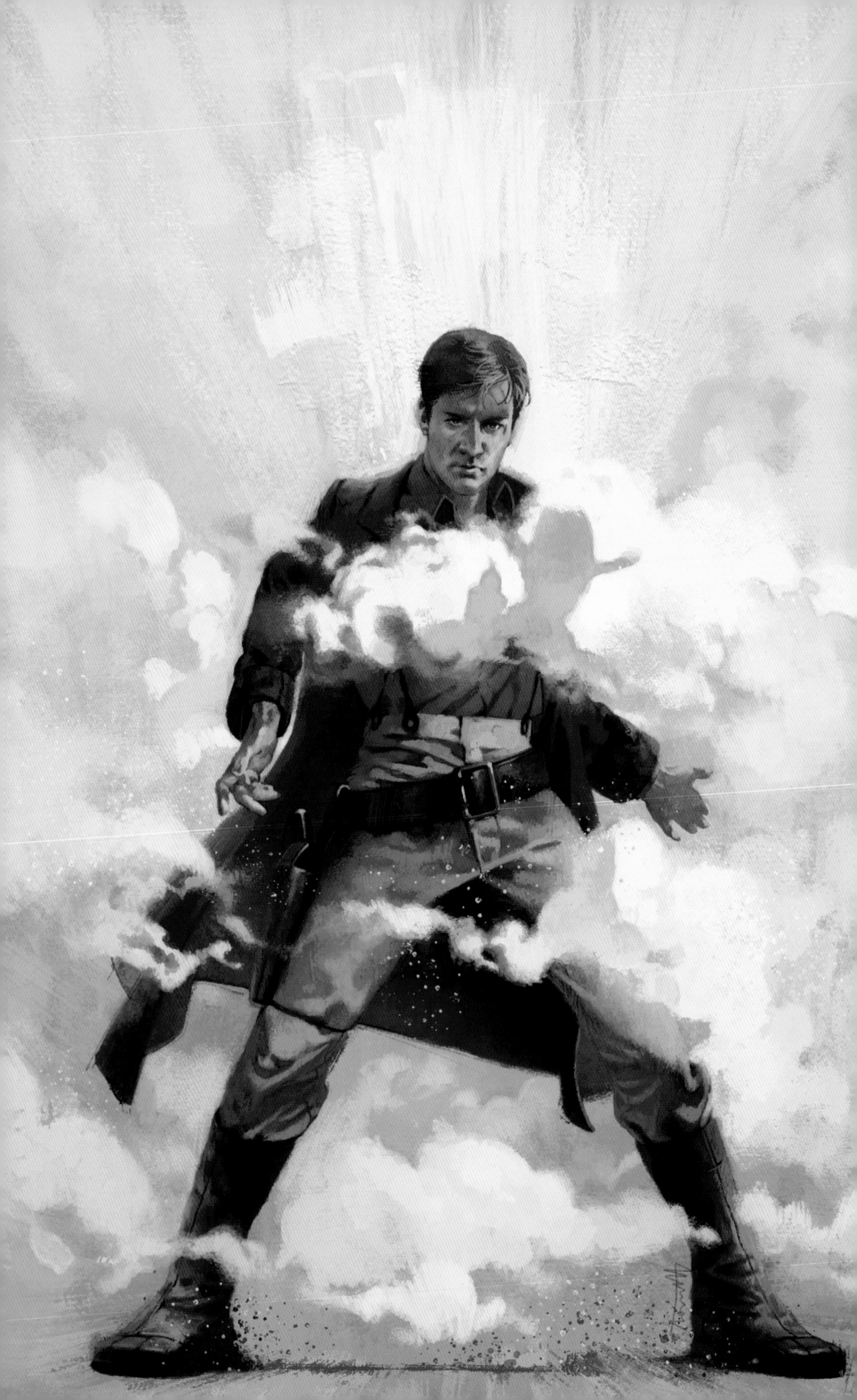

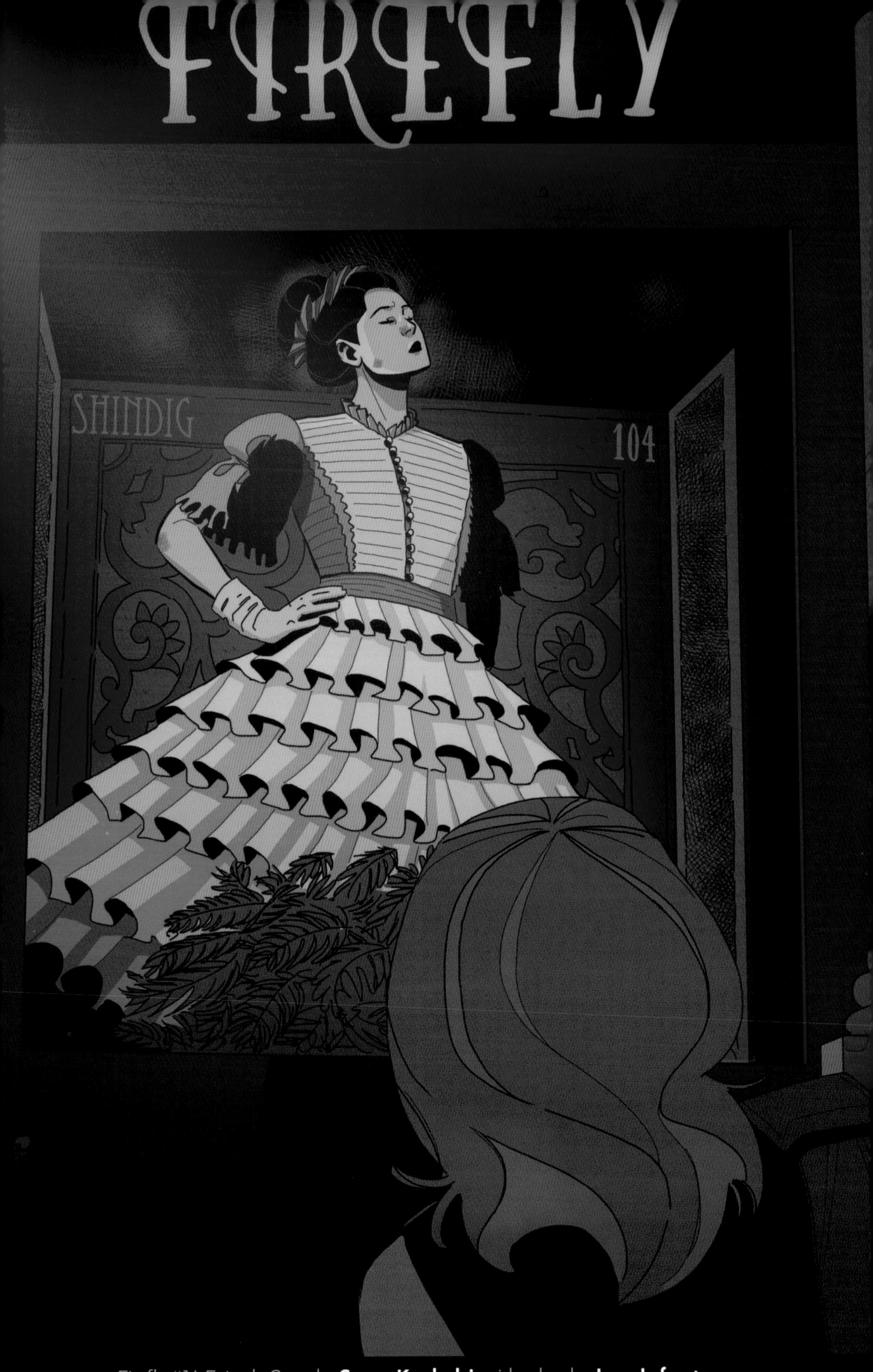
FIREFLY
SHINDIG
104

Firefly #16 Episode Cover by **George Kambadais** with colors by **Joana Lafuente**

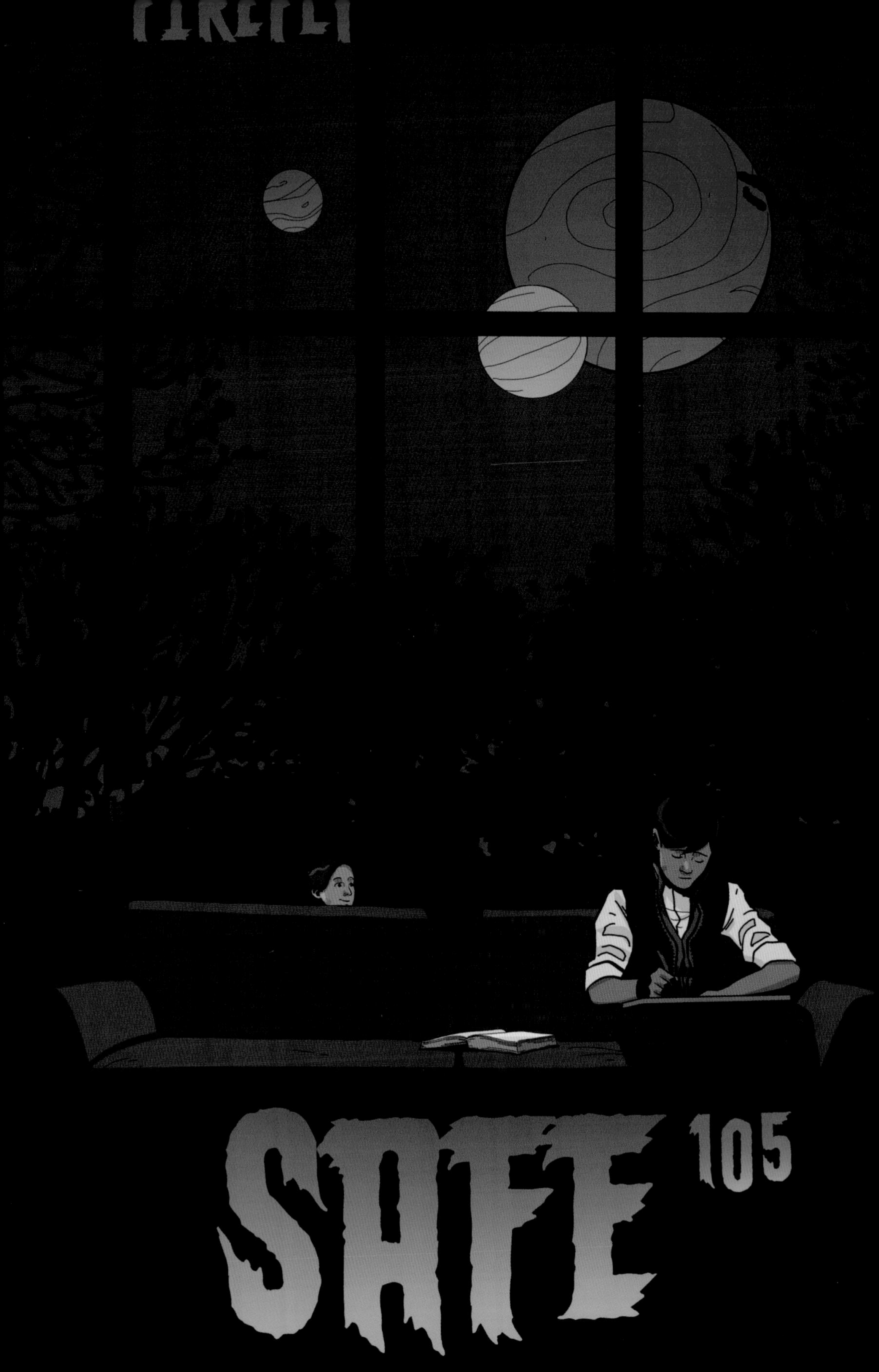
SAFE
105

Firefly #17 Episode Cover by **George Kambadais** with colors by **Joana Lafuente**

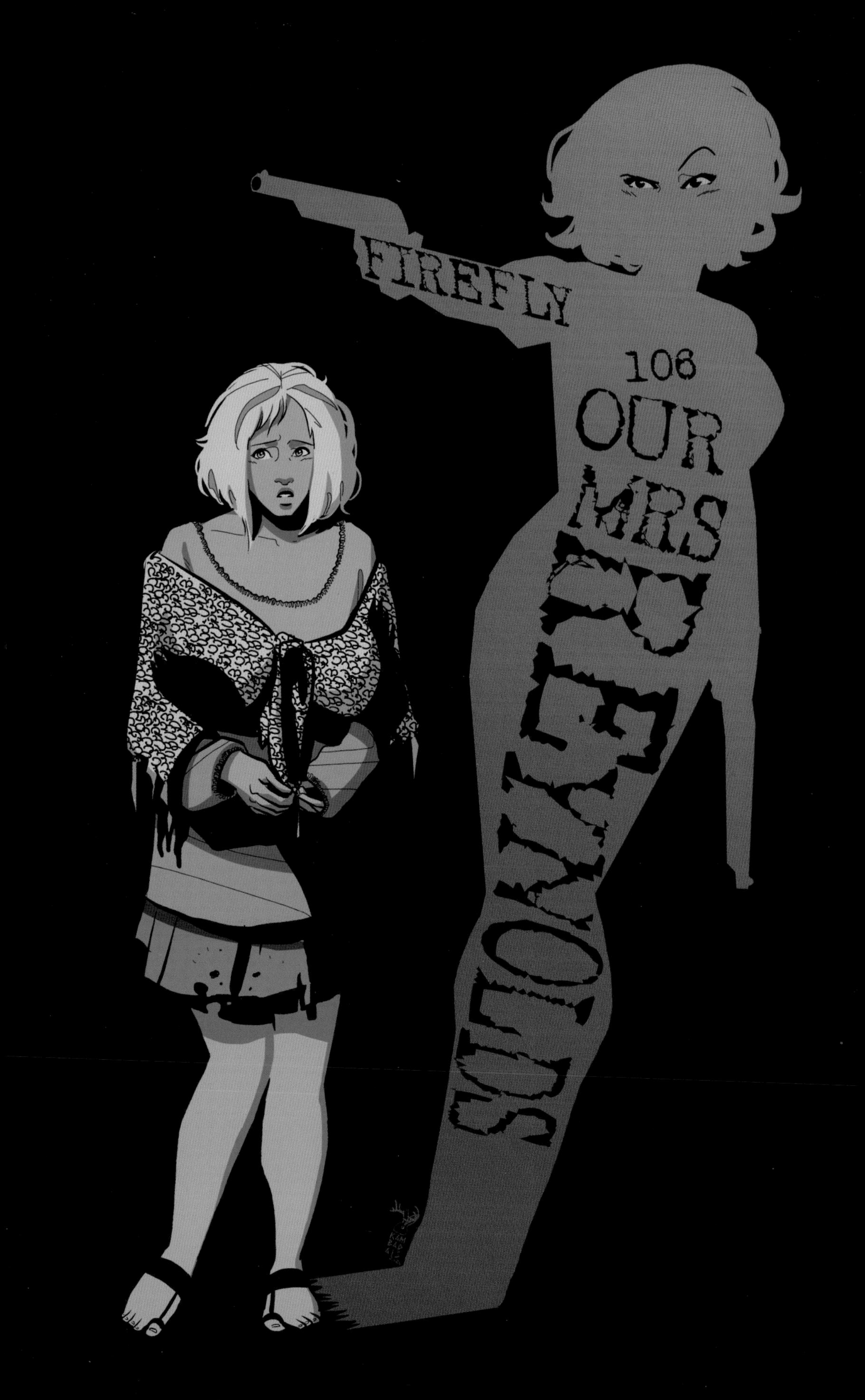
FIREFLY
106
OUR MRS REYNOLDS

Firefly #18 Episode Cover by **George Kambadais** with colors by **Joana Lafuente**

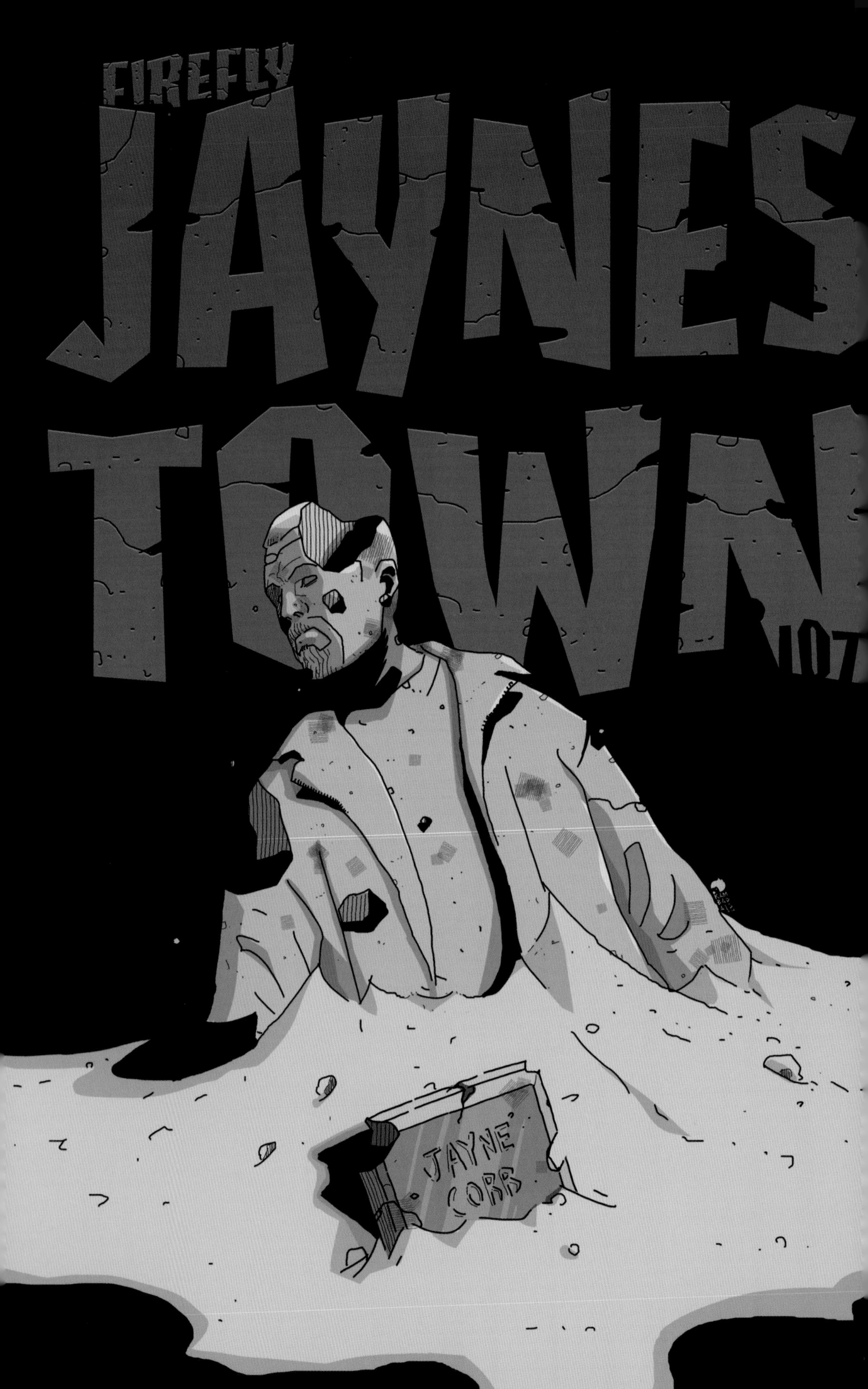
FIREFLY
JAYNES
TOWN
JAYNE
COBB

Firefly #19 Episode Cover by **George Kambadais** with colors by **Joana Lafuente**

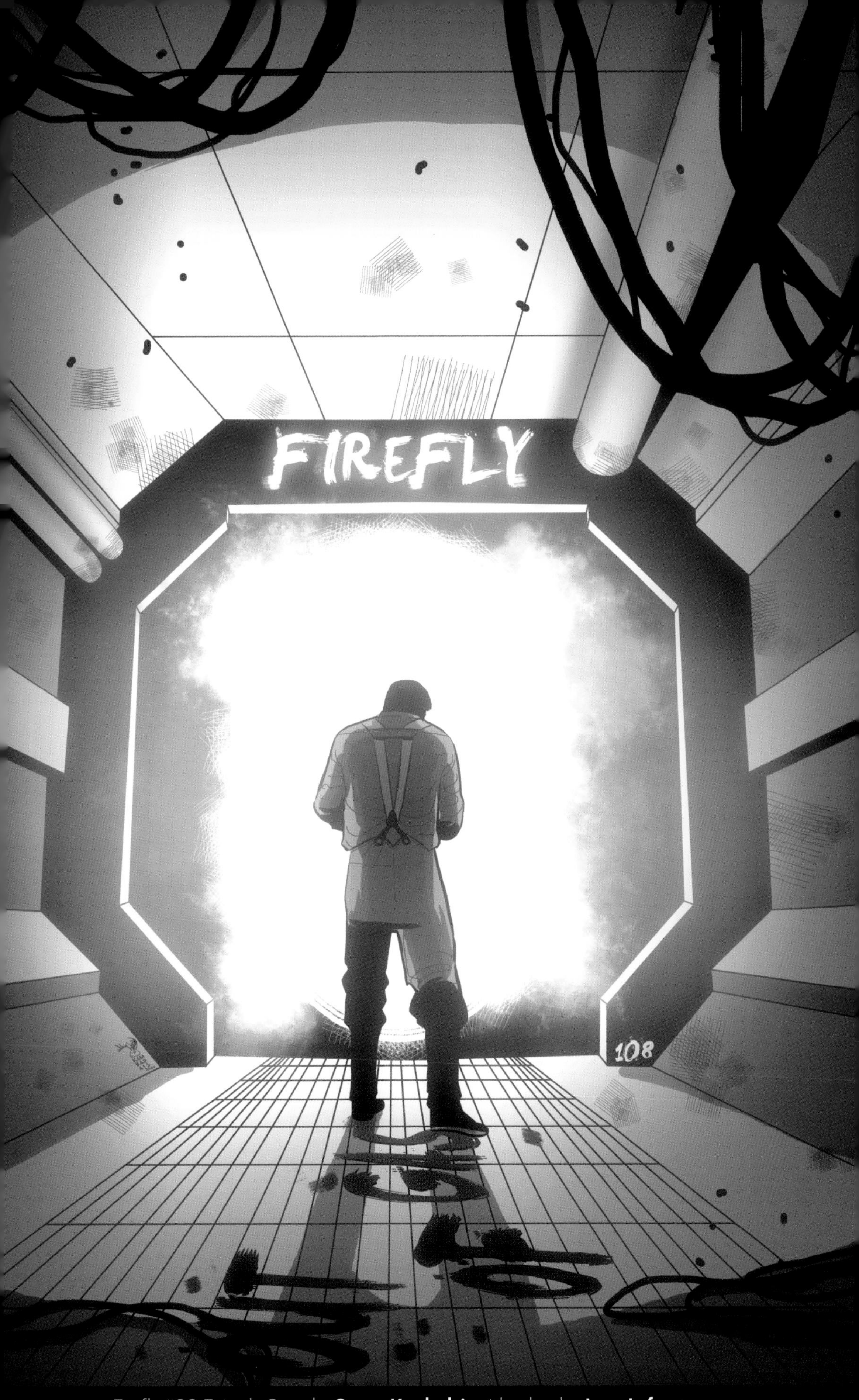
FIREFLY
108
Firefly #20 Episode Cover by **George Kambadais** with colors by **Joana Lafuente**

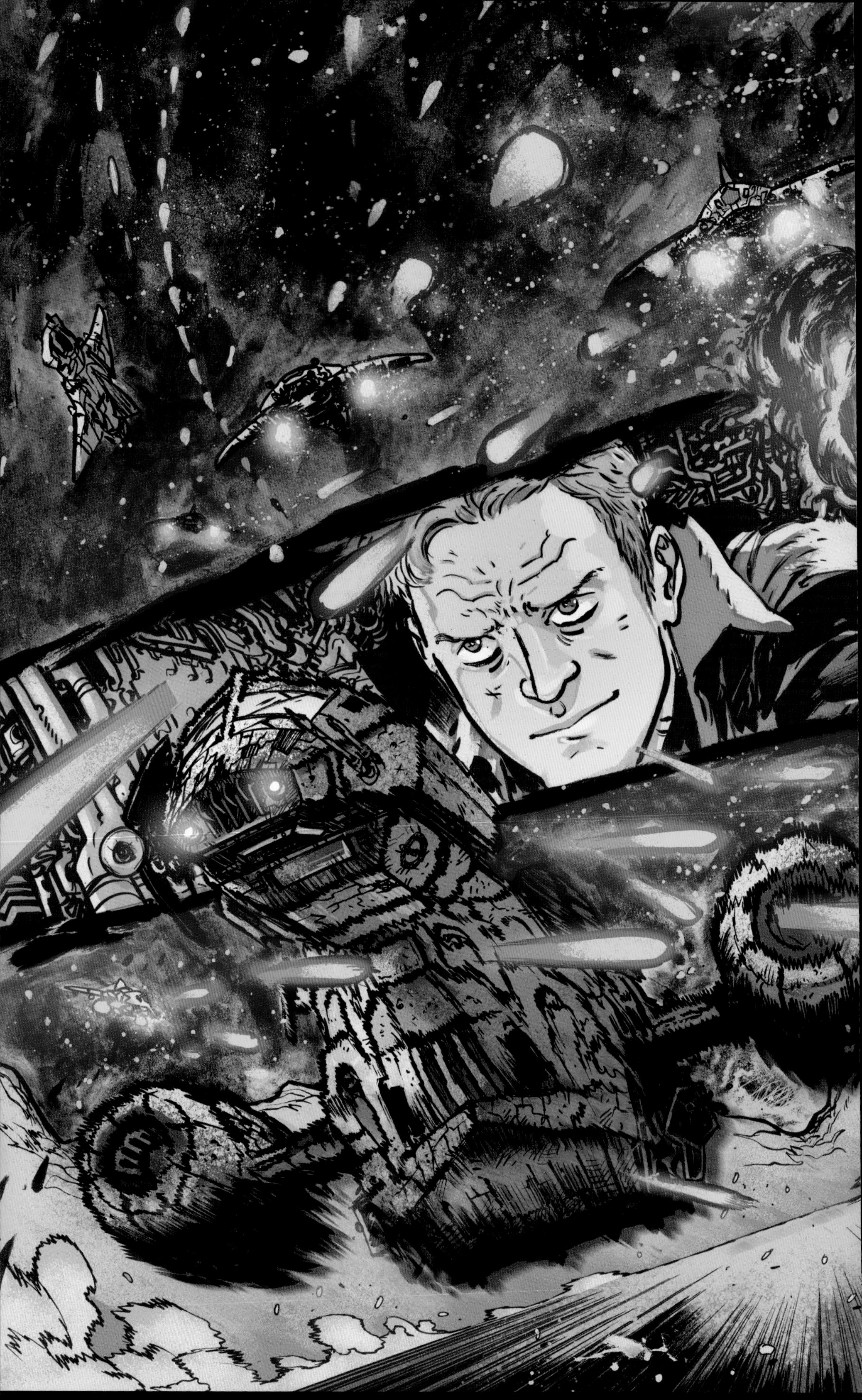

Firefly #16 Variant Cover by **Daniel Warren Johnson** with colors by **Mike Spicer**

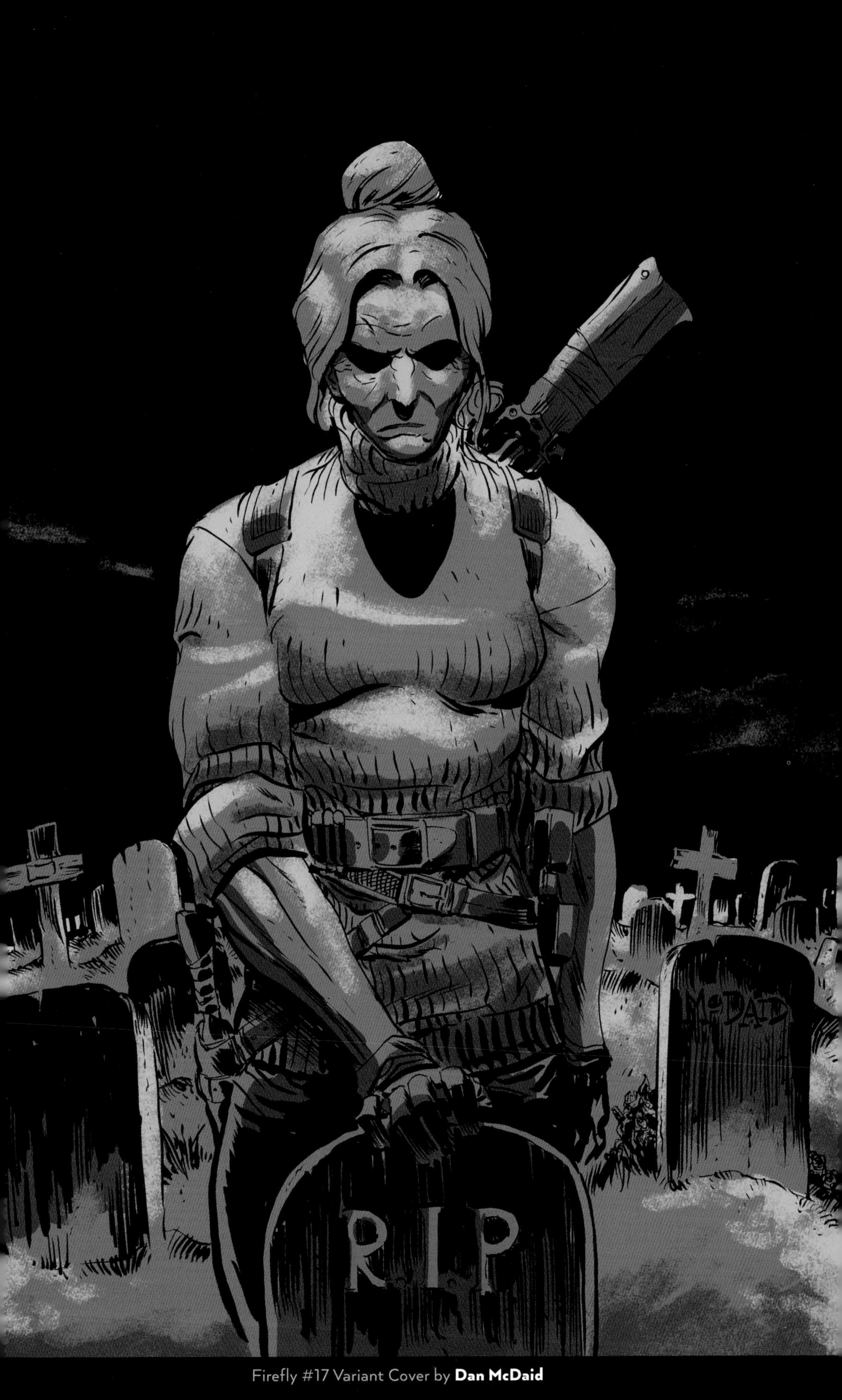
McDAID
R.I.P.
Firefly #17 Variant Cover by **Dan McDaid**

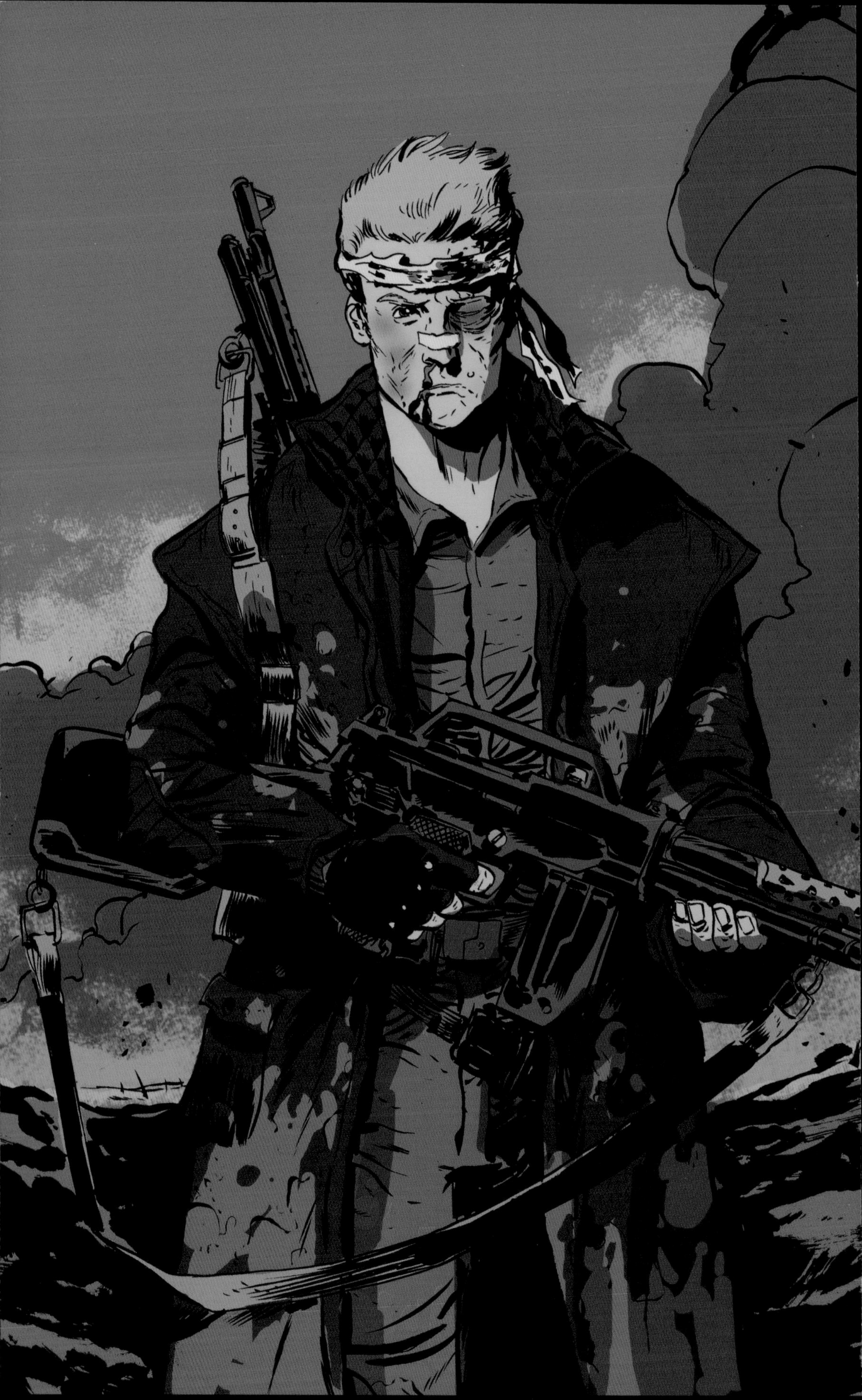

Firefly #18 Variant Cover by **Dan McDaid**

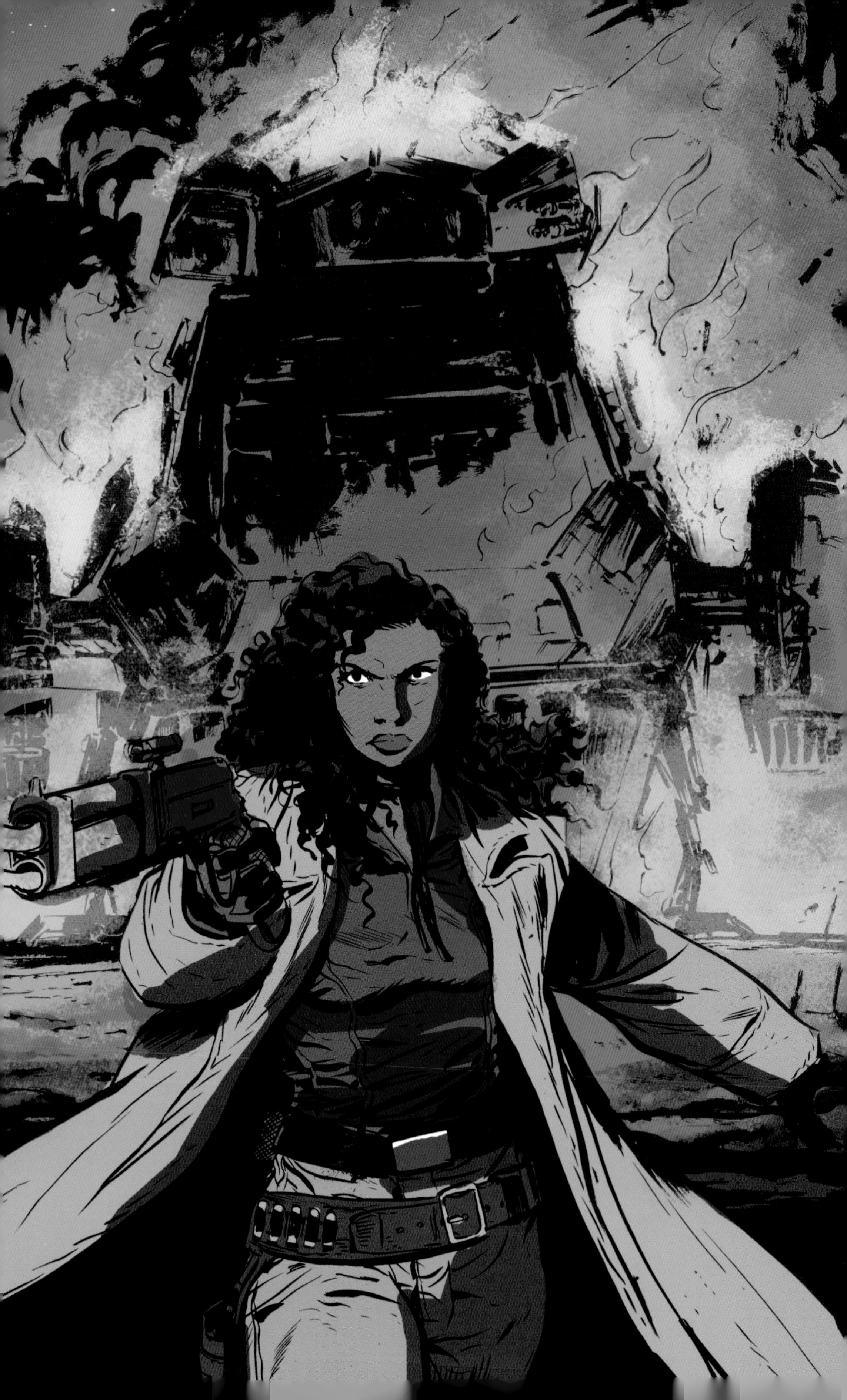

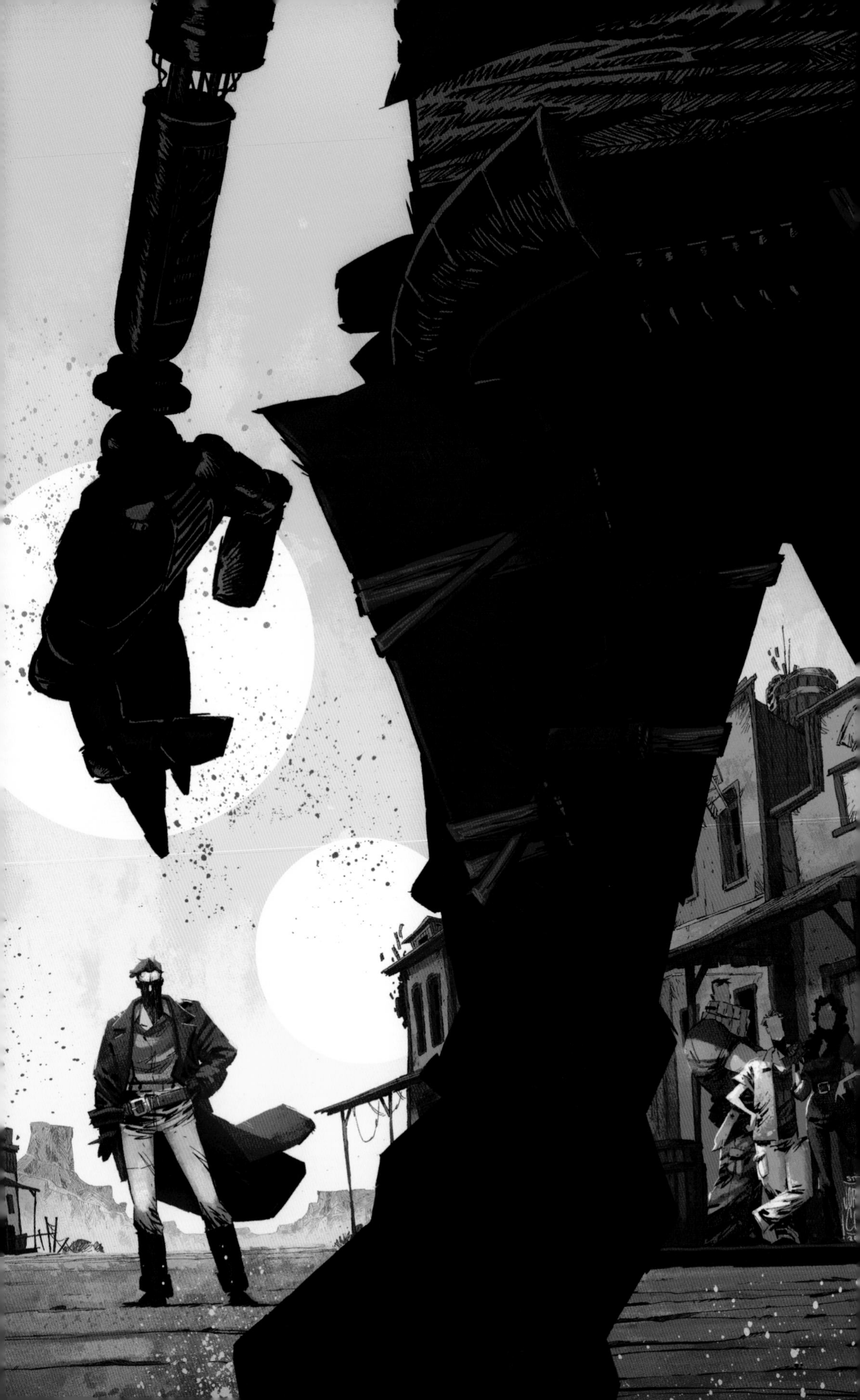

WHAT MAKES US SPECIAL

OH, I GOT

HEATHENS

APLENTY

RIGHT HERE.

DEAD.

AWFUL IN MY SKY.

NO

POWER

IN THE

VERSE

CAN

STOP

ME.

YOU'RE

WE AL

喧闹 起来

喧闹 起来

Curse your sudden but

INEVITABL

BETRAYAL

WHY DO

WE SHOO

HER FIRS

Maybe I'm not a fancy gentleman like you with your very fine hat. But I do business. We're here for b

I brought you some supper. But if you'd prefer a lecture I have a few very catchy ones prepped.

Ship like this will be with you 'til the day you die. That's 'cause it's a death trap.

Ain't heard back yet Didn't she shoot you one time?

BEING RIGHT

It's a real burden

Truly nifty har!

Truly nifty har!

I'm in a tricky position. I guess you know Got me a boatload of terribly strange

Here's a little concep

MAN OF HONO

IN A DEN OF

THIEVES.

Sergeant Malcolm Reynolds. Now you still a sergeant, sir? Still

Big tough veteran.

Only I think you're still a

That big w

IF YOU DIE CAN

HAVE YOUR SH

Preacher, don't

Quite specific

I brought you some supper. But

if you'd prefer a lecture I have a

few very catchy ones prepped

SIN AND

HELLFIRE.

喧闹

CAN'T STOP THE SIGNAL...

FIREFLY

LEGACY EDITION BOOK ONE

"...has everything *Firefly* fans would expect from the House of Whedon.

—AIN'T IT COOL NEWS"

BOOM!
LEGACY EDITION
WHEDON
FIREFLY
BOOK 1
JOSS WHEDON
Zack Whedon • Brett Matthews • Patton Oswalt • Will Conrad • Chris Samnee
firefly™
LEGACY EDITION BOOK ONE

Legacy Edition Book One Cover by **Nimit Malavia**

BOOK ONE COLLECTS

Serenity Volume 1: Those Left Behind
Serenity Volume 2: Better Days
Serenity: The Shepherd's Tale OGN

From Joss Whedon (creator of *Buffy the Vampire Slayer*), Serenity rides again, in these official sequels to the critically acclaimed show *Firefly*, collected for the first time under one cover!

Featuring stories by Joss Whedon, Emmy Award-winning comedian Patton Oswalt, and Eisner Award-winning artist Chris Samnee, buried histories and secret identities are revealed, along with all the heist-takin', authority-dodgin', death-defyin' space-cowboyin' you've been missing from your life, as this ragtag crew of mercenaries, outlaws, and fugitives travel the stars in search of their next adventure.

Legacy Editions collect every issue of the most popular BOOM! Studios series in chronological order and in a newly designed, value priced format for the very first time.

AVAILABLE IN STORES NOW

BOOK TWO ALSO AVAILABLE NOW

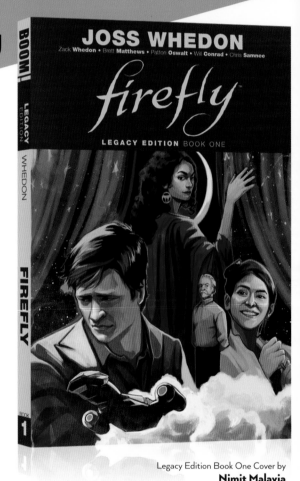

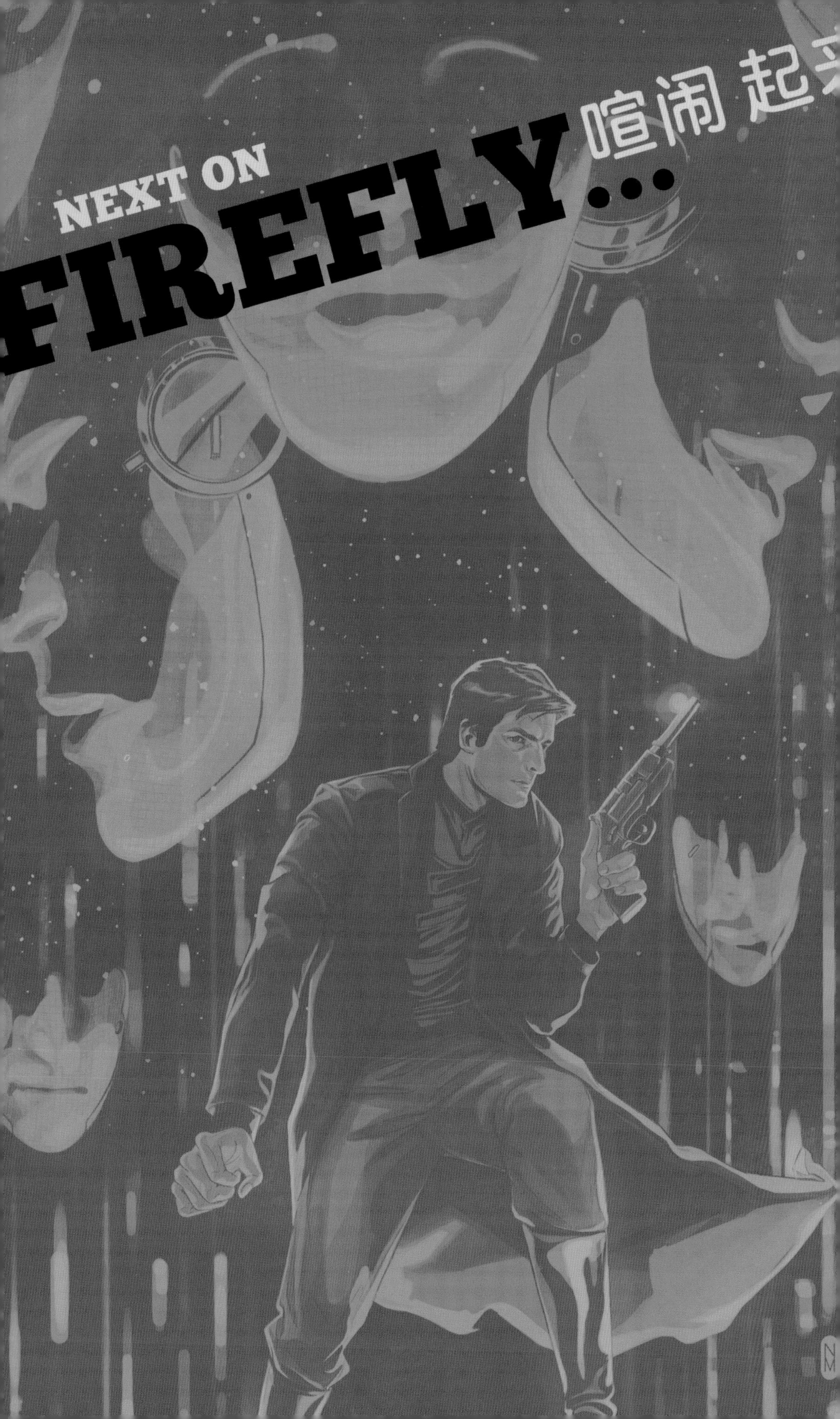
NEXT ON
FIREFLY...
喧闹 起

DISCOVER
VISIONARY CREATORS

THE WOODS
JAMES TYNION IV • MICHAEL DIALYNAS
VOL 1
THE ARROW

"The Spire is fantastic! My kind of genre free-for-all."
—BRIAN K. VAUGHAN (Saga)
THE SPIRE
SIMON SPURRIER
JEFF STOKELY
ANDRÉ MAY

MARK WAID • PETER KRAUSE
IRREDEEMABLE
AFTERWORD BY GRANT MORRISON

MARK WAID • JEAN DIAZ
INCORRUPTIBLE

MICHAEL ALAN NELSON
DAN MORA
GABRIEL CASSATA
HEXED
THE HARLOT & THE THIEF VOLUME ONE

ABNETT & CULBARD
WILD'S END
FIRST LIGHT
"IT'S REALLY GREAT!"
JEFF LEMIRE

James Tynion IV

The Woods
Volume 1
ISBN: 978-1-60886-454-6 | $9.99 US
Volume 2
ISBN: 978-1-60886-495-9 | $14.99 US
Volume 3
ISBN: 978-1-60886-773-8 | $14.99 US

The Backstagers
Volume 1
ISBN: 978-1-60886-993-0 | $14.99 US

Simon Spurrier

Six-Gun Gorilla
ISBN: 978-1-60886-390-7 | $19.99 US

The Spire
ISBN: 978-1-60886-913-8 | $29.99 US

Weavers
ISBN: 978-1-60886-963-3 | $19.99 US

Mark Waid

Irredeemable
Volume 1
ISBN: 978-1-93450-690-5 | $16.99 US
Volume 2
ISBN: 978-1-60886-000-5 | $16.99 US

Incorruptible
Volume 1
ISBN: 978-1-60886-015-9 | $16.99 US
Volume 2
ISBN: 978-1-60886-028-9 | $16.99 US

Michael Alan Nelson

Hexed The Harlot & The Thief
Volume 1
ISBN: 978-1-60886-718-9 | $14.99 US
Volume 2
ISBN: 978-1-60886-816-2 | $14.99 US

Day Men
Volume 1
ISBN: 978-1-60886-393-8 | $9.99 US
Volume 2
ISBN: 978-1-60886-852-0 | $9.99 US

Dan Abnett

Wild's End
Volume 1: First Light
ISBN: 978-1-60886-735-6 | $19.99 US
Volume 2: The Enemy Within
ISBN: 978-1-60886-877-3 | $19.99 US

Hypernaturals
Volume 1
ISBN: 978-1-60886-298-6 | $16.99 US
Volume 2
ISBN: 978-1-60886-319-8 | $19.99 US

BOOM! STUDIOS™

AVAILABLE AT YOUR LOCAL COMICS SHOP AND BOOKSTORE
To find a comics shop in your area, visit www.comicshoplocator.com
WWW.**BOOM-STUDIOS**.COM